WHAT PEOPLE ARE

A BETTER WORLD IS POSSIBLE

We are in a place we have never been before. We are facing a series of interconnected systemic crises that put both humanity and the planet in serious peril. This book not only clearly describes the problem but, most importantly, points to the solution. The "rules of the game" need to be radically changed and this will only happen if enough people, speaking with a clear enough voice, demand such a change. This book is not, therefore, a "worthy" text on economics, but a vital handbook for our survival!
Stewart Wallis, Executive Director, New Economics Foundation

We have to take our power and demand that our governments act boldly to tackle the environmental crisis; create a global economy that serves everyone; create truly inclusive democracy at all levels; and stop wasting lives and money on war. This book will inspire, challenge you and make sense of how the system works. It's your handbook for a bottom up revolution. Read it and play your part.
Baroness Helena Kennedy QC

Bruce Nixon's book is a powerful call for a peaceful and constructive mass revolt by the people of the world. He shows that the present way our lives are organised threatens the suicide of our own species and the further destruction of many others. His analysis points clearly to what we need to do to change it. I hope the book will be widely read and acted on.
James Robertson, "The grandfather of green economics"

At this time of ecological and spiritual crisis Bruce Nixon's book is a voice of sanity, wisdom and common sense. His vision presents a

genuine and positive way forward for humanity.
Satish Kumar, Editor of Resurgence, founder of the Small School and Director of Programmes at Schumacher College

Sustainable development isn't about saving whales or polar bears; it's equally about saving us from extinction. Bruce Nixon's work redirects us, with conviction, force and clarity, to that urgent goal.
Kevin McCloud, journalist, television presenter and WWF ambassador

I am grateful to Bruce Nixon for his wisdom, clarity and intention about making this a better world. We have no choice in these troubled times but to read and take seriously what he has to say. Thank you, Bruce, for your strong, timely and eye-opening message.
Sandra Janoff, PhD, Co-Director, Future Search Network, USA

This book is one of those rare things – a fascinating explanation of the interlocking global crisis in finance, climate, energy and food which leaves you at the end feeling hopeful and empowered.
David Boyle, author of *The Tyranny of Numbers* and *Money Matters*

We are in the midst of an economic crisis, but it is not the one covered in the media every day. The real crisis arises from the irreconcilable clash between efforts to maintain and increase growth in GDP while at the same time as managing ever more serious ecological crunches, from climate change to the loss of ecosystems. Bruce Nixon sets out the dimensions of the crisis we face and reaches the inescapable conclusion that we cannot hope to solve the multiple and related challenges in front of us unless we alter our view of economics. Read on to find out how a better world is possible, and how we need to change things to get there.
Tony Juniper, campaigner, writer and advisor

This book jolts us to recognize that we can't go on doing things as we do. This needs to be said. Its many examples of proven sustainable ways of doing things also need to be more widely known. This is a book that should be widely read.
Christopher Day, eco-architect and author of *Places of the Soul, Consensus Design: Socially inclusive process*

Bruce Nixon has provided a comprehensive assessment of why we need to change the way business and government operate to meet the needs of future generations of people, plants and creatures. After reading A Better World is Possible: What needs to be done and how we can make happen, *one is left with a sense that with some joined up thinking and, above all, co-operation anything is possible.*
Pete Riley, Campaigns Director GM Freeze

There are a lot of books out there that provide you with a complex intellectual analysis of the dual climate and economic crises – and leave you alone to mourn the political vacuum, while lamenting humanity's imminent demise. Bruce Nixon's book, though, is a breath of fresh air. It provides you with an easy to follow analysis about the human and environmental crises we face, but goes beyond this to articulate what a better world might look like. Most importantly, he tells you what ordinary people can do about it. It's a must-read toolkit for those of us wanting to see a more sustainable, just and equitable world.
Deborah Doane, Director, World Development Movement

Bruce Nixon dares to name the real nightmare that we all try to retreat from, hiding behind a false god called 'the market', stale ideologies or, simply, self-denying withdrawal. It is not often that we find a visionary writer, prepared, after detailing the problems, to go ahead and risk offering "A way out". Coming from a profound humaneness, this book is a must read for all those who engage in changing the present unacceptable, unsustainable world. Having forgiven ourselves for horrendous wrongs done by one set of ancestors to another, often

carried forward to the present, we can, together, South and North in our rainbow reality, build a glittering world of fairness and justice.
Olaseinde Makanjuola Arigbede, National Co-ordinator/ Animator, United Small and Medium scale Farmers' Associations of Nigeria

In a world of increasing population, diminishing natural resources and challenges posed by climate change, business-as-usual in our food and farming systems is no longer an option. This book starkly outlines the situation we are in – but also importantly the changes we can make, at citizen, community, national and international levels – to create more sustainable ways of producing and consuming the food on our tables.
Peter Melchett, Policy Director, Soil Association

I am very happy to endorse this book. You have addressed the context of our challenges well, and put across compelling evidence that things must change. But, importantly, what you give readers is a sense of realistic opportunity – that as citizens we really do have an opportunity to engage with positive activity to help change our lives for good. Books like yours are essential reading for challenging times ahead, giving us all an opportunity to shape a future vision based on community and personal empowerment.
Myles Bremner, Chief Executive, Garden Organic

A Better World is Possible

What needs to be done and how we can make it happen

A Better World is Possible

What needs to be done and how we can make it happen

Bruce Nixon

Winchester, UK
Washington, USA

First published by O-Books, 2011
O-Books is an imprint of John Hunt Publishing Ltd., Laurel House, Station Approach, Alresford, Hants, SO24 9JH, UK
office1@o-books.net
www.o-books.com

For distributor details and how to order please visit the 'Ordering' section on our website.

ISBN: 978 1 84694 514 4

A CIP catalogue record for this book is available from the British Library.

Design: Stuart Davies

Printed in the UK by CPI Antony Rowe
Printed in the USA by Offset Paperback Mfrs, Inc

CONTENTS

Introduction

Another world is possible, she is on her way. On a quiet day, I can hear her breathing.
Arundhati Roy

A period of extraordinary change

I began writing this book two years ago. The sub-prime crisis and credit crunch were emerging, tipping the world into an unprecedented breakdown in the flawed financial system, followed by deepening recession. George Bush Jnr. has gone, replaced by Barack Obama. His election, as the first black American President, and his acceptance speech moved millions around the world and gave new hope. It remains to be seen whether he will be able to implement his bold plans for change given the difficulties he faces. In the UK, New Labour has gone. The Lib Dem Conservative coalition, promising new politics, fresh ideas and openness to feedback, has imposed the deepest cuts since WWII. But the strategy is not radical or evidence based. The West is hugely indebted to China and India, clearly now the dominant powers.

Warnings about climate change and the threats to all life on the planet have grown louder. Public awareness has grown, though not enough. Governments, diverted by the financial crisis, still fail to take the necessary actions to avoid environmental catastrophe. We are truly living in interesting times; change unfolds at an astonishing pace. Paradoxically, response to the biggest threat to our survival is frighteningly slow and superficial.

Worldwide poverty, hunger, disease, injustice and inequality continue. Pledges given by rich nations remain unfulfilled. Money which should be created only by central reserve banks is largely created by debt, to the benefit of bankers. It is a system that robs us and transfers wealth from those who create it to rich and powerful elites. The lack of well-informed, active, inclusive democracy at every level allows it.

People all over the world are angry about what is essentially a rip-off – lost livelihoods and homes, diminished savings and pensions, indebtedness, recession, poorer chances of work and constant insecurity. They've given trillions to bankers who caused the crisis, withhold credit for enterprise and continue to pay themselves excessive salaries and bonuses.

What has happened over recent decades is an outrage. Yet we allowed it. Change rarely comes about from within a system. It comes from outside. That has to be us.

The two key arguments of this book are:

The whole global system has to be transformed to serve everyone, everywhere.

We, ordinary people, need to turn our anger into effective action to bring about radical change.

We face the biggest challenge in our history. Climate change is one symptom of our failure to live in harmony with the Earth and all life on it, including each other. These 5 issues confronting us are inseparably linked:

- **Climate change** is possibly out of control and irreversible and possibly only 70 months before we reach the tipping point.
- **Peak everything** not just Peak Oil.
- **We are destroying the ecosystem** on which all life depends, poisoning the Earth, the air all creatures breathe and the water of which life is made.
- **Poverty and economic injustice**
- **Violence, war, terrorism and the threat of nuclear annihilation**

We need to transform the system, rather than trying to fix it. We need to change it for the benefit all. We need far more representative and inclusive democracy from local to global levels. We need to transform the debt money system and taxation. Above all we need the hope and inspiration of a great new endeavour combined with practical action. Many people know that something is deeply wrong and have had enough. There are alternatives to this unsustainable, unjust system fuelled by debt money and war.

We could be at the beginning of a new age in which we cherish the Earth's resources and diversity, an age of sustainability, fairness, economic justice and peace – an age of less greed, selfishness and more responsibility. The urgency of the crisis could lead to nations and their leaders learning to respect difference, find common ground and work together for the well-being of all humanity. We could at last realise we are all interdependent and part of a miraculous, beautiful and interconnected web of life. In that way, we'll save ourselves, just in time, from the potential disasters of climate change and nuclear obliteration.

It is our choice. It won't just happen. We certainly cannot leave it to politicians. It depends on every one of us, 6.7 billion people, using our power. We cannot afford to indulge in despair or cynicism and pretend we are powerless. We are not. We have a unique opportunity to transform our world. Everyone is needed to participate and play their part. ***All of us have to get involved in politics!***

The purpose of the book is to help create the mass movement needed to prevent catastrophic climate change, save our planet Earth, create a sustainable and just global economic system and put an end to war. I offer this book as a resource for people all over the world who want to act to transform the system. To use your power, you need to be well-informed. This book is full of information – choose from the contents what you most need to read.

Part One: Making Sense of the Situation We are In. To change things for the better, we first need to *understand the underlying system*. We shall not succeed in bringing about transformation if we are system blind. I'll open eyes to the system, how it works, its consequences and the key underlying issues. By expressing my views I hope to help you form yours.

It is a myth that the issues are too complicated for the average person to understand. It is vitally necessary to understand this increasingly complex, interconnected, constantly changing ***living system***. Our understanding of the miracle of life will always be incomplete. There will be fresh insights every day. There can be no certainties. We are all on a journey and need open minds. Out of control politicians with big egos and big ideas are dangerous. Margaret Thatcher's TINA *"There is no alternative"* is false. Solutions always bring unintended consequences – hence, the importance of applying the precautionary principle, risk assessment and due diligence. To reach wise decisions it is essential to involve all stakeholders and a wide diversity of people.

Part Two: A Vision for a Better World: Possibilities for a better future and what needs to be done. Here, I describe constructive ways forward, key proposals and good models that already exist. Above all, we need to focus on ***Creating Possibilities.*** Many people I meet are experts on why we cannot change things for the better; maybe they tried, now weary and discouraged. We need to be aware that ***breakdowns nearly always herald breakthroughs!*** That's if we choose to make it so. Breakdowns are normal and happen all the time. We need leaders, like you, who have hope and are focused on ***how we can,*** not why we can't. This part of the book offers all kinds of exciting possibilities for a better, more sustainable, fairer, non-violent world. However, it is most important that you dream and create your own possibilities. Here is another amazing possibility: that we, the majority of 6.7 billion people on the planet, realise our power to transform things for the better and take the necessary action. I set out actions that everyone can take to turn the situation round. I invite you to play your unique part in a perfectly achievable transformation.

Will we to go down in history as the Age of Stupid? In March 2009 I attended one of the countrywide premieres of the *Age of Stupid* film. It was one of the most terrifying, moving and empowering events I have experienced – truly "people power" in action. The campaign was created and organised by two bold women, Franny Armstrong and Lizzie Gillett with their large team. The film helped get millions all over the world on to the streets to put pressure on their governments and demand they do the right thing to replace the Kyoto agreement that expires in 2012.

On Saturday 5th December 2009, more than 50,000 people of all ages came together in the Wave, organised by the Stop Climate Chaos Coalition to demand action on climate change, the biggest ever UK climate change march. I am glad I was part of it. The Wave called on the UK Government to take urgent and effective action. We encircled Parliament. Government did respond.

The UN Climate Summit in Copenhagen, COP15 looked like the best chance we had to save ourselves and future generations. The outcome was bitterly disappointing. For the first time representatives of 193 nations, including 110 world leaders, met with climate change as the single issue. An accord was reached but no binding agreement. The process was flawed. Hopes were not high for COP16 in 2010 and little was achieved. Be prepared to campaign again to make sure our governments do ***much MORE.***

We need a continuing mass movement. Arm yourself and your family and friends with this book. Use it as your handbook. Inform yourself about the whole system and what you can do to transform it and create a better, sustainable, fairer and non-violent world for the benefit of all. Get lobbying! We have to believe in ourselves and that anything is possible and *"Yes, we can!"*

The book is partly a record of how the human story unfolded over these past two years. So, I have dated each chapter to place it in its time, updating as necessary.

References. I have not provided a long list of references. Today, it is easy to source or update data by using your Internet browser. References are only given where permission was needed.

Part One

Making Sense of the Situation We are In:

How, we, 6.7 billion people, are robbed and our futures are endangered by a few

Chapter 1

A Time of System Breakdown but also of Hope

Begun October 2008

We live in a beautiful world much of which is a paradise. Life is full of possibilities, especially for people in the prosperous North. Scientific discoveries, medical advances and new technologies offer wonderful opportunities for greater well-being, if used for human needs and shared widely in the world rather than to make a few very rich people even more rich and powerful.

For ordinary working people in countries like the UK, life is far better now than fifty years ago when I was a student in Liverpool. We only have to see a film like *"of time and the city"* by Terence Davies, showing scenes of Liverpool just after WWII, to appreciate the depths of poverty that existed then in British industrial cities in the mid twentieth century. Go back a century and poverty, ill-health and conditions in factories were even more desperate. Victorians experienced constant epidemics. Parents frequently had to watch helplessly as their children died. In 1851 the mean age of males in Britain was 25.78 years. The average lifespan in 1840, in the Whitechapel district of London, was 45 years for the upper class and 27 years for tradesman. Labourers and servants lived only 22 years on average.

Most of us have so much to be grateful for.

If the only prayer you ever said was thank you, it would be enough.
Meister Eckhart

When we focus on the simple things that give us joy, everything falls into place and we are at ease. These are our families, our children, grandparents, having meals with friends, good neighbours, living in a community, love and generosity, the beauty of countryside and miracle of nature, our gardens, beautiful places, buildings, music and dance and much more. The same things are enjoyed by people in what we call poor countries, where people are often more philosophical. They cannot understand why we need so many possessions.

However, there is a shadow side. Our world can be hell on earth. People in poor countries cannot be happy when they are unable to grow food, have no land, are starving, at risk of flooding, where there are no basic services, people are dying for lack of health care and medicines and there is no safety from violence and war and they are subject to an onslaught of missiles and bombs raining down on their homes and communities. It is distressing, when we are aware of all the avoidable disease, poverty, insecurity, injustice, violence and the unfulfilled lives. How can we be happy ignoring this, especially when our lifestyle and inaction is largely responsible?

As I started writing in October 2008, the breakdown had begun. It is a far greater wake-up call than 9/11. It is the realisation that we've been robbed and our future on the planet is endangered by an economic system that benefits a few rich and powerful people but has disastrous consequences for the rest. We are the victims of a giant experiment – a big "con". We've been taken for "suckers".

We, 6.7 billion people, need to feel our outrage and anger.

The fear and anger we prefer to avoid needs to be felt and turned into action. It is astonishing that we allowed it all to happen. There were many warning voices. Who is responsible? The honest answer is we all are. Many of us, in the prosperous West, played our part. We got involved in the excitement. We consumed and got more affluent, though more stressed and no happier. The poor majority in the world bear little responsibility for it. We were seduced by the possibilities for making more money, having more and more stuff at amazingly low prices and a whirlwind of new, constantly developing technology. Technology brought enormous benefits but is also part of spend, spend, get rich quick addiction and out of control capitalism.

We, in prosperous democracies, are in the best position to change it. We need to start in our own country. Although civil liberties have been eroded in the past 13 years, we don't live in such fear of the consequences of dissent as people in many poor countries do. It's our responsibility to show courage and take action.

It's worth looking back to learn. Many people, all over the world, have woken up to the reality of the past thirty years: the system must be changed! But governments and corporate leaders don't *"get it"*.

The financial crisis and the rapidly growing recession are doing most harm to "ordinary" people, especially the poor majority all over the world. Free market capitalism is not, as claimed, a "trickle down" system, lifting the poor out of poverty. It is a "trickle up" system through which the poor, and not so well off, make a few people enormously rich. It makes the gap between the rich and poor increasingly wider. It has failed to solve the enormous problem of poverty. One billion people are hungry. It is plundering and degrading the Earth on which all life depends. It is not, as claimed, a self- correcting system. Or at least, the self-corrections have devastating effects. It is out of control. However, these events, distressing as they are, are symptoms of a greater crisis. And they distract us from the bigger threat. Governments, using our money, are rushing to patch up the financial system and prevent depression, re-establish "business as usual", without changing the fundamentals.

The City of London, instead of doing what it's there for, aided and abetted by government, engaged in ingenious schemes and devices to *"create money out of thin air"*. Then, government used taxpayers' resources to bail out the people who mismanaged these institutions. It continued to allow UK citizens to be robbed through tax avoidance and evasion schemes and offshore havens. Instead of seeing the underlying perverse economic system and tackling that, instead of seeing the threat of climate change as the highest priority, government squandered resources on an illegal Iraq war and a questionable war in Afghanistan, without providing our troops with adequate equipment.

A complete loss of integrity. An epidemic of scandals has caused us to lose faith in people we should be able to trust – at the top of business, in banking, government, Parliament and the MPs who represent us. A widespread lack of integrity has been exposed.

Human beings face the biggest threat in their history. The biggest crisis is ***not*** the collapse in the financial system, causing estimated losses of around $2,800,000,000,000. The greater threat is climate change and destruction of the ecosystem on which all life depends. Like Peak Oil, the economic collapse, awful as it is for many people, is a symptom, a warning that our time is up unless we take bold and urgent action. It is diverting our attention. Our current way of life is unsustainable and simply has to change. Because oil is embedded in almost everything we consume, Peak Oil will ultimately force the change upon us. There may be a temporary remission now, but in the longer term the price of oil will inevitably escalate as supply is outstripped by demand.

All of this, coming together, amounts to the biggest challenge we have ever faced. It would be better to take vigorous action now, rather than when it is too late.

The Gravest Threats to Humanity

- Climate change – unpredictable, possibly out of control and irreversible and the dire consequences for 6.7 billion people
- By the end of the century average temperature could have risen 5 degrees and seas by 1 to 3 feet
- Consuming more than "spaceship Earth" can provide. Human population isrising. By 2050 it is expected to reach 9bn – whilst most other species are declining
- Destruction and degradation of the complex ecological system on which all life depends
- The "Western" consumerist way of life
- "Mono-culture of the mind" as Vandana Shiva calls the "one and only one way" we in the West impose on the world
- Hidden control of food and commodities by a few giant companies and their influence on world and national government
- Pandemics caused by industrialisation of animal husbandry and its cruelty
- Poverty, injustice, starvation, avoidable disease and stunted lives – 1bn hungry people
- Growing toxicity: what we eat and drink, absorb through our skins, the air we breathe and electronic smog
- Violence – war, civil war and nuclear proliferation, the threat of nuclear catastrophe and nuclear terrorism
- Lack of inspired, principled, servant leadership, fit for the 21st century

We need to realise that all of us must be servant leaders. Transforming the world requires us to transform ourselves.

Breakdowns always offer the possibility of breakthroughs. The global crisis may turn out to be a blessing. We need to understand this: *breakdowns can lead to breakthroughs.* As the old paradigm dies, new opportunities are created. Living systems are like that. This breakdown is challenging the unsustainable, free market dogma that has flourished for thirty years. This breakdown opens the way for radical transformation and greening our economy.

There is a better way as I hope to show. People are motivated by a vision of something better, not fear and gloom. That just leads to dysfunctional behaviour like denial, depression, inaction or confrontation and violence. It is not a hopeless situation. A far better future is to be had. We need to create our own vision of the future we desire. That is how the most successful leaders, leaders who have changed the world, transformed their organisations or built new ones, have done it: by honestly confronting the full reality of the situation, communicating and articulating an inspiring vision of what is possible, providing hope and empowering people to take wise action. That is what all of us need to do. All of us can be leaders. We need to learn how.

"Yes we can!" Like many others, I was up late, watching, listening to the exciting drama of Barack Obama's election. I joined millions all over the world, watching Afro Americans, and just Americans, celebrating together a historic victory, singing, dancing, crying and jumping for joy. It was a milestone in the long struggle of Afro Americans to emerge from slavery, discrimination and feeling or being thought inferior. His message ***"Yes we can!"*** spoken by their grandmothers for over 200 years is an inspiration to people everywhere. We are truly one world!

The good news is that major breakdowns often throw up great leaders. That may be happening now. Barack Obama, from a relatively humble background that gives him empathy with ordinary people, provides a good example to all of us. He is the first black President of the United States. This alone should give us hope. He won by involving record numbers of hitherto disengaged Americans. The youth vote, Afro Americans, Hispanics and the not so young all got engaged. He involved them in his campaign and he got them out to vote. He raised a quarter of his $600m campaign fund, the largest ever, from ordinary people. He used the "Fifth Estate". He created a more democratic process, using the Internet and texting that suited young people. That achievement alone is an inspiration. He is now in regular e-mail contact with that vast constituency, using its members not only as a sounding board but to provide constant feedback on his performance.

US Open Government Directive. On his first day in office Obama issued his Open Government Directive, stating that his administration should be transparent, participatory and collaborative:

> *My Administration is committed to creating an unprecedented level of openness in Government. We will work together to ensure the public trust and establish a system of transparency, public participation, and collaboration. Openness will strengthen our democracy and promote efficiency and effectiveness in Government.*

In his victory speech on 6 November 2008, Barack Obama singled out one woman as someone who embodied the spirit of his election win. Ann Nixon Cooper, aged 106, was born when women and black people were not allowed to vote. In a BBC interview, she spoke about the enormous changes she had witnessed during her lifetime. She feels nothing but relief that things have changed as much as they have. Some day maybe we'll all be one, she reflected.

Obama gives hope to the world again, especially to oppressed peoples. ***"Yes We Can!"*** is a beacon for taking personal responsibility and the cause of better democracy throughout the world. He has been clear that it will be a long hard struggle. Black Americans know that from experience. He is committed to listening to people, including them in the process, telling the truth and taking thoughtful, considered action in a disciplined, deliberative way. In appointing his own team, he refers back to Abraham Lincoln's example of appointing former adversaries to his Cabinet, a "team of rivals" that helped him in the Union's darkest hour.

Barack Obama provides inspiration for a world that desperately needs it – *The Audacity of Hope,* as he titled his second book. His inspiration could not have come at a better moment. However, the United States of America is an extremely divided nation. He knows he'll disappoint. We are always in danger of expecting too much of one leader. Instead, of expecting too much of one person, all of us need to lead. In a crisis situation as complex as this, the collective leadership and creativity of all humanity is needed. Margaret Wheatley defines a leader as *"Anyone willing to help."* That's my definition too. We all need to express inspiring possibilities as a positive intention.

The human story is a long struggle to emerge out of oppression, poverty, chaos, intolerance and violence. Some would say it is a dialogue between good and evil – generosity and greed, love and hate below which is fear. It is also a story of unintended consequences and disappointment. We fail to learn from history; we quickly forget. If only leaders learned from history. Ever since we emerged on the planet, we have been on a journey of discovery and experimentation. It is all a mystery. Each of us has to give it meaning and find our unique purpose. I believe we are progressing, constantly experimenting, constantly learning from failures, often lurching from one extreme to another.

Maybe we are at the end of a thirty year long nightmare, inspired by the doctrines of Milton Friedman, grasped by

Margaret Thatcher and Ronald Reagan without intellectual rigour or integrity, taken even further by George Bush, Tony Blair and Gordon Brown. We forgot the lessons of the Great Crash of 29 October 1929 and the Great Depression that followed and undid all the measures introduced by FDR to prevent that happening again. At Bretton Woods, the American negotiator rejected some of the most important ideas of John Maynard Keynes, designed to prevent a repetition. Milton Friedman's doctrines of monetary policy, taxation, privatisation and deregulation informed policies of governments around the globe, including the USA, the UK, Canada, New Zealand, Chile and, after 1989, many Eastern European countries – to their people's cost.

These doctrines were forced on poor countries, as a condition of access to markets, aid and loans – the latter have led to enormous burdens of debt and interest repayments. For many, this was a disaster. Linked with Bush's message of *"freedom loving peoples"* and so-called democracy forced on entirely different cultures, his doctrines gave a few people freedom to make a lot of money at the expense of everyone else. Amongst the casualties have been many jobs and steady demise of reliable pension schemes.

Not with our consent

Experiments based on extreme, untested theories have been conducted at the expense of "ordinary people", inflicted on us without our informed consent, by leaders, many of whom lack the essential qualifications for global leadership – humility, integrity, ecological and environmental education, awareness of the need to involve people in change, openness to learning, and an understanding of how to resolve conflict. Often they have been unwilling to tell us the truth. Global media monopoly keeps people misled and badly informed.

We have been guinea pigs for these experiments! The

process has brought us to the brink of the greatest disaster of all time. But that realisation can open our eyes, help us decide: ***"never again"*** and make it a time of opportunity. This time we have learned more and it could be different. Hopefully we are less naïve. It can be a hopeful time again.

The disastrous Iraq war begun without a UN resolution, the necessary risk assessment or long-term strategy, fought on a false premise, against the advice of experienced experts, was an "eye opener" to millions. It was also a disillusioning experience for the millions who marched to protest against it. We should not give up.

We need a different set of guiding principles at this stage in our evolution when we are more than ever one world. Unlike many of its advisers and citizens, our government failed to grasp the importance of ecology, the "precautionary principle" or the need for rigorous risk assessment before letting loose potentially dangerous technologies, or making strategic decisions affecting the environment and the future of humanity. We are entitled to expect leaders to act with due diligence. Joe Klein's interview with Barack Obama for TIME on 3 November 2008 was widely reported:

> *What seems important or clever or in need of some dramatic moment a lot of times just needs reflection and care.*

Barack Obama

New Labour was often dangerously ignorant and unyielding to the best advice. It failed to see the ironies of using violence to end violence and creating more debt to solve a crisis caused by excessive debt, or the alternatives (Chapter 10). Will the Lib-Dem Conservative coalition be different? We need leaders with open minds who see themselves as servants and put listening, honesty, integrity and the public interest before all else.

Wilful leaders have to be restrained. They are like wild horses and we have to tame them. We need participatory democracy that gives people real involvement. We cannot afford any longer to be discouraged, disengaged and uninformed. Leaving it to "them" is not an option. The crisis will not be resolved unless we citizens take our power, support and use the many NGOs to bring about change, seek reliable sources of information to inform ourselves, lobby our MPs and push government and big business relentlessly!

If we are not angry we need to be! We must become active world citizens, organise, protest, use the Internet, demonstrate, use civil disobedience if necessary and insist on a proper world democracy. The often secretive decision-making process monopolised by governments and big corporations, who dislike contrary voices, is dysfunctional. Business is there to serve people, not itself. Governments need to serve people, not business. We cannot allow wilful leaders to put politics, corporate interests or their personal egos before the needs of people and planet.

Sleaze and corruption are endemic. How can senior politicians take a strong stand for the interests of citizens, and protect us from Big Business, when there may be lucrative jobs for them once out of office? It was reported that Tony Blair would earn around £2 million a year in his part-time role providing "strategic advice and insight" to JP Morgan, the US investment bank. In addition the deal for his memoirs was reported to be worth at least £5 million. It is alleged that members of the House of Lords, that absurd name for an outdated second chamber that reinforces our class system, take cash to change legislation. In the dying days of the last Parliament, the fiddles became notorious – abusing their expenses, which they tried to hide, voting themselves out of step pay increases, vastly expensive pensions, in contrast to the deteriorating pensions most citizens face.

Politicians need principles, integrity and courage. That must include intellectual integrity, telling the truth as honestly as they can. This is barely possible within an adversarial party political system in which representatives slag each other off and are "whipped" into toeing the party line. Given the political system and media that we have, speaking and acting with integrity takes massive courage. But all confidence in our leaders will be lost if they don't do it.

Because of human nature, we need powerful institutions that force us to do the right thing and act with honesty.

The purpose of this book is to encourage "ordinary" people to believe they can change the world for the better. It is becoming increasingly clear that everyone needs to get involved in politics. No leader, however gifted and inspiring, can do it without citizens' support. That support must include ***challenging*** our leaders. Disagreement, diverse and conflicting views are essential to avoid disastrous, wilful courses of action like those of George Bush and Tony Blair. They acted without due diligence and integrity.

When Greenpeace activists were arrested for painting a slogan on a chimney at Kingsnorth coal power plant, the High Court ruled it was warranted in order to prevent the much greater damage that would result from global warming. The World Development Movement (WDM) calculated that a new power station at Kingsnorth would create 30,000 climate refugees. WDM argued that this would be unjust to the developing world and should not be allowed to happen.

Al Gore says we have reached the stage where civil disobedience is needed to prevent the construction of coal plants that do not have carbon capture. We know that effective carbon capture is a long way off being proven or commercially viable. Like nuclear power, it could merely store up severe problems for future generations. Isn't it extraordinary that we have to do these things to prevent our own governments, which should be protecting us, from endangering the future of humanity?

Pressure works. It is all very well to say just get on with things and take individual action. That on its own is not enough. We have to bring about system change. That means campaigning, being an activist. It was public pressure, through Friends of the Earth and other campaigning groups, that changed the UK Climate Change Act, raising the 2050 CO2 reduction target from 60 to 80 per cent and the inclusion of aviation and shipping. Constant pressure has forced companies to react.

Activism is my rent for living on the planet.
Alice Walker

Changing the global economic system requires us to transform democracy and rethink human rights. Protection from the consequences of an economic system that results in climate change needs to be part of the Universal Declaration of Human Rights, as Mary Robinson argues. As Ecuador has done, we also need to acknowledge the rights of nature and our fellow species and not treat them as inferior and merely there to serve our needs. Democracy has to be unlocked everywhere if the world is to be transformed. Democracy can only work if citizens are fully informed. Democracies like ours need to lead the way.

We need a new inspiration for our lives, beyond consumerism and greed, the possibility of a sustainable, just world and an end to violence as our way of dealing with conflict and difference. This is a book for people who, in their hearts, want to make this happen. That is almost all of us, if we knew how and believed we could make a difference. We can do this, as well as earn a living and bring up our families. We just have to prioritise the unique contributions we want to make. It means each of us knowing who we are, identifying what most matter s to us. We need to know our purpose in being on this Earth.

I aim to open eyes. The corporate and conventional view gets overwhelming exposure, through huge advertising budgets, infiltration of government and politics, enticements, increasing control of education and research, withholding information, punitive treatment of whistle-blowers, wielding the law as a weapon, and media domination. Until recently, what amounts to corporate corruption or criminality, dressed in a blue suit, went almost unnoticed and unpunished, unlike working-class criminality. I am far from anti-business, but against corporate abuse of power and an economic system that is both harmful to smaller and local businesses and endangers our lives and well-being on a massive scale.

Human beings are inherently creative. We have survived by adapting. When we see the need for change, we begin to transform the system and create something new. This time it must be done much faster! The vast majority care about their fellow human beings. The most powerful influence in the world is love. You see this in families and all the good, caring things people do in their communities. We need to apply love to the great global transformation.

Chapter 2

Understanding the Financial Crisis

Begun December 2008

When the capital development of a country becomes a by-product of a casino, the job is likely to be ill-done.
John Maynard Keynes

Never in the field of endeavour has so much money been owed by so few to so many.
Mervyn King

Setting the scene

Extraordinary affluence: Robert Peston's description of two examples of extraordinary affluence, summarised here, sets the scene for this chapter. Indian businessman Mukesh Ambani built a 27 storey tower in Mumbai to house his family and staff. His wealth was valued at US$15.5bn (according to Forbes), making him the richest man in Asia and the world's seventh richest. Lakshmi Mitt, Indian steel magnate, paid £57m in 2004 for an eighteen bedroom mansion in London (Peston, R, 2008).

In contrast, 62 per cent of Mumbai's population live in slums. India has massive poverty. Most people in Mumbai, to which many poor people have migrated, live in slums and shantytowns. They cover only 6.8 per cent of the city's land yet 62 per cent of the population live in them. Much of this poverty is caused by dispossessing poor people from their lands to make way for industrialisation, denying them the means to feed themselves. A ghastly example of some consequences of India's rapid economic growth is *in North East India, where "... vast subterranean coal fires burn out of control beneath towns and villages in the Jharia coalfields in Jharkhand state. The air is filled with smoke and poisonous gas as fires smoulder in the ground from underground coal seams which are spontaneously combusting over an area of several hundred square kilometres. Children mine coal here day in day out, and half a million people are being moved out of their ancestral villages to make way for the coal mines fuelling India's growth." (Unreported World: India, Children of the Inferno, 2009)*

The worst financial crisis since the Great Depression

As I continued writing in December 2008 the worst financial crisis since the Great Depression was unfolding. It was brought about by the greed of a few reckless people, lack of competence and integrity, and governments and business leaders with an uncritical belief in unproven economic theories. $10.8trn worth of global equities had been lost. The world's financial institutions faced losses of $2,800,000,000. These are unimaginable figures, more than enough to implement the UN Millennium goals and save the world from the consequences of climate change and Peak Oil. Just $500bn would have been enough to cancel all "Third World" (that condescending phrase) debt.

National debt. Robert Peston said we borrowed too much. The ratio of our record £4000 billion consumer, big company (especially through private equity) and public-sector debt to our annual economic output or GDP is just over 300 per cent. Householders borrowed £1200 billion in mortgages alone. (Peston, R, 2008). In January 2009 UK national debt reached £697.5bn, 47.5 per cent of £1473bn GDP. The Centre for Policy Studies claimed that government figures for national debt, wrongly excluded the cost of public sector pension liabilities, the hidden costs of New Labour's flagship Private Finance Initiatives (PFI) contracts and debts incurred by Network Rail. When these are taken into account total national debt was three times what government claimed. We were not the most indebted. The per cent figures for other large economies in 2009 were US 60.8, France 63.9, Germany 64.9, Italy 104, Japan 170. US national debt had grown steadily since the end of WWII and was expected to reach $11trn.

The cost of rescue. Governments committed $2trn to be injected into the banking system. The proposed US economic rescue bill reached $800bn to $1.3trn. The UK government gave £39bn to three of our biggest banks – Royal Bank of Scotland, Lloyds TSB and HBOS – by buying shares in them to provide new capital. Some commentators predicted UK government borrowing could reach £120bn by 2010/11, or 7.8 per cent of national output.

The general picture was clear. Deeply in debt, we'd pay for it in higher taxes, public expenditure cuts and recession. Mervyn King, Bank of England governor, described it as the worst financial crisis since WWI.

How it happened. The financial crisis was brought about by excessive lending and debt, reckless selling and mergers, gambling by bankers and the creation of ingenious, opaque devices that made the financial market too complex to understand or control: short selling, "securitisation", derivatives, hedge funds and private equity. The failures of the US credit agency and UK's Financial Services Agency all contributed to the collapse. As systems become increasingly complex, they become increasingly unstable. Even the banks could not understand the system and that became the problem. They could not value their assets, assess their risks nor trust each other. So they were reluctant to lend. In 2001 bank dependence on net wholesale funding from other banks and financial institutions was nil; by 2007, it had become £625bn. That boosted property values too much. When all this was realised in August 2008, trust collapsed.

It first began to show in the USA. The "sub-prime crisis" was caused by unscrupulous lending to people who did not have the income to buy a home. That inevitably led to large-scale repossessions and contributed to a depressed housing market. Imprudent lending led to the failures of mortgage lenders, insurance companies, a world-wide "credit crunch" and collapse of the banking system and the stock market crash. The spreading of risky debt around the banking system contributed to its complexity and made banks reluctant to lend to each other.

Recklessness was encouraged by a culture in which huge remuneration and bonuses were regarded as acceptable – though not by the general public. It was allowed by inadequate regulation and supervision. The taxation regime disproportionately favours the very rich and large businesses at the expense of small businesses, middle classes and the poor and allows extensive tax evasion and tax havens. London drew in super-rich people and entrepreneurs, including 116,000 "non-doms", who were allowed to avoid paying their proper share of tax. That further inflated an already escalating property market. It fostered a culture of breathtaking greed, justified by the theory that it helped make the UK prosperous.

Do we really want our country to prosper in such a way? It has had a corrupting effect on whole of society and spreads like a virus.

These policies make it hard for "ordinary" people to buy a home, especially first-time buyers, people on low incomes, including essential workers, living in big cities and rural areas where prices have been driven up by wealthy buyers. An escalating housing market puts families under huge pressure to earn enough to pay their mortgages. This has personal and social consequences. With the encouragement of banks, their lax lending policies and cheap credit, the nation became over-indebted. Often both partners with children had to work full time, many working excessive, if not intolerable hours with further consequences for children and marriages. Then properties became worth less than the mortgage. This is not real wealth, based on productive industries, skilled work of which people feel proud, businesses creating human well-being. Social mobility continues to be elusive and our children are amongst the unhappiest in Europe.

"Ordinary" taxpayers and savers foot the bill for government interventions needed to stabilise the system. It is low and middle income taxpayers whose contribution to taxes is disproportionately high. The rich and super-rich pay disproportionately low rates of tax and employ experts to minimise or avoid tax and keep their money offshore. Furthermore, low interest rates, introduced to revive a failing economy, hit hardest small savers, who outnumber mortgagees, pensioners and local government investments. We are still paying for obscene bonuses.

Taxes are "perverse" in the sense that rich people pay least proportionately. The already very wealthy are best able to benefit from the City's expertise and ingenuity not only in getting richer but also in tax avoidance and evasion, offshore tax havens and money laundering. This is expertise in making even more money out of money, rather than creating real wealth. It includes buying and selling companies as if they were possessions, gambling on the stock exchange. These practices make life even more insecure for ordinary people and are an avoidance of responsibility to society and fellow human beings.

This makes people angry; the robbing of the poor to bail out the rich.

> *The free market preachers have long practised state welfare for the rich...*
>
> **George Monbiot**, *Guardian*, 30 September 2008

President Bush inherited a small surplus of $240bn; Barack Obama inherited a deficit of over $1.2trn. The US Treasury debt was believed to be $4trn or 30 per cent of US GDP. In October

2008, Eurozone governments pledged around $3trn to restore confidence in the banking system. The UK Government's package of measures aimed at rescuing the banking system would make $692bn available. The total UK money rescue plan involved some £600bn. Banks would get a £46bn cash injection that might rise to £75bn, compared with total annual public spending, including Health and Education, of £618bn. Britain's deficit was likely to reach £90.1bn in 2009/10.

Breathtaking irresponsibility, lack of awareness and criminality. Financial sector payments made up some two-thirds of the bonuses across the entire British economy. Total bonus payments in 2007 hit £28bn. According to the Office for National Statistics (ONS), bonus payments in the UK financial sector had more than trebled since 2003. This was for just over one million employees in the sector but heavily skewed towards the high-powered executives who regularly received seven-figure bonuses.

Lack of awareness and responsibility was breathtaking. In the City sums like £7000 were spent on a single bottle of champagne. There were reports of AIG Insurance, bailed out by US taxpayers, spending $440,000 on a lavish corporate retreat. Barclays bankers at were said to be flying to Italy for a £500,000 three-day corporate trip to a five-star hotel on Lake Como. There were similar reports of eighty bankers entertaining 100 clients and their partners at the 16th century Villa d'Este in Cernobbio and over one hundred Barclays Private Equity staff enjoying a break at £1800 a night in the French Riviera.

In December 2008 an astonishing example of criminality appeared, the alleged $50bn /£33bn fraud, involving a hedge fund run by Bernard Madoff, former chairman of the NASDAQ stock market. Banks affected included Britain's RBS, Spain's Santander and France's BNP Paribas. According to the US Attorney, Mr Madoff told several employees that the $17.1bn hedge fund business was a fraud that had been insolvent for years. He reportedly said, *"a giant Ponzi scheme,"* it finally collapsed like a stack of cards.

The salaries, bonuses and pensions of bankers and others responsible for the global financial and economic meltdown were scandalous. Risky short-term transactions rewarded at the expense of beneficial long-term investment. The basic pay of Bob Diamond, who runs the City arm of Barclays Bank, was £250,000 in 2007, but his total pay including bonuses and shares was £21m. In January 2008 he received £14.8m from another incentive scheme. Many of these huge rewards are hidden. Sir Fred Goodwin, who resigned as chief executive of the Royal Bank of Scotland to receive £20bn cash from government, earned £5.375m in 2008. He waived his right to a £1.2m payoff but was entitled to an annual pension of £579,000. RBS made the biggest corporate annual loss in history – more than £24.1bn, partly because of the unwise decision to buy ailing ABN Amro at a peak price! Despite the catastrophic failure of RBS under his stewardship, he refused to give back any of his likely pension pot of almost £30 million. City bankers like these seem completely out of touch with ordinary people and their feelings of anger. Why are such people awarded knighthoods?

There is a common pattern in human affairs. "Whistle-blowers" are ignored until it is too late and punished. Paul Moore, the former head of risk at HBOS, was fired for warning his board of the risks of their "overeager sales culture". It is now revealed that the Royal Bank of Scotland was involved in enormous schemes, some £25bn to cut its tax bill and avoid some £500m of tax annually. The latest revelations claim that Barclays made close to £1bn profit a year from a series of elaborate deals so complex that HM Revenues and Customs struggles to unravel them. A whistle-blower said that such schemes were central to Barclay's business.

Stealth and sleight of hand. Chancellor of the Exchequer, Gordon Brown, a decent man with good intentions, was deeply involved in building London City as the kind of global financial centre it has become. It is widely believed that he thought he could, with ingenuity and sleight of hand, disguise tax increases, for example by increasing National Insurance contributions. His early tax changes undermined pension schemes and made them even more vulnerable. Now ordinary people suffer the consequences. Flaws in our democracy allow this kind of behaviour. Proper scrutiny in Parliament would have prevented it. Like many of us at the time, he was trapped in a flawed mindset. We are all on a steep learning curve and need open minds.

The UK Government boasted our economy was the 4th richest in the world. As a result of Thatcher and New Labour policies, the UK became the fourth richest economy. But it is an unbalanced economy, too dependent on North Sea oil and gas while it lasted, too dependent on arms manufacture, retail and financial services. Manufacturing now accounts for only 13 per cent of our economy.

In 1979 when Margaret Thatcher came to power, she was confronted with the need to transform a Britain that had become one of the poorest countries in Europe. As decline in our manufacturing industries left thousands without work, she set up incapacity benefit, intended for people near the end of their working lives. But that has led to an unintended legacy of dependency, with many people under thirty signing on continuously. In Northern cities like Liverpool and Manchester, as many as a quarter of the population are living on benefits. New Labour, despite strenuous efforts largely failing to tackle poverty, left an unsolved problem for the new government.

It is now clear what has emerged. Like New York, London City became a global centre for making money out of money and the most expensive city property in the world (now displaced by Moscow). Its prosperity was built too much on ingenious and opaque devices to make rich people richer, enabling them to avoid tax. The City, rather than fulfilling its proper role of supporting enterprises that create real wealth, played the major part in creating the current crisis, credit boom and bust and making homes unaffordable. New Labour presided over a period of growth dependent on excessive consumer spending, record levels of personal debt. It contributed to an even more unequal society.

Gordon Brown loosened control of the City. He wisely made the Bank of England independent of government in 1997, but stripped away its regulatory powers to supervise banks and other providers of financial services, transferring them to a newly created Financial Services Authority (FSA). This took away its most important function and did not work. The FSA was cut off from essential information and had too little power.

The roots of the crisis

> *If banks feel they must keep on dancing while the music is playing and that at the end of the party the central bank will make sure everyone gets home safely, then over time the parties will become wilder and wilder.*
> **Mervyn King** 10 June 2008

> *As long as the music is playing, you've got to get up and dance.*
> **Chuck Prince**, outgoing CEO of Citibank

Chuck Prince was being honest about himself. It would take greater courage to call a halt to the dance. The collapse of the global banking, with all its reverberations, has its roots in untested economic theories, originating in the USA, supported by most Western governments and imposed by global institutions as ***the*** way to increase prosperity and raise the poor out of poverty. It is a world run by an elite of mega rich and powerful people who worship the *"Great Gods"* of continuous economic growth and free market capitalism. These theories were not validated, nor generally questioned, until now.

"Mono-culture of the mind". The world has been subjected to what Vandana Shiva calls *"Mono-culture of the mind."* After World War Two, the USA wanted to keep its factories busy. They re-invented the *"buy now pay later"* consumer society that brought on the 1929 crash, adding built-in obsolescence, and subliminal advertising to create dissatisfaction and wants that were more powerful than needs. A new form of capitalism unfolded. However, in 1945 after a conference at Bretton Woods, regulatory measures were adopted that were intended to prevent a repetition of the Great Depression of the Thirties. A system of rules, institutions, and procedures were set up to regulate the international monetary system. The forerunners of the World Bank and the International Monetary Fund (IMF) were set up. A relatively benign period ensued in which incomes generally improved.

However, in the Eighties, economist Milton Friedman's controversial ideas on a free market economy, monetary policy, taxation, privatisation and deregulation began to be widely adopted by leaders such as Ronald Reagan and Margaret Thatcher. These ideas were imposed on poor countries by the World Trade Organisation (WTO), World Bank and IMF, often with disastrous consequences (Chapter 4).

Total System Failure. A process had begun that ultimately led to the current crisis and what Joseph Stiglitz calls system failure. It also contributed to massive, accelerating unsustainable economic growth. The process is described in his article in Vanity Fair, January 2009. For parts of the following analysis I am indebted to his thinking.

The truth is most of the individual mistakes boil down to just one: a belief that markets are self-adjusting and that the role of government should be minimal.

Joseph Stiglitz

As a result of policies started by Margaret Thatcher and continued by New Labour, a "flexible labour market" meant worsening terms for employees and job insecurity. The UK's much admired company pension schemes for employees, especially final salary schemes started to collapse. Business invaded everything and "service" was secondary.

In his book *Who Runs Britain,* Robert Peston argues that under New Labour a small group of super-rich dictated large amounts of government policy. They were given access to Downing Street and the Treasury to a new extent. Nothing like it occurred under Margaret Thatcher. In return for comparatively small financial contributions to the Labour Party, they were given what amounted to exemption from the obligation to pay taxation. The effect was to create private wealth on a scale not been seen since before World War One.

Debt was a key piece of the jigsaw. Our apparently growing prosperity was based on benefiting from other countries' (China, India, Japan and Saudi) propensity to save – their thrift paid for our big binge. By borrowing from them, we systematically transferred their savings to fund our growth. The rub is that much of our country is now owned by them. We have to pay growing interest and ultimately repay the debt. These extremely clever people and our leaders were not wise enough to see this. Unfortunately there is no correlation between being extremely clever and being wise. That's the lesson for us, 6.7 billion people: we can't leave it to them!

The rocket scientists of finance they employed were amongst the cleverest people on Earth, but their technology was complicated and fragile. It was bound to end in tears.
Evan Davies, *City Uncovered,* BBC2, 14 January 2009

Summary
The roots of the crisis and the dismantling of regulation

- President Richard Nixon devalues the dollar, which begins to undermine the system set up at Bretton Woods, at the end of WWII.
- President Reagan, ex B movie star, presides over a process of financial deregulation, removing Paul Volker as Chairman of the Federal Reserve Board and appointing Alan Greenspan.
- Mrs Thatcher begins similar policies in UK. The destruction of the real economy begins and the seeds of a bubble are sown.
- The long-term effect in USA is a massive infrastructure legacy for Barack Obama to address. Mrs Thatcher bequeathed similar problems here in UK.
- Privatisation and hasty, cheap sell-offs of taxpayers' investments make a few people extremely rich.
- Privatisation does not necessarily lead to better value or service to the public.
- Tony Blair continues the process, privatisation by stealth, introducing competition and business concepts into public services, health, education and prisons.
- Mutual savings banks, building societies, banks and insurance companies become PLCs, raising capital by borrowing on the financial markets. Former members are tempted by shares and windfalls. Banks merge and small savings banks and mutual societies are swallowed up by big banks.
- Ownership of companies becomes more remote as they are taken over and larger and larger transnational corporations are formed. Changes in ownership

become more frequent.

- It becomes a game like Monopoly, without responsibility for people's needs, work or lives.
- Larger means more remote from communities and their needs.
- The advent in the 1980s and 1990s of Private Equity not publicly traded or listed on a stock exchange, the boom in "leveraged buyouts", "corporate raiders" and "hostile takeovers".
- "Leveraged buyouts" impose huge indebtedness that bears down on companies and leads to deteriorating terms for employees including their pension schemes.
- Western countries export manufacturing to developing countries and the UK economy becomes too dependent on retail and financial services. We cease to know how to make things. Some areas of the country become deprived waste lands.
- Boom and Bust: The Hi-tech bubble is followed by the housing bubble.
- Self-regulation by banks and corporations becomes the credo.
- After intense lobbying Congress repeals the Glass-Steagall Act that had separated commercial banks (that lend money) from Investment banks (that sell equities) to prevent conflicts of interest. This was a catastrophic error.
- Gordon Brown took away the regulatory powers of the Bank of England giving them to a weak FSA.
- Slowly, Britain's once admired employee pension schemes were eroded, in some cases raided.

Thus the scene was set.

How the banking crisis and global recession emerged

- Banks start lending irresponsibly, their senior people awarding themselves huge bonuses based on short-term earnings.
- Banks are next allowed to increase their debt – to capital ratios which inflates the housing bubble.
- Tax cuts and lower interest rates add further fuel to the fire.
- Incentives such as stock options encourage top management to adopt short-term attitudes; huge bonuses for bankers encourage risky investments.
- Complicated instruments such as derivatives – "weapons of mass destruction" as Warren Buffet calls them – are created by banks; these make supervision difficult. "Gambling" becomes widespread.
- Securitisation – "rocket securities"– is the next innovation, invented in USA and adopted by Lehman and Northern Rock. In both cases, under a certain kind of arrogant leadership, it leads to meltdown.
- "Sub-prime mortgages" are offered to poor people who have little chance of being able to keep up payments and the resulting large-scale defaults and foreclosures precipitate the crisis.
- These developments and the complexity of inter-bank lending lead to a complete lack of confidence within in the banking industry and the so-called credit crunch.
- On both sides of the Atlantic, particularly in USA and UK, flawed incentive structures, an inadequate regulatory system and inadequate supervision e.g. USA credit rating agencies and the UK Financial Services Authority (FSA) allow a situation to develop that they were designed to prevent.

- Takeovers by Private Equity investors increase leverage (indebtedness), hence ultimately increasing costs, and reduce the availability of company information.
- "Structured finance" is used by bankers to put billions and billions of dollars and pounds in offshore havens, many in British crown colonies like Antigua, the Bahamas, British Virgin Islands, Barbados and the Caymans, to avoid billions in tax.
- The US and Western economies become dependent on cheap goods and huge borrowings from thrifty China, Japan, India and Saudi Arabia. USA and UK have become hugely indebted to these countries.
- Consumer and business borrowing reach unprecedented levels.
- UK and US government borrowing debt reaches unprecedented levels too.
- Before the bubble bursts UK house prices, particularly in the south east, reach the highest levels. Housing becomes increasingly unaffordable for young first-time buyers and essential workers.
- Governments bail out the banks whilst banks continue to hold lavish parties and meetings and pay out money to shareholders. Failed bank bosses still collect huge settlements. The taxpayer will pay.
- Meanwhile there has been a massive collapse of confidence, leading to recession, job losses, further defaults on mortgages, damage to pension schemes, major falls in the value of equities in the stock markets which damages rich and poor.
- The bail outs do not actually result in essential lending to businesses because the banks have made too many bad loans.

- The FTSE 100 index (cut will have) recorded the worst annual performance in its 24 year history when markets closed on New Year's Eve 2008, notching up a near 33% decline. Nikkei index in Japan closed at its lowest in 26 years.
- In early March 2009, whilst the recession continued, the Bank of England cut its interest rate to 0.5%, the lowest in its 315 year history, and the Bank and UK government agreed to use "quantitative easing" to put £75bn to £150bn extra money into the economy.

Notes: for full definitions of these terms go to Wikipedia.

Hedge funds "A hedge fund is an investment fund open to a limited range of investors that is permitted by regulators to undertake a wider range of investment and trading activities than other investment funds and pays a performance fee to its investment manager." Wikipedia – Hedge Fund.

Leveraging "Leveraging in finance, or gearing, is borrowing money to supplement existing funds for investment in such a way that the potential positive or negative outcome is magnified and/or enhanced. Financial leverage (FL) takes the form of a loan or other borrowings (debt), the proceeds of which are (re)invested with the intent to earn a greater rate of return than the cost of interest. Wikipedia –Finance.

Private equity "Private equity is an asset class consisting of equity securities in operating companies that are not publicly traded on a stock exchange". Wikipedia – Private Equity.

Securitization is a structured finance process that distributes risk by aggregating assets in a pool (often by selling assets to a special purpose entity), then issuing new securities backed by the assets and their cash flows. The securities are sold to investors who share the risk and reward from those assets. It is similar to a sale of a profitable business ("spinning off") into a separate entity. Wikipedia – Securitization.

Short selling "Short selling or "shorting" is the practice of selling a financial instrument that the seller does not own at the time of the sale." Wikipedia – Finance.

An unbalanced economy was created, that eroded our ability to make things, took away pride in doing well by doing good, destroyed communities, de-skilled people and created massive insecurity. Amongst the legacies of the Reagan/Thatcher era is a huge infrastructure problem which, in the USA, Barack Obama is now seeking to address. In the UK, using Private Finance Initiatives (PFI) and Public Private Partnerships (PPP) to address this legacy has added to and disguised the debt burden.

Do privatisation and these devices provide value for money? These crucial questions remain unanswered. Government has not published evaluations, not ones I am aware of, as to whether the privatisation of railways, health services, hospitals, prisons and schools, their construction and refurbishment, London Underground refurbishment and many other initiatives have been or are value for money. Similarly extensive outsourcing (hospital cleaning services for instance) PPP and PFI have not been properly evaluated. Government used its majority with the Tories to force things through, often against the advice of cross-party parliamentary committees. The New Labour era was characterised as privatising by stealth.

Let's be clear. A corporation is legally required to serve its shareholders, ***not*** stakeholders or the public. Directors are good at serving themselves. It is naïve to have other expectation. Therefore, we cannot accept blanket theories that privatisation offers better value. We need rigorously independent evaluation.

Underlying it all is making decisions from ideology instead of relentlessly seeking what works. Margaret Thatcher, no doubt with the best of intentions and facing massive economic problems, inflicted unproven theories on the country. George

Monbiot's article *You are being fleeced in the biggest, weirdest rip-off yet: a widened M25* (Monbiot, G, 2009) exposes the excessive cost and absurdity of PFI schemes and the propensity to create ingenious devices to hide the truth. Under PFI, he explains, private companies build public infrastructure – roads, bridges, schools, hospitals, prisons and the rest – then lease it back to the state for 25 or 30 years. Over 800 deals have been signed since the scheme was launched in 1992. They committed the taxpayers to spending around £215bn. For new hospitals built under private finance initiatives, it has been estimated that the NHS in England faces a total bill of £65bn including rising charges of more than 10 per cent of their turnover.

He continues, Government argued that because private companies are more efficient than the state, PFI is cheaper than public procurement. But that does not appear to be so. PFI schemes must be tested against a yardstick called the public sector comparator. However, as government underwrites the scheme, the greater part of the risk falls on taxpayers, negating the rationale of PFI. Furthermore because of greater risks during recession, banks backing PFI infrastructure projects increased their margins, in some cases by 500 per cent. The irony is the government now lends cheap money to the banks, who then charge us very high rates of interest for the use of our own cash. These banks are now mostly or partly owned by us. Taking the example of the M25 expansion financed through RBS, George Monbiot points out that we, the taxpayers, will be bailing RBS out twice; providing the bail out ***and*** paying the interest rates, bankers' fees, including salaries and bonuses. RBS (in other words you and me) already has £10bn invested in PFI schemes in this country, for which we are paying extravagant rates. And as PFI schemes are counted as public sector debt, he asks why the government doesn't just cut out the middleman and fund the project itself? For how such projects could be financed without debt see Chapter 10.

People are angry and afraid. Almost every business was reporting falling profits. BA's CEO described *"incredibly difficult trading conditions"* and *"the bleakest trading environment ever."* Unemployment was predicted to reach 3.3 million the end of 2009. The financial collapse impacts on the savings, pensions and livelihoods of ordinary people and large numbers of people have entered negative equity. Repossessions increased by 71 per cent compared with the same months in 2007.

Putting it all into perspective, of 6.7 billion people in the world, 1 billion are hungry. Sixty per cent of humans live on just 6 per cent of the world's resources. Twenty-two million Africans have AIDS. From the perspective of poor and developing countries, the North has shown a callous disregard for the consequences of their greed for the majority in the world. This has been going on for a long time. But by December 2010 the number of people living on less than $1.25 a day will be about 90 million higher because of the far-reaching impacts of the financial crisis. The food price hike from 2005 to 2008 pushed an additional 130 million people below the $1.25 a day poverty line, according to the World Bank. Recent oil price increases pushed an estimated further 25 million into poverty.

Markets are efficient; but only to a point. Investing in a sustainable future is not in the short-term interests of directors and shareholders. Free enterprise does not allocate resources according to a nation's or the world's long-term priority needs. The market rides roughshod over poor people all over the world. Privatisation has brought refreshing innovation, enterprise and efficiency. It also gave away national assets, paid for by taxpayers, at knock-down prices and made a few people very rich. Privatisation, without rigorous strategic frameworks and regulation, leads to short-term gain at the expense of long-term value. It has probably been poor value for money and has accumulated enormous debts for the nation. Paying for public infrastructure investments through Private Finance Initiatives

(PFI) and Public Private Partnerships (PPP) was a device to get round limits set by the public sector borrowing requirement. How much will we ultimately pay under these devices?

We were warned. Sir Fred Goodwin or Gordon Brown liked to argue that none of this could have been predicted. There were plenty of warnings. We did not listen. Over the decades, clear-sighted people like Mahatma Gandhi, Albert Einstein, John Maynard Keynes, Ernst Schumacher, Kenneth Boulding, Kenneth Galbraith, Herman Daly, Hazel Henderson, George Soros, Joseph Stiglitz, Peter Hawken and Warren Buffett warned us what would happen. Reagan mocked Carter, when he campaigned about Peak Oil in the Seventies, with an artful, *"There you go again!"*

> *God forbid that India should ever take to industrialisation after the manner of the West. The economic imperialism of a single tiny island kingdom (the UK) is today keeping the world in chains. If an entire nation of 300 million took to similar economic exploitation, it would strip the world bare like locusts.*
>
> **Mahatma Gandhi**, 1928

In 1972 *The Limits to Growth* report, commissioned by the Club of Rome, warned of the consequences of a rapidly growing world population and finite resource supplies. It used the World model to simulate the consequence of interactions between the Earth and human systems. Five variables were examined: world population, industrialisation, pollution, food production and resource depletion. An updated version, *Limits to Growth: The 30-Year Update,* was published in 2004. In 2008 Graham Turner published a paper called *"A Comparison of 'The Limits to Growth' with Thirty Years of Reality"*. It examined the past thirty years of reality with the predictions made in 1972 and found that changes in industrial production, food production and pollution are all in line with the book's predictions of economic collapse in the 21st century.

But most leaders, with their celebrity mentors and compliant economists, were too much in the grip of exciting money-making games, technological innovation and the consumer society to heed these warnings. The rest of us were simply managing as best we could, trying to make a living, keep our jobs, bring up our kids, often paying for child care with two parents working, with no time or energy for much else.

All of this has happened on a global scale. The behaviour of the richest countries towards poorer ones is scandalous. We colonised and exploited poorer countries for centuries and still do. The globalised economic system, based on sourcing for lowest-cost, is an updated form of colonialism. Transnational corporations are the new empires, their economies larger than many countries. So- called *"free trade"* is patently *"unfair trade"*. It generates huge quantities of CO2. Military interventions supposedly to install *"democracy"*, lacks credibility. The West supported oppressive regimes, led by dictators and murderers like Pinochet and Saddam Hussein, because they were favourable to Western economic and political interests. We overturned Mohamad Mossadegh's enlightened democratically elected government in Iran because of our oil interests.

The goal of Western foreign policy has been to secure its political and economic interests: oil supplies, other vital resources and markets for big business. Someone said:

> *Would Bush and Blair have gone to war against Iraq, if its main export was bananas?*

We are all up to our necks in this system. We are there by proxy. Business and government do the dirty work, on our behalf, that gets us cheap products, oil and food. We choose to ignore it.

The past thirteen years were wasted. It is a classic case of how, when leaders are "system blind", they completely fail us.

Instead of building a more sustainable, future orientated and balanced economy, they squandered 10 per cent of our wealth on war. We ended up with an economy too dependent on financial services, retail and munitions. Lagging behind other developed nations, the UK failed to make long-term investments to tackle climate change, provide a sustainable transport system and a secure, sustainable supply of electricity, heating and energy. Generally deferring to business interests, Government was far too slow in taking far-sighted decisions. It did not recognise the need for a new paradigm. Nor did it provide sufficient strategic vision with actions to back it up. Government must be pressured into doing so.

At last disastrous theories are being challenged but not sufficiently. It will still be *"business as usual"* unless masses of people take a stand and make sure there is a fundamental change in the system and not a superficial "fix". I shall show in Part Two that there are alternative ways of dealing with this crisis, that do not involve massive government borrowing, and ways of preventing such a crisis in future. Remember, institutions do not change radically from within. It is outrageous that the G8 or G20, representing only the wealthiest, largest, and most powerful economies in the world, think they can meet, in a dire emergency, and decide the future of peoples living in 195 countries without involving them. They require outside pressure. It has to be people pressure!

People of the world must insist so-called *"world leaders"* and *"business leaders"* do what's right. I put these terms in quotes because, too often, they don't lead. These misnomers have disempowering effects. Doing what is "politically possible" is an excuse for doing too little. People are outraged; their eyes open to the folly of the past thirty years. Global institutions have imposed an unsustainable economic system on the world. Business and government are there to serve. Leaders should be *Servant Leaders,* instead of self-serving. Our government not only stood by; it fully participated and played a major part of it. Will we allow this to continue?

We ***all*** need to be the world leaders. Collectively, we are better qualified and wiser.

Governments must be pressured into doing the right thing. Millions protested against the Iraq war in approximately 800 cities around the world including 3 million in Rome. A million took to the streets of London, the UK's biggest ever demonstration. Yet Blair, without due diligence, a proper risk assessment or post-conflict strategy, went ahead with an illegal war, without a UN resolution. That was a defining moment for the British people. We cannot let this be repeated.

The UN Climate Summit. In December 2009, leaders from 192 countries gathered for the UN Climate Change Conference in Copenhagen to decide the fate of our planet. On the 5th December 2009, in London and elsewhere, millions marched and put pressure on governments to transform things for the better. The result was disappointing but it was a step forward: there were some outcomes and hopefully much was learned. The signs are that the Lib Dem Conservative Coalition may not have learned the need for radical systems thinking, not ideology. There will be much more for us to do afterwards and throughout the coming years.

It is up to us again.

Chapter 3

We, 6.7 Billion People, Need to Feel Our Anger

October 2008

That anger can provide the energy for fundamental change; we need to transform democracy

These questions keep coming to me:

> *When we are threatened with the biggest disaster in human history, how can we, the majority of 6.7 billion people on the planet, allow our lives to be threatened by a small minority lacking the most essential qualifications for global leadership?*
>
> *Are we, 6.7 billion people, as much as anyone, responsible simply because we do not get engaged? We knew but we did nothing. We chose to leave it to "them". We pretended there was nothing we could do. How will we be regarded by future generations?*

Then I think of our octogenarian local hero:

> *Progress is not made without persistent effort, ignoring setbacks. We are lucky in that campaigning is not life-threatening in England! But not campaigning could be!*
>
> **Zena Bullmore, MBE**, Chairman of Dacorum Hospital Action Group

As I started this chapter, a world recession had begun. Anxious people were cutting their spending and trying to make their precious savings more secure. As unemployment rose, people were afraid of losing their jobs, worrying about their pensions and relatively small investments. Savings were often 40 per cent down, pensions severely affected and houses were being repossessed in increasing numbers. British Chambers of Commerce said unemployment might rise to 3 million by the end of 2009. Many small businesses all over the country are still struggling to survive. It is still hard to get credit to cover running costs and now people face public sector cuts and fear a double dip recession.

I met a lot of angry, frightened people, depressed about the global situation and feeing there is nothing they can do. Beneath depression, often there is anger. As I delivered leaflets and posters for Transition Town Berkhamsted, I listened to retired people, elderly people, carers, local shopkeepers and other small business people. Whether interested in our transition town or not, they had a lot to say. I visited a neighbouring village, about to lose its Post Office and maybe, as a result, their only shop. I found more worried people including the manageress of the pub. All over the country communities are undermined, small shops, pubs and post offices are closing at an alarming rate. Around 27 pubs close per week. Over the past ten years, independent booksellers have declined from 5000 to about 500. 2000 local shops are closing each year. The National Federation of Sub Postmasters predicted 3000 post offices would shut, leaving a network of 9000. The idea of a public service seems to be forgotten. Since 1990, 40 per cent of bank branches have closed. 42 per cent of English towns and villages no longer have a shop of any kind. Government could find billions for bankers and war but not for investment in Royal Mail or a Green New Deal.

In March 2009, it was proposed to use Post Offices to provide banking services we can trust. A coalition of trade unions, business leaders, pensioner and pressure groups called for a new Post Bank, to provide financial services to people and businesses not served by high street lenders. They argued Post Bank would secure the network's future, create 11,000 jobs and establish the form of relationship-banking *"abandoned"* by the country's biggest banks.

Local businesses make up 99 per cent of UK business. They are engines for innovation, growth and job creation. Fifty per cent of their turnover goes back into the local community compared with 5 per cent from supermarkets. Small companies were not responsible for the financial collapse. Their aggregated savings exceed their debt.

Being able to walk to local shops saves CO2 emissions and helps create healthier people and happier communities. Superstores put local shopkeepers out of business. So people have little alternative to using them. Superstores make a huge contribution to CO2 emissions by encouraging people to drive to get a lower price. Their distribution system results in enormous transport emissions. Mirroring the global system, of which superstores are part, all the social and environmental costs are not in the price.

In our town, most small retailers have succumbed to competition from supermarkets, big chains and online shopping. It is a real loss. They are part of the rich fabric of our communities. Many provide advice and small items not available from superstores. We lost an excellent fishmonger, replaced by an ice cream bar. Our independent book shop has gone, replaced, significantly, by a security and safes business. Of two local food shops that remained, one has just closed; the other is struggling. Both have offered healthy organic and ethically sourced food, won countless national awards and contributed with generosity to our community and its health.

Small retailers face unfair competition. Small local shops cannot survive whilst it is easier to drive than walk, safer to drive than cycle. Large retailers provide free, easily accessible parking. Councils argue that business rates are set by

Government and they can't give preferential rates to small businesses. In a recession the chances of survival are even worse for small retailers specialising in ethical and organic food, which only costs more because externalised costs are excluded. Organic sales in the UK have fallen by 30 per cent.

Of course it is the underlying system that created this situation. An inquiry is needed into the unfair competition suffered by small retailers ***from*** supermarkets and not merely supermarkets' relationships with suppliers and farmers. Italy, France and Germany have passed legislation to restrict large stores in favour of smaller shopkeepers. The Lib-Dem Conservative coalition has just announced the go-ahead for a new code of practice governing relations between grocers and suppliers enforced by a Supermarket Ombudsman proposed by MP Tim Farron with all-party support. This does not go far enough. Small retailers need special support from councils in the form of dedicated car parking and fairer rates. Once again, creating a healthier society ultimately saves money.

There is growing awareness of the urgency of food security. Locally produced food, direct from farmers or in local markets and farmers markets can be fresher, more nutritious and cheaper. Stressed people with limited budgets need affordable, easy and convenient options. A government with joined up thinking, serious about climate change, Peak Oil, social costs and fair competition must enact legislation to provide tax incentives, lower business rates, designated parking and other forms of support for small local retailers and organic food. They need to enable better local bus services and infrastructure that makes it more attractive to shop locally and travel on foot or bicycle.

There is massive distrust and cynicism. Perhaps the biggest blow to trust in the political system was when we and our representatives in Parliament were misled and the country was taken into an illegal and ill-conceived war, opposed by vast numbers of citizens. People believe their needs and wishes are ignored by government and local government; consultations are shams. The East of England Plan proposed a vast increase in new housing in our small town and across the local borough over the next 30 years. Little thought was given to providing adequate infrastructure, what is needed to address climate change and Peak Oil or the extreme impacts on small, established communities, some of which may double in size. Our local general hospital is closing, the land to be sold, despite enormous objections and protests by the Dacorum Hospital Action Group, supported by the two local MPs. People now must drive further, through a congested route, causing more emissions.

Inspiring leadership and citizen involvement are lacking. Local politicians are not rising to the biggest leadership challenge: to offer an inspiring vision and bold strategy to tackle our highest priority, *the environmental crisis*. Nor do they understand the need to involve people. People protest vigorously if they feel strongly, but have no faith in consultations. To the despair of councillors, few people participate in consultations. ***Councils don't get it: they consult but don't involve people from the start, a vital difference.*** A major problem is that a town of 22,000 people has virtually no autonomy to decide its future. Decisions taken by Berkhamsted Town Council are frequently overruled by the Borough, in turn severely constrained by central government. We need local democracy that really involves local people and engages their creativity and energy.

The Principle of Subsidiarity needs to be applied. We have the most centralised government in Europe. New laws and important strategic decisions are often passed through rapidly without adequate scrutiny. More decisions need to be pushed down. Local people are the experts on what they need. Subsidiarity is an ***organizing*** principle: matters are best handled by the smallest, lowest or least centralised competent authority. We need to demand government transfers more power to communities. See Chapter 11: *Unlocking Democracy*.

British towns have become "clone towns". *"Clone Town Britain"* was invented by the New Economics Foundation (nef) in their famous report. What I have described is typical of the whole country with rare exceptions. Most towns are ruined by overdevelopment, chain stores and supermarkets, out of town warehouse stores, with all the inevitable traffic, CO2 emissions and pollution. Historic high streets have been spoiled by ugly, garish shop fronts, poor architecture and cheap building. We have lost much of the traditional architecture and historic individuality that make towns delightful. Our communities are damaged by the loss of unique high street shops. People cannot see the sense of it all, especially when Peak Oil and Climate Change make it important for people to drive less and walk or cycle more.

At the root of *Clone Town Britain* is an unsustainable global economic system that puts economic growth, cheapness, making money and the interests of big business and developers before the needs and well-being of people. Everything is becoming clearer as we see the drama unfolding. Most ordinary people know there is something deeply wrong with a system that destroys so many good companies, jobs and communities, creates massive insecurity, damages people's pensions, turns so many skilled people into call centre workers, causes ill-health and makes a few people extremely rich. It is primarily about cutting costs, price competition that harms suppliers, global sourcing – *"a race to the bottom"*. It's all about making money, not providing healthy food, quality products, good service and good value. Governments and business leaders must see that the system needs to be *fundamentally* changed.

The bias for "big ideas". Wanting to appear to be getting something done, politicians are attracted to big "solutions" provided by big business. These are imposed by central government instead of devolving power to local people and enabling them to solve their problems. An example is the

Pathfinder demolition programme and *Housing Market Renewal* leading to "tinning up" large swathes of good Victorian terraced homes in Northern cities like Liverpool, Manchester, Oldham, Salford and St Helens. The flawed rationale was that it would lead to economic renewal. Some 850,000 homes were to be involved in this scheme. Residents say they were kept in the dark until the last moment. It devalued their homes, broke up communities, resulted in few new affordable homes and caused considerable hardship for many people. The main beneficiaries were not local people but developers, councils and housing trusts.

The so-called urban "Renaissance" by Business Improvement Districts created huge shopping complexes in former public spaces now owned and controlled by large property companies, and pose threats to civil liberties and local democracy – Liverpool One, Blue Water, Cardinal Place Victoria, Paddington Waterside, London's Westfield shopping centre, Metro Centre Gateshead and Cardiff Bay. They destroy the unique character of place; they sweep away much loved buildings. These big ideas were imported from the USA and contributed to a greater increase in poverty under New Labour than under Mrs Thatcher. Read about how the needs and wishes of local people were ignored in Anna Minton's revealing book, *Ground Control: Fear and Happiness in the Twenty-First Century City.*

Too few political leaders are qualified for the job. They don't have the necessary holistic or ecological education. They lack experience of leading people or leading change. They don't understand what it is to be a ***servant leader***; how change comes about; how to include people; how to reach good decisions by listening to diverse views; how to get people to take responsibility by devolving power. Government lags behind. It doesn't do what the majority of enlightened citizens want. They withhold information; to be blunt, they lie, are stubbornly defensive, unaware they are in denial. They underestimate the public. They hold on to power and centralise. They concede reforms reluctantly because it means letting go. Too often, they overreact to dramatic media reports. They deal with symptoms instead of underlying causes. They rely too much on business for briefings, rather than people with in-depth on-the-ground experience, or those who have done research into what works. Political power, manipulation and adversarial, often abusive, debate are no way to reach wise decisions.

The behaviour of political leaders is unedifying and sets a bad example. "Big hitters", "big beasts" and "bully boys" get promoted. They behave like bruisers. Remember the treatment of David Kelly? Politicians are constantly playing the blame game and "trashing" their "opponents" instead of working together to create a new possibility. It is a deplorable spectacle, aided and abetted by the media, especially television and radio interviewers with their silly *"Who's to blame?"* It is all about winning the argument, rather than seeking truth and discovering what works. Most of these leaders have a patriarchal, combative, "macho" mindset when a different blend, including more feminine values, is needed. We are entitled to expect better. Again we have a choice; we voted them in.

In today's world, genuine participatory democracy is a necessity. To bring about the necessary system change, we need to *"get the whole system into the room"*. Not only do we need to reform our own democracy; global democracy is needed. Government has not understood the need for processes that involve people in bringing about a great transformation.

Elite gatherings like the World Economic Forum in Davos, the G8 or G20 are simply unacceptable. It is outrageous when small groups of rich, powerful people, out of touch with how most people live, strongly influenced by big corporations, make vital strategic decisions for the world. At a recent G20 meeting, there was only one representative from the whole of Africa. Distasteful gatherings of political and business leaders, media tycoons and celebrities in places like the Rothschild villa in Corfu corrupt democracy. Political leaders are too susceptible to blandishments. We cannot bring about fundamental change when governments are more influenced by corporate interests than those of people. It's bound to lead to flawed solutions.

We have only a "sort of democracy". We are extremely lucky to live in one of the better democracies, compared with countries run by tyrants, where corruption is extreme and order has broken down. Yet it is only a relative democracy, unfit for the enormous challenges the whole world faces. Our democracy should be a beacon. It is not, especially in the areas of genuine involvement, human rights and civil liberties. Our liberties are always under threat: e.g. plans, many now abandoned, for a massive data base monitoring e-mails, phone calls and Internet use; the National Identity Card and National Identity Register storing vast amounts of personal data; plans to compromise data privacy; allowing government to alter any Act of Parliament and cancel rules of confidentiality to use information obtained for one purpose to be used for another.

The media and press play a major part in obstructing change and keeping things as they are. For democracy to work, citizens need to be well-informed. Rupert Murdoch's papers can sway the outcome of elections. We need informed analysis and positive news about good models, solutions, best practice from all over the world. Marx referred to religion as *"the opiate of the people"*. Today, the media fills this role. It depresses people and diverts energy from addressing the real priorities. Leaders, who should focus on long-term priorities and bold strategic action, constantly respond to daily media sensationalism. That said the UK media do expose some things that business and politicians would prefer to keep from the public. They rely on sensational headlines, unbalanced opinion and gossip about leaders and celebrities in the battle to survive. The media do not give prominence to the radical ideas that would transform the situation. I intend to do that in Part Two.

We collude with this system and we pay for it with poor government. We could buy better papers.

Reform rarely comes from within a system. It happens on the boundary, driven by pressures from outside. We have to make it happen through relentless pressure. Reforming our democracy is agonisingly slow. Governments are reluctant to concede power. We need a far greater degree of enlightened participation and involvement. We must get proper proportional representation.

The twentieth century produced perhaps a dozen or so great leaders e.g. Mahatma Gandhi, Franklin Delano Roosevelt, Winston Churchill, Jawaharlal Nehru, Mikhail Gorbachev and Clement Attlee and Nye Bevan, who brought in the NHS. We need leaders like these who can inspire and enrol citizens in a great endeavour. We need political leaders with the vision, integrity and holistic education essential for national and global leadership. When bold, far-sighted vision is required, a tactical 4-5 year political mindset is too short. Prime Ministers need to tell the nation the stark truth about the severity of our situation and provide an inspiring vision and a clear well thought out strategy.

So, again, why do we, 6.7 billion of us, put up with it? Why do we allow a small number of people to impose their will? Why are most of us so acquiescent? Vast numbers of people in Western countries are disengaged from party politics and increasingly turn to campaigning through non-governmental organisations (NGOs) and independent research organisations. These can be extremely successful in bringing about change, especially when they collaborate in coalitions. The Jubilee 2000 Coalition brought about debt cancellation for very poor countries and the Green New Deal Coalition is making an impact.

The good news: we could be on the threshold of a benign

revolution. There is an alternative to the consumer society: an economy that focuses on sustainability, the well-being of people everywhere, economic justice and ending violence. Part of the answer must be a "steady state economy", especially in mature developed countries. That need not lead to unemployment. On the contrary, a Green Economy can provide all kinds of new opportunities for forward thinking entrepreneurs, worthwhile employment and prosperity.

A growing consensus for change. In a recent Fabian-YouGov poll in the UK, 70 per cent agreed that "those at the top are failing to pay their fair share towards investment in public services" and 55 per cent of those polled blamed reckless lending by the banks for the credit crunch. Eighty per cent believe that bonuses should "reward long-term success rather than short-term performance". A recent Harris poll found public opinion "strikingly consistent" across Europe, Asia and the US, with large majorities protesting that the gap between rich and poor has grown too wide: 74 per cent in the UK and 78 per cent in the USA. Clear majorities in all the countries polled said that taxes should be raised for the rich and lowered for the poor.

Breakthroughs. The Green New Deal Coalition put forward proposals, published by the New Economics Foundation (nef), full of exciting, radical, well thought out ideas, elaborated on in Chapter 9. The phrase, Green New Deal, has entered the vocabulary all over the world.

The United Nations Environment Programme (UNEP) launched a Green Economy Initiative. It calls for comprehensive, joined-up action by politicians throughout the world. In the USA, Barack Obama signed a Green Stimulus Initiative planning to invest $15bn annually in renewable energy over the next decade, thus creating 5m new jobs if reactionary forces will let him! The US Apollo Alliance, an alliance of business and unions which has existed for many years, offers a ten point plan. The Green for All Group in the Center for American Progress is a coalition of the Sierra Club and United Steel Workers Union, set up to build an inclusive green economy strong enough to lift people out of poverty. By advocating local, state and federal commitments to job creation, job training, and entrepreneurial opportunities in the emerging green economy, especially for people from disadvantaged communities, it fights both poverty and pollution at the same time. The UK Local Government Association called for a Green New Deal, urging Government to spend at least 20 per cent of their economic recovery package on green programmes: *Putting people first – Creating Green Jobs.*

"The largest movement in history". In his recent book, *Blessed Unrest: How the Largest Social Movement in History is Restoring Grace, Justice and Beauty to the World,* Peter Hawken reckoned there may be as many as a million such organisations in 243 countries, some of which are available on the WiserEarth website.

Someone said:

There are two great powers; USA and people power.

There is strength in numbers, if we are organised properly. Dr Olaseinde Arigbede, an activist working to empower small African farmers says:

If you are not organised, you cannot make change.

We cannot afford to be disengaged. The situation is far too serious and urgent to leave it to political and business leaders. We cannot depend on them to have the vision and values needed, to be sufficiently aware to act with integrity, do the right thing and do it soon enough. We have to hold them to account and insist on a better democracy in which citizens are properly represented and politicians are fully accountable. Global institutions must represent and serve equally all the people of the world.

With our immense knowledge and resources, all the advances in science, medicine and technology, we can create a world in which everyone enjoys a good education, health, freedom from violence and the opportunity for a fulfilling life. The UN Millennium Goals ***could be*** fulfilled. There is no shortage of anything. The problem is how the Earth's resources are distributed, used and wasted.

We may be at a "Tipping Point" if enough of us get actively involved. There could not be a better moment in history to bring about a complete change in a global economic system that is both broken and unsustainable.

Chapter 4

We Face the Biggest Crisis in Human History – Growth is Not Working

January 2009

Introduction

> *Anyone who believes exponential growth can go on forever in a finite world is either a madman or an economist.*
> **Kenneth Boulding**, economist

Collectively, we face the biggest crisis in human history: the possibility of abrupt and irreversible climate change. Of course there are dissenting voices. But even if climate change is not caused by human activity, which seems unlikely, there is still a problem. Every day there is more news about the potentially devastating effects of climate change. Floods in England first brought it home to us. Changes in our climate are increasingly apparent although relatively minor compared with the effects on other countries. The premier of the Maldives has plans to build up its land mass and ultimately to evacuate. Many other islands and low lying areas face a similar future.

Moreover, oil is running out and will become increasingly expensive.

Imagine a World; Imagine London, Your City, Town or Village

- Without abundant cheap oil – think of all those products derived from petrochemicals including plastics – oil is embedded in almost everything we consume
- Our climate has changed dramatically
- Seas have risen by a metre – remember London is in a flood plain!
- Food is expensive; widespread food, water and resource shortages are leading to desperation and conflict, wars and migration
- But also imagine the possibilities for a far better world and way of life!

In the West, we have enjoyed over a century of unprecedented growth and prosperity based on astonishing technological innovation made possible by abundant supplies of cheap oil. Now we are at a turning point. We'll need to turn our inherent creativity towards creating a new kind of world that is very different and better for everyone.

The emerging situation is far more complex than climate change and Peak Oil. These five issues are inseparably linked.

The big issues:

- Climate change
- Peak Oil
- Destruction of the ecosystem on which all life depends
- Poverty and economic injustice
- Violence, War and the threat of nuclear annihilation

A cynic might say we, in the "West", are only waking up as

climate change and Peak Oil start to hurt us, no longer just other people in remote countries. Climate change is a symptom of a malaise that is broader and deeper. We need a moral and spiritual re-awakening. As Meg Wheatley says, *"It's our turn to help the world."*

The following figure gives the general picture:

We're Taking More Than Our Fair Share

- Since the early seventies our consumption has steadily exceeded the Earth's bio-capacity by more and more. Today by 30% and increasing every day
- World population is now 6.7 billion and by 2050 it's estimated to be 9 billion. Poverty makes it grow.
- 60 per cent live on 6% of the world's resources
- The wealth of the world's 475 billionaires is $1trn and their combined income is more than that of the bottom half of humanity
- 1 billion people are hungry and the number is growing
- UK and EU account for 12.5 tonnes of CO2 (average) per person per year; Australia 28; US and Canada some 20; China 4; India 2 and sub-Saharan Africa less than 1 tonne
- Much of developing countries' emissions are created in making things for us – China 25% World demand for energy set to rise 53% by 2030
- London's footprint is 125 times its surface area. If everyone consumed like Londoners, we would need 3 planets, 5 at the Los Angeles rate of consumption!
- UK's food and farming footprint is nearly 6 times our food growing area
- The move from rural to city: 47% city dwellers in 2000; over 50% in 2007; 60% by 2060

- Mega cities (over 10M): 1950 = one; 2000 = 19; 2015 = 23; 15 in Asia – many surrounded by extreme poverty. China expects to build 400 new cities by 2010
- Cars: China 15.5m in 2002; 156m by 2020, i.e. 20m increase per year
- Massive waste: we throw away a third of our food. East Anglia has only 10 years landfill space left. We scatter waste around the world

These figures are pre-recession but the message is unchanged. We are on a path to ecological bankruptcy.

The global economy and our lifestyles will be transformed. The economic crisis could be a blessing, an opportunity to create a more sustainable, fairer and happier world. The recession is going to save our bacon for a while by reducing consumption and hence emissions and use of non-renewable resources. The need for new work may open eyes to the opportunities in innovative industries to green our economies and accelerate power generation, transport systems and the development of vehicles that do not use fossil fuel. But the transition is already having harsh effects on many people.

Belief in rapid economic growth is unsustainable. It is one of our blind spots. It is destroying the biosphere on which all life depends. We need a Great Transition to bring about a twenty-first century Industrial Revolution and a steady state economy. In the following sections of this chapter, I shall attempt to make sense of the five interconnected issues that face us: climate change; Peak Oil; destruction of the ecosystem on which all life depends; poverty; and violence, war and the threat of nuclear annihilation.

Section A: Climate Change

Every day the warnings get stronger.

The Government's Stern Review set out dire consequences and warned that the global cost of climate change to business and governments could reach 20 per cent of world Gross Domestic Product (GDP) if nothing is done. Without action, greenhouse gas emissions are projected to almost double by 2030. With no policies to curb pollution, the most likely increase in temperatures is 5C by 2050. In 2007 the Intergovernmental Panel on Climate Change (IPCC) forecast that sea levels might rise by 28cm (11 inches) to 43cm (17inches) by 2100, although 59cm (nearly 2 feet) is a possibility. This is not just a problem for millions in poor countries like Bangladesh. It is already a problem for us. Around 5 million people live in flood risk areas in England and Wales and many coastal areas, in East Anglia for example, face great anxiety about their future. Unstable climate, heat waves and hurricane strength winds will increase. Hundreds of millions will suffer water shortages; up to 30 per cent of species risk extinction and food production will be hit. Christian Aid say climate change is already killing 300,000 a year in poor countries.

Has climate change already gone beyond the point of no return? The New Economics Foundation (NEF) argues that, as of July 2010, we have only 77 months before we reach a crucial tipping point.

No excuse for failing to act. In March 2009, a group of marine experts meeting in Copenhagen suggested that IPCC scientists had made a drastic underestimation of the problem and oceans were likely to rise twice as fast. Low lying countries will be particularly affected but low lying areas of Britain, such as the Thames Estuary, will suffer. Over 2,500 climate experts from 80 countries, at an emergency summit in Copenhagen, concluded that there was now *"no excuse"* for failure to act on global warming. Failure to agree on strong carbon reduction targets in political negotiations could bring *"abrupt or irreversible"* shifts in climate that *"will be very difficult for contemporary societies to cope with."* They said carbon emissions have increased more than anyone thought possible, and the world's natural carbon stores could be losing the ability to soak up human pollution.

Amongst Possible Threats Are:

- A 4C temperature rise could turn swaths of southern Europe into desert
- Sea levels rise twice as fast as official estimates predict
- Modest warming unleashes a carbon "time bomb" from Arctic soils
- A failure to cut emissions renders half of the world uninhabitable
- Rising temperatures kill off 85 per cent of the Amazon rainforest
- There could be mass starvation and mass migration to the North

Several experts at the conference warned that temperatures are likely to soar beyond the 2C target set by European politicians. *"The 2C target is gone and 3C is difficult. I think we're heading for 4C at least,"* one said. Politicians have failed to take on board the severe consequences of failing to cut world carbon emissions, according to Brown's economic adviser, Nicholas Stern. Acting now would be far cheaper than to delay. And this could provide much needed jobs for many people. Scientists issued a plea for world leaders to curb greenhouse gas emissions or face an ecological and social disaster. Veteran climate campaigner James Lovelock predicts 5 degree higher temperatures, 1 to 3 feet rise in sea levels, mass migration and a reduction in population to 1 billion because of the Earth's inability to feed the human population.

"A perfect storm". Professor John Beddington, UK Government chief scientist, warned that growing world population will cause a *"perfect storm"* of food, energy and water shortages, a crisis with dire consequences. Demand for food and energy will jump 50 per cent and for fresh water by 30 per cent, as the population reaches 8.3 billion by 2030. Population growth is a major issue that can only be tackled by eliminating dire poverty and giving women choices. When women are given education and the opportunity to escape poverty, they want fewer children.

The seas absorb CO2 and since the Industrial Revolution seas have become 30 per cent more acidic. CO2 emissions are increasing the acidity of the seas. That may result in mass extinction of marine life. Together with overconsumption of fish, that affects food security. Also we do not know how the whole marine ecosystem will be affected. There may be limits to the extent that seas can absorb our emissions too. These are further reasons why we should reduce our emissions. As ever, we interfere with major ecosystems at our peril.

The scientific consensus is that the environmental crisis is primarily man-made, largely caused by CO2 and methane. Even if, as some argue, it's mainly down to solar activity, we still face a crisis. Emissions are constantly rising because of our growing demands, the rising expectations of poorer and developing countries and steadily growing population. Population is estimated to rise to 9bn by 2050.

This table demonstrates the size of the problem! Generally, oil producing countries, affluent people and wealthy countries pollute most; poor countries and people are worst affected.

CO_2 Emissions Per Capita Tonnes of Some Countries 2004

Qatar	69.2
Kuwait	38.0
United Arab Emirates	37.8
Luxembourg	24.9
USA	20.4
Canada	20.0
Norway	19.01
Australia	16.3
Saudi Arabia	13.4
Japan	9.84
UK	9.79
Germany	9.79
New Zealand	7.8
China	3.84

The current estimate is that the world average emissions per person needs to be no more than 2 tonnes

India	1.2
Pakistan	0.81
Bangladesh	0.25

Most African countries well below 1.00 to minute

Source: Wikipedia quoting *United Nations Millennium Development Goals Indicators*, 12 September 2007.

The USA, with 5 per cent of the world population, emits 25 per cent of world greenhouse gases, and with 30 per cent of the world's automobiles contributes 45 per cent of the world's automotive emissions. Environmental Defense, an advocacy group, says unless China, India, the USA and UK take this seriously, the damage done to the world will soon be trebled.

UK's carbon footprint is NOT the official figure. The UK has exported most of its manufacturing with all the associated pollution to poorer, developing countries less able to operate sustainably. Otherwise our emissions would be twice as high. David McKay's excellent book, *Sustainable Energy: Without the Hot Air*, reveals that the UK's carbon footprint is not the official 11 tonnes of CO2 per person but about 21 (Mackay, D, 2009). This is because we now make very little. The official figure does not count all the "stuff" we import, made in other countries. But for those obliging countries, and ***if we didn't cheat, we'd have twice as big a problem!***

What are the main sources of emissions?

The six CO2 equivalents governed by the Kyoto Protocol are carbon dioxide, methane, nitrous oxide, hydro fluorocarbons, per fluorocarbons, and sulphur hexafluoride.

The following figures give clear indications of the priorities for where cuts are need and provide a guide for government policy, businesses and individual choices. However, before getting into this subject we need to address the concept of embedded oil and CO2.

Oil and CO2 and are embedded in just about everything we consume and do. For example, emissions embedded in IT, Telecom and consumer electronic equipment imports to the USA in 2006 were 3.5 times larger than all emissions from electric power generation in California and are rapidly growing. Whilst UK emissions fell by 5 per cent from 1992 to 2004, emissions from consumed goods and services grew by 18 per cent. Emissions embedded in the Internet are the equivalent of 22 million cars.

The main sources of UK emissions, based on 2006 figures, were energy industries (38.9 per cent), transport (24.2 per cent), other industries (17.7 per cent) and residential (14.4 per cent). Government accounts for 8 per cent of CO2 emissions. These figures and the chart below indicate where the priorities for action lie.

The Independent Committee on Climate Change says there is

big potential to cut emissions in business and the public sector, and save money through reduced energy bills. In many cases, required actions are simple, and low cost. They include switching off computers and lights overnight. Overall savings of almost £900m and 9 MtCO2 annually would be achievable if cost-effective measures were introduced:

- Almost three-quarters of this through better management of energy (e.g. optimising heating start/finish times and motion sensitive lights).
- Much of the rest through investing in more efficient heating and cooling systems and the most efficient lights and appliances (currently relatively expensive).
- In addition there is scope for some 2 MtCO2 from renewable energy in buildings, likely to be at a higher cost now but an important part of delivering carbon savings.
- Savings of around £500m per year by 2020 are feasible from improved processes in industry, more efficient heat generation and more energy efficient plant designs; this would save almost 6 MtCO2, and further 1 MtCO2 possible through greater use of Combined Heat and Power (CHP).

UK per cent Emissions of CO2 by IPCC Source Category 2006

Energy industries (public electricity and heating 33.1)	38.9
Road transport (including cars 12.4)	21.7
Manufacturing and construction	14.8
Residential	14.4
Commercial and institutional	3.9
Industrial processes (materials)	2.5
Other transport (including air, rail, national navigation)	1.8

Fugitive emissions from fuels	0.9
Agriculture and forestry	0.8
Military (aircraft and shipping)	0.5
Other (Waste treatment and disposal 0.1, land use, land use change and forestry on balance nil)	0.1

Source: *AEA Energy and Environment*

Food as such is not included in these figures. See Food section, below.

A radical rethink is needed. These figures make it clear that our whole way of life and doing business needs a radical rethink. Clearly the first four sources above are top priorities. Our current way of life is unsustainable. It is based on continuous economic growth, an unfair global trading system, pursuing the apparent lowest cost, wherever that can be sourced and at whatever cost to people and planet. Producing energy from renewable sources, reducing emissions from energy production, using less energy and using it economically are the top priorities.

We need a new basis for calculating cost and a new approach that taxes the ***unsustainable*** at source and incentivises and rewards the ***sustainable.*** The New Economics Foundation is amongst many organisations proposing alternatives, see Chapter 9.

Of course conclusions are not straightforward because of the complexities of the system and uncertainties in assessing the outcomes of alternative actions. For example the idea of labelling food and goods with their carbon footprint is a practical nightmare. There are confusing differences in figures available from different sources. Figures are changing all the time. But there are general principles we can apply when making choices and the more we understand the better. The *Ecologist* is perhaps one of the most reliable guides for citizens.

Construction, Demolition and Regeneration

These are major sources of CO2 emissions, harmful pollution

and use of non-renewable resources. We cannot carry on at the present rate. Environmental impact assessments are essential before deciding on new construction. According to *Concrete Thinking – for a sustainable world, 2006,* worldwide "cement manufacturing accounts for approximately 5 per cent of CO2 emissions. When all greenhouse gas emissions generated by human activities are considered, the cement industry is responsible for approximately 3 per cent of global emissions. China produces 37 per cent of the world's cement, followed by India with 6 per cent and the US with 5 per cent. Most facilities in China rely on inefficient and outdated technologies; these plants contribute to 6 to 8 per cent of the CO2 emissions in China. The cement industry has made progress and since 1972 has improved energy efficiencies by 33 per cent."

A policy of conservation, upgrading and reusing older buildings is more sustainable from many aspects, including social, cultural and aesthetic. The relative sustainability of different materials, such as wood, steel and concrete, sourcing locally wherever possible, and using local labour needs to be assessed in every case. Generally, using steel, especially recycled steel, and wood, appears to be far more sustainable than concrete.

Food

Food accounts for nearly a third of the UK's climate footprint, i.e. CO2 and methane emissions. Meat and dairy are half this problem. The Soil Association say soya fed to pork, poultry and dairy cows in the UK has displaced an area of rainforest the size of Devon and Cornwall – see Rainforests below. Clearly our shopping choices are extremely important.

Supermarkets contribute 20 per cent of UK CO2 emissions. A substantial part of their contribution, and that of warehouse stores, is their countrywide and worldwide sourcing and distribution systems and the need for customers to travel to out-of-town sites. In many cases people have no alternative now as local shops are driven out of business by the unfair competition created by supermarket and warehouse shopping and other factors described earlier. We need to create a level playing field for small shops. It is another example of the folly of cheap prices and big companies externalising substantial social costs. This whole system needs to be radically rethought. It's unsustainable.

Household greenhouse gas emissions from food account for almost twice those produced by driving. Most, 83 per cent comes from the food production processes, rather than food miles 11 per cent and retail wholesale 6 per cent.

Food production	83 per cent, (37 per cent CO_2, 20 per cent methane, 26 per cent nitrous oxide)
Transport – farm to customer	11 per cent
Wholesale/retail (refrigeration and lighting).	6 per cent

It also depends very much upon what you choose to eat.

Meat	4800g per 300g pack
Tomatoes	2800g per 300g punnet
Cheese	2600g per 300g pack
Eggs	1650g per half-dozen box
Milk	1050g per litre bottle
Salmon fillets	500g per 250g pack wild caught
Potatoes	240g per 1kg pack
Apples	110g per 4 apple pack
Onions	60g per 750g
Carrot	45g per 1kg

Using animals to produce food is extremely uneconomical since food animals require large amounts of plant foods to live and grow. It is a poor investment one; we get back as little as 5 per cent of what we put in. In environmental terms, this is an enormous waste of resources; fossil fuels, fertilizers, cleared land, all with their own greenhouse impact, are required for grazing or feed-crops. Instead, growing plant foods for direct human consumption (although this has its own environmental impact) would require much less of everything to feed the same human population.

Excess meat consumption is a major source of Western ill health such as heart disease and, because it takes precedence over local food production, Third World poverty and hunger.

The impact of livestock on global warming, whether from their digestion, manure, respiration, or crops required for their feed, lies in the sheer number of them. As 6.7 billion human beings, and rising, increasingly demand animal products, the global livestock population soars. In 2004, the global livestock population numbered over 22 billion: more than 3½ times the human population of the planet, and of which the overwhelming majority were animals bred primarily for food. The number grows each year by an average of around 3 per cent or 550m animals.

A diet rich in meat is unsustainable. Farmed animals produce 18 per cent of world greenhouse gases, including 37 per cent of world methane. Meat and dairy products make up a third of humanity's intake of protein. Only 5-25 per cent of the nutrients going into producing meat are converted into edible meat making it the most inefficient way of providing protein. Of all meats, beef is the least sustainable. Red meat production emits 2.5 times as much CO2 as chicken. The methane and the nitrous oxide released from manure are worse still – see the chart below. The amount of CO2 involved depends on how the animals are reared. Cattle feed is far more polluting than natural pasture. Plans for giant cattle farms appear not to take all this into account.

Livestock contribute more to global warming than transport, according to the UN Food & Agriculture Organisation (FAO) *Livestock's long shadow: Environmental issues and options.* Its impact includes emissions directly from animals, as well indirect. Global warming is caused by three main "greenhouse" gases: carbon dioxide, methane and nitrous oxide, each with different greenhouse potency. By international convention, the impact of all gases in measured in "CO2 equivalent" to allow the overall impact on the environment to be compared.

Livestock's Contribution to Global Warming

- **Carbon dioxide:** Animal farming indirectly contributes carbon dioxide through deforestation for pasture and feed-crop land, and burning of fossil fuels for feed production, farm and slaughterhouse operations, manure management, cold transportation and refrigeration. Livestock also directly produce carbon dioxide by respiration.
- **Methane:** Methane (a greenhouse gas 23 times more effective at warming the globe than CO2) is produced by farm animal manure. It is also produced by the enteric fermentation (belching and flatulence) of cattle, sheep and other ruminants.
- **Nitrous oxide:** Livestock activities contribute nitrous oxide (a greenhouse gas 296 times more potent than CO2) mainly through manure, nitrogen fertilizer production and nitrogen fertilizer application.

Large-scale livestock production also contributes to the destruction of biodiversity, loss of species, fish stocks and forests, land degradation, erosion, river pollution, water shortages and to poverty, by taking land from poor people. Methane emissions, mainly coming from cattle and refuse dumps, are rising. On a positive note, these can be exploited for producing heat and power and growing tender vegetables as is being done beside a sugar factory in Norfolk. Eating less meat and consuming less milk and dairy products, or going further and changing to a vegetarian diet, is probably one of the most effective things anyone can do to halt climate change.

Calculating how much CO2 is involved in different purchase options is complex. That is true for choosing what fish to buy. Fish farms can be particularly destructive. Shrimp farms have destroyed 30 per cent of the world's mangrove swamps, many of which are vital to prevent flooding of low-lying areas. We simply have to do our best to keep well informed about these issues and make informed choices.

New Scientist, *Dinner's dirty secret*, 10 September 2008, provides an excellent source for this complex subject. It says the only sure option is to become vegetarian! Organically grown crops have a much smaller carbon footprint. So, as a general rule, going vegetarian or organic will help most. Growing your own and buying local, fresh produce and eating in season will help further and be healthier. Another option is to shift from red meat and eat occasional chicken, eggs and fish, preferably organic. As to whether a vegetarian diet provides enough nutrients, Christopher Weber at Carnegie Mellon University in Pittsburgh, Pennsylvania says plant-based diets are probably nutritionally superior to diets deriving a much of their calories from animals.

It is a crazy world where organic food costs more yet does less harm. A sensible policy would be to tax non-organic and subsidise organic to reduce its price.

My view is that we must considerably reduce our consumption of animals and fish, perhaps making them an occasional or weekly treat. This is more achievable, balanced, makes for better health and is better for diversity, eco-agriculture and organic farming methods. Think what would otherwise happen to our large areas of our countryside if we did not have animals grazing there. What would we do without all the materials and products made from animals such as their wool, by-products like leather, which is so much healthier for our feet than oil-derived plastic?

Homes

Our houses now consume about 27 per cent of UK electricity, a lot of which is needlessly wasted. It is now easy to build "zero-carbon" homes, such as the German Passivhaus or even better ones produced in Denmark, for little more than the cost of a standard house. By 2016, all new UK homes will be required to have nil net carbon emissions (Level 6).

George Monbiot reckons it would take 1,700 years to replace our housing stock at the current rate of building, even if that were desirable! The big issue is the existing stock of what he calls our "leaky homes." Like other European governments, ours needs to play a major role providing research subsidies, financial support, incentives, infrastructure and properly enforced standards and regulations. Prices will then come down as demand increases and jobs will then be created. But, our government is not doing enough.

Individuals

Individuals are directly responsible, through their consumption, for 44 per cent of CO2 emissions and indirectly far more.

Rainforests

Rainforest destruction is the largest single source of carbon emissions after energy, contributing up to 10 times as much as aviation. The Stern Report warned that rainforest destruction alone would, in the next four years, release more carbon into the atmosphere than every flight from the dawn of aviation until 2025. A huge amount of deforestation takes place to make way for crops to feed cattle, food crops and now biofuels for export to rich countries. Destruction of forests also leads to loss of species, damage to the lives of forest peoples, massive erosion and further poverty as in Haiti where good soil is flowing into the Caribbean Sea.

Figures from the Oxford-based Global Canopy Programme (GCP) show that deforestation accounts for up to 25 per cent of global emissions of heat-trapping gases, while transport and industry account for 14 per cent each.

Rainforests are nature's capital. Trees are precious; they are carbon sinks that absorb our CO2. We are living off our capital. We need to live off the income; not destroy capital. Poor people in poor countries need incentives to protect forests and alternative ways of earning that do not force them to cut down trees in order to survive, including grants of land. Indigenous people are being shown how to make a far better living by protecting and using the forest sustainably, for example by taking the latex from trees instead of felling them. These areas should not be destroyed to grow crops or cattle to feed rich Westerners with their unhealthy diets, or for biofuels. We should leave rainforests in India and Latin America to indigenous peoples who understand how to manage them, if they and we are to survive. We must change our habits and lobby for take global action to stop this process.

Transport

The transport sector contributes 26 per cent of UK carbon emissions. Looking at all modes of transport, a study by Oxford University's Centre for the Environment showed that rapidly increasing air travel accounted for 70 per cent of the sector's climate change impact and 13 per cent of the UK's total impact, while cars were responsible for 25 per cent and public transport for 3.5 per cent.

UK Transport
Which is greenest?

	Grams of CO2 per passenger kilometre
Ship (transatlantic luxury cruise liner, full)	1611
Domestic short-haul flight (including effects at altitude)	300
International short-haul flight (including effects at altitude)	248
Average petrol car	210
International long-haul flight (including effects at altitude)	201
Average diesel car	199
Motorbikes	107
Bus	89
Rail	60
Coach	20

Sources: *Ecologist*, Which is greenest? July/August 2008; Monbiot, G, 2006, *Heat: How to Stop the Planet Burning,* Passenger Transport Emissions Factors, IPCC, 1999; IPCC report, *Aviation and the Global Atmosphere*, 8.3 3.4

Figures for hybrid, electric and hydrogen cell powered vehicles are not included.

The most energy efficient modes of passenger transport. David MacKay's book, *Sustainable Energy: Without the Hot Air*, a major source of information in this section, shows that the most energy effective modes of transport, as measured by average kWh per 100 passenger km, (A kWh is the amount of power consumed/generated over a period of one hour.) in order are:

- 10 or below: cycle, walk, electric train full
- 20 or below: electric high speed train full, electric scooter, underground train full, coach full, trolley bus, electric car 2 passengers, diesel HST full, tram, electric car full, under-

ground system, car full
- 30 or below: sea bus
- 40 or below: bus is just above 30

Cycling and walking are the healthiest though not yet safest ways to travel. Little energy is embedded in cycles. Figures for trains depend on speed; very high speeds mean higher figures. The figure he gives for a Range Rover is about 114 kWh per 100 passenger km, well above a 747, and close to an Ocean Liner about 121 kWh per 100 passenger km. To put things into perspective, the amount of energy saved by switching off your phone charger, 0.01 kWh per day, is exactly the same as driving an average car for a second! Not to say that turning off such devices is not worth doing. It all adds up.

Hydrogen fuel-cell cars. David MacKay says considerable development is needed before this technology becomes viable. Their current energy consumption of nearly 70 kWh per 100 passenger km is well above a Boeing 747, around 50 kWh per 100 passenger km. Currently converting energy to and from hydrogen is inefficient and requires 80 per cent to 200 per cent more energy than in a baseline diesel bus and 220 per cent more than for an average car (MacKay, D, 2009).

Freight transport. Energy requirements for different forms of freight transport in energy used per kilometre – kilowatt-hour per ton-kilometre (kWh/t-km) of freight moved not including vehicle weight in least order:

- Rail and then ship: At or below 0.1 kWh/t-km
- Road: just below 1.1
- Air: 1.6

(MacKay, D, 2009)

Global shipping accounts for 1.12bn tonnes of CO2, or nearly 4.5 per cent of all global emissions of the main greenhouse gas.

The UN IPCC report suggests that shipping emissions, which are only now being taken into account by UK and European targets for cutting global warming, will become one of the largest single sources of man-made CO2 after cars, housing, agriculture and industry.

Shipping's damaging pollution. Shipping in the form of ferries, cruise liners, container ships and oil tankers pump out harmful chemicals because of the dirty fuel they use. They burn cheap, dirty, high-sulphur fuel. Shipping is responsible for 18-30 per cent of global nitrogen oxide pollution and 9 per cent of sulphur dioxide. Sixteen of the world's largest ships can produce as much lung damaging pollution as all the cars in the world. It is estimated that there are 100,000 such ships and their number is growing rapidly as a result of European and North American nations' global sourcing from Asia in particular. The chemicals they emit can cause cancer, heart disease and asthma. This could cause a million deaths worldwide over the coming decade. James Corbett, professor of marine policy at the University of Delaware, estimates a rising annual death toll of 64,000; 27,000 in Europe and 2000 in Britain. Another source attributes 60,000 deaths annually in the USA to this cause. The costs to health services run into billions; big business externalising costs again. The UN International Maritime Organisation has allowed this situation but pressure for action is mounting. The USA has imposed buffer zones in 2010. The EU has similar, less adequate plans. Norwegian shipping company Eidsesvik has developed *Viking Lady*, a ship powered by a fuel cell using liquefied gas which causes far less pollution.

However, shipping is more fuel efficient than road transport. If we used higher quality fuel it could be could be far less polluting. Reducing road transport and getting it off or reducing fossil fuel use is a high priority (MacKay, D, 2009).

Aviation. Globally, aviation is responsible for about 650 million tonnes or 2 per cent of CO2 emissions, rising 3-4 per cent annually. Pollution from high flying jets is up to four times more damaging to the environment than the same amount released from chimneys and exhaust pipes. The mix of gases injected into the icy atmosphere from high flying aircraft are two to four times more damaging than from other sources, particularly at night. There is little prospect of substantially less polluting aircraft in the near future. Improvements in design and the use of biofuels, posing a threat to forests and food growing, will be wiped out by growing air traffic. There can be little doubt that emissions from aircraft in the major developing countries will pose an increasing threat to efforts to combat climate change.

The Green Car Congress report dated 24th November 2008 outlined the UK Campaign for Better Transport's comprehensive transport policies for cutting greenhouse gases from the UK transport by 26 per cent by 2020. The future of trains, freight, hydrogen fuel cell buses, hybrid and electric cars, car share schemes are all described in Chapter 8: *Greening the World*.

Urban areas

Urban areas are responsible for 75 per cent of greenhouse gas emissions and the world population is moving from country to city. Often a deplorable situation, especially poverty stricken and insanitary slums, is created, as in Mumbai. However, cities ***can be*** designed to be highly sustainable, for example Curitiba in Brazil. There is more about both in Part Two, Chapter 13: *Sustainable Cities, Towns and Communities.*

Waste

Waste and waste disposal, including toxic nuclear waste, are major worldwide problems involving extensive national and international transportation. We ship vast quantities of scrap metals and waste overseas. Sometimes it is sent back as unacceptable. As waste is "gold" we may regret this one day. The UK, the wasteful man of Europe, is running out of space for dumps. UK figures are improving, but East Anglia has only 10 years' space left and the UK faces huge fines unless it can meet European Union Landfill Directive targets to reduce the amount of waste that gets dumped in landfill by 2013. The cost of landfill is enormous but under present arrangements, local councils do not have the funds to recycle more of it which, together with using it to generate heat and power, would be more economic and sustainable. Incinerating waste, favoured by some local authorities, is highly toxic. The UK has targets to recycle 40 per cent of household waste by 2010 and 50 per cent by 2020 but Wales' aims are far more radical: 70 per cent recycled by 2025 and zero waste by 2070. In 2008, St Arvans became the first zero waste (*zero-wastraff*) village.

What needs to be done?

Reversing climate change. Globally, we need to rapidly cut rising global CO2 emissions, largely resulting from using fossil fuels, to a sustainable world average of 2 tonnes per person. By 2050, the EU and UK need to get down to at least 3 tonnes, an 80 per cent reduction on 1990 levels. Three tonnes or a 90 per cent reduction now looks safer.

What We Need to Do

- The world needs to cut rapidly rising emissions to a sustainable average of 2-3 tonnes per person, probably only 2 tonnes.
- UK and EU need to get down from 12.5 tonnes to 3 tonnes by 2050, an 80 per cent reduction; many experts now argue for 2 tonnes, a 90 per cent reduction
- Developing countries say: rich countries created the problem; have the technological capability; and need to set an example and assist with aid and technology

- We need a new, sustainable, global economic model based on human needs, not corporate power and debt
- The fairest solution is a personal CO2 limit of 2 tonnes for every person on the planet.

It's time to give something back

This section gave clear indications for businesses, governments and individual citizens. The policies to achieve these goals are described in Part Two.

New Labour's achievements

Although New Labour was desperately slow to develop a coherent strategy, it deserves credit. Ed Miliband, as Secretary of State for Energy, was very different from his predecessors. Like Lord Adonis, Transport Secretary, he was a breath of fresh air.

UK Climate Change Act, 2008, enacted 2 December, set legally binding targets for greenhouse gas emission reductions through action in the UK and abroad of at least 80 per cent by 2050, and reductions in CO2 emissions of at least 26 per cent by 2020, against a 1990 baseline. The 2020 target was reviewed soon after Royal Assent to reflect the move to include all greenhouse gases and the increase in the 2050 target to 80 per cent. At the last minute, after a successful popular campaign, emissions from aircraft and shipping were included. The act outlined key provisions and milestones. Many experts regard this act as a model for other nations. However, they doubt these targets will be met, given Government's lack of clear and comprehensive policies and strategies, conflicting and inadequate plans and actions and targets still not backed up with adequate, consistent funding and rigorous enforcement of regulations.

Government also deserves credit not only for a host of smaller initiatives, such as Environmental Impact Assessments

(EVAs), targets for generating renewable energy and standards and regulations for new building. But again, the latter are inadequately implemented and monitored.

Funding for electric and plug-in petrol-electric hybrids. In April 2009, a £250m plan was announced to promote low carbon transport over the next five years, including funding for electric and plug-in petrol-electric hybrids and £20 million for a network of charging points. An analyst at Spyder Automotive suggested that by 2020 a quarter of cars could be electric. AA president Edmund King said our cities could be revolutionised but infrastructure, incentives, clean energy and affordable, practical vehicles would be needed. Electric and plug-in petrol-electric hybrids were expected to go on sale in two years' time but are likely to be very expensive initially.

Carbon budgets. In April 2009, Alastair Darling announced a target to cut carbon emissions by 34 per cent by 2020. Most experts thought that not enough and 40 per cent is needed. The budget laid down in five year tranches, carbon budgets designed to bring down our emissions by 80 per cent by 2050 with an interim target of 34 per cent by 2020. He also announced a £1.4bn package of measures to reduce carbon emissions and create a low-carbon economy amounting to 9.6 per cent of total spending commitments.

Carbon capture and storage (CCS). In April 2009, Ed Miliband announced that in future new, coal-fired power stations must be fitted with carbon capture and storage (CCS) equipment to remove 90 per cent of CO2. It would be pumped out into disused oil wells in the North Sea. Later, the technology will have to be installed in existing coal power stations. A similar bill was going through the US senate, helped by the UK's action as it would be conditional on the technology being sufficiently adopted elsewhere in the world. Britain set an example to countries like China and India. However, there are considerable doubts about the cost, feasibility and speed with which carbon capture can be introduced.

Smart meters. On 11 May 2009, Government announced plans to install in every home by 2020 smart meters that will record customers' gas and electricity use and let consumers see how much energy they are using thus helping them to save energy costs. 26 million electricity meters and 22 million gas meters will need to be fitted at a cost of £7bn. Smart meters will end the need for meter readers, meaning big savings for energy firms who hope bills will fall.

The UK Low Carbon Transition Plan. In July 2009, Ed Miliband launched this exemplary plan, and the ***Great British Refurb Plan*** for our 7m "leaky" homes (see Chapter 13: *Sustainable Cities, Towns and Communities* for details). After years of campaigning by environmental groups, in March 2010, he announced the excellent ***Household Energy Management Strategy*** programme, effective from April, 2010, offering incentives to improve the energy efficiency of the UK's 22m homes. These include generous feed-in tariffs and a loan scheme to help people install a range of small-scale renewable energy technologies such as such as PV solar panels where conditions are suitable or ground source heat pumps, biomass boilers and insulation.

Ofgem predicts that by 2020 electricity is likely to rise 20 per cent, bringing average household energy costs to £2,000 a year. Also, future supplies are in jeopardy. Anyone fitting a typical £12,500, 2.5kW PV system to their existing home will initially be paid 41.3p per kilowatt hour (kWh) generated, rising with energy prices. The Department of Energy and Climate Change (DECC) said homeowners who install photovoltaic panels could earn £900 a year when they first put in the technology, along with saving £140 a year on their bills. It was calculated that on average the offer from government would pay you £1,000 a year for the next 25 years, in return for an upfront investment of £12,500. Since people move house on average every nine to 12 years, householders may not have a long enough to pay back the loan before they move. So loans may be attached to the house to overcome the financial barriers and upfront costs people face in making their homes greener. The scheme also ensures householders save more on their bills than the cost of the repayments. A Pay as You Save programme was tried out on 500 homes in a £4m pilot.

Green Investment Bank. In March 2010 Alastair Darling announced plans for a "green investment bank" to finance clean energy projects in the UK, with initial funding of £2bn. This may be continued by the coalition.

High Speed Railways. Suddenly we were blessed with someone with the imagination, chutzpah and charisma to succeed. Lord Andrew Adonis announced visionary plans for "High Speed 2", creating high speed lines between London and Glasgow via Edinburgh, Newcastle, Leeds, Manchester and Birmingham. A tunnel under the Pennines linking Leeds and Manchester will cut the journey from 55 to 15 minutes. London to Birmingham journey time will be cut from 90 to 45 minutes. Meanwhile London Paddington to Swansea will be electrified. All this could have a transforming effect on the economy of the UK by linking together our key cities and regions. It would also link those cities to European cities. He gained cross-party support so that these plans would be implemented whatever the result of the elections.

By rejuvenating great Victorian regional cities, the concentration of our economy on the South East and London City may at last be broken. Perhaps the City will at last be doing the job of providing money for a rejuvenation of our economy instead of creating money out of thin air for a small minority of mega rich! All that unsustainable development of more housing in the overburdened South East may become unnecessary and recognised as folly! Housing in the regions could be recognised as an asset requiring refurbishment instead of demolition. This should mark the end of heavily polluting short-haul air travel within the UK and Europe. £20bn, well spent, could partly be paid for by progressively heavy taxing short-haul air travel and abandoning plans for enlarging runways and motorways (Hutton, W, 2009).

It has to be said, however, that this comes shamefully late in the day and should have happened twenty years ago. By 2025 Britain may have built 400 miles of high-speed rail, roughly what France will do in a year, whereas Europe has 3,480 miles of railways on which trains can travel at 150 mph or more; 2,160 more miles are under construction and another 5,280 are planned totalling 10,000. Meanwhile Britain has 68 miles. We missed the opportunity thanks to lack of imagination, prejudice against rail and the success of the air lobby.

Lessons from New Labour

The only point of looking back is to learn. In response to the biggest crisis in human history there was a failure of leadership. We were warned that the UK would suffer severe power shortages unless bold action was taken. There was no bold strategy. Inconsistent policies bewildered people and made them cynical. It was a wasted opportunity. The nation's attention was diverted, its resources and energy diverted, by war. Now it is diverted by the debt crisis.

Government Failed to Enlist the Nation in a Great Endeavour

- Faced with the biggest environmental crisis in history, they failed to offer an inspiring vision and bold strategy for our future – no Plan B
- There were fundamental splits in government policy and inadequate plans, funding, regulations and enforcement to back up targets

- Our response compared unfavourably with other European countries
- We were shamefully slow to invest in public transport improvements
- Government frequently ignored its expert advisers and was too much influenced by vested interests
- Many ministers are ecologically uneducated
- Failure to see the business advantage of investing in renewables – industry highly critical of the inadequate and stop-go nature of Government support
- Persistent bias towards Mega fixes rather than distributed localised solutions
- Many ill-conceived schemes e.g. the Car Scrappage; Carbon Trading Schemes bungled, exploited to make profits and used dishonestly; Renewables Obligation Credits (ROCs) described as "deeply flawed"

Cautions – National and International Plans and "Hot Air"

I must declare that I am strongly opposed to the nuclear option, for reasons I shall explain later. I want to write with honesty and integrity. It is essential to keep an open mind.

There is considerable confusion about various solutions. Some people believe that UK and global emission targets can be met without using nuclear or coal, by using renewable resources such as wind, wave, tidal, water, solar on roofs and solar in deserts together with greater efficiency, reductions in consumption and reductions in waste. It seems highly probable and desirable given the disadvantages of coal and nuclear power, discussed later.

For solar power to work, countries like the UK without plentiful sun would need to be linked to other countries. To overcome intermittency, countries like those around the North

Sea, with plentiful wind and water power, will be linked together in a network. The overriding challenge for both solar and wind energy effective is to make both storage and energy grid networks over vast distances viable. Both can be done. And, yes, it will all come at a considerable cost.

US Energy Secretary Steven Chu says:

> *The challenge is to make solar energy cost-effective. The amount of energy hitting the Earth – if you looked at it, if you could convert (with photovoltaic cells) 20 per cent of the Sun's energy into electricity you would need 5 per cent of the world's deserts. This is not much land. So the opportunity is enormous. The question is whether we can make it cost-effective. You have to transport this long distances because people don't live in deserts.*

Similarly, on wind:

> *The good news is that many of the areas with good wind are where there aren't many people, so there are fewer objections to wind farms. The bad news is that there aren't many people. So we are planning to look at how you get an interconnecting (transmission) system, to allow us to develop these great resources.*

But, as Stern said, the cost will be nothing compared with the cost of not doing it or delaying action.

Opening Europe's largest onshore wind farm, Whitelee in Scotland, Scottish First Minister Alex Salmond announced that it is to be expanded further. He believes that half of Scotland's power needs can be met from wind power. Incidentally, Scotland has enacted the world's strongest legislation to tackle climate change to cut the nation's CO2 emissions by 42 per cent by 2020. Their Climate Change Bill sets emissions reductions targets of 80 per cent by 2050, including emissions from international aviation and shipping. It also requires the Scottish

Government to set legally binding annual cuts in emissions from 2012. However, to put this in perspective, David MacKay believes that to achieve complete decarbonisation of our electricity supply system by 2030 we'll need about a 100-fold increase in wind farms in Britain and a five-fold increase in nuclear power. That's the scale of the challenge if we're serious about getting off fossil fuels.

A sensible way forward seems to be for each country or region to decide on a plan, based on its natural and bioregional advantages and what it chooses to spend, chosen from several options. David MacKay sets out a number of options for the UK with or without nuclear. The Principle of Subsidiarity needs to be applied.

The case against nuclear power

The precautionary principle should apply. You will know that many former opponents are either now on the fence or have come down in favour of the nuclear solution. They believe the situation is now so dire that it has to be part of the solution. Because of the potential hazards for the ***whole world,*** I believe that new investment by any country in nuclear power should be an international decision. Meanwhile countries like ours should set an example.

An issue for referenda. I believe the issues, particularly regarding the nuclear option, with enormous potential long-term dangers to life, are so important that citizens should decide on a plan for Britain, through a referendum, provided they have been *fully* informed of all aspects of the issues. That still leaves the international implications unresolved, but at least Britain would be setting an example that could influence the world.

Nuclear power produces 16 per cent of the world's electricity and drives several hundred nuclear submarines. Many of the power stations are nearing the end of their lives. Nuclear power is an option with too many unknowns, health risks and security problems. There is still no solution to the problem of how to dispose of highly reactive waste that will remain for a thousand years and more, a toxic legacy for future generations. Reports suggest that European Pressurised Reactors (EPRs) may produce many times more radiation than previous ones. Also, compared with renewable solutions, nuclear power will contribute too little, will be available too late and is too costly. What is more, how can we, with credibility or integrity, oppose other countries such as Iran developing their own nuclear capability if we persist in similar action?

Nuclear power generation poses unacceptable and unresolved risks, as was seen in the Chernobyl disaster in 1986, which was the result of a flawed reactor design that was operated with inadequately trained personnel and without proper regard for safety. The risks which could be devastating are **uninsurable**. The 2005 Chernobyl Forum report said that some seven million people were receiving or eligible for benefits as "Chernobyl victims", which means that resources are not targeting the needy few per cent of them. Remedying this presents daunting political problems, however. Nearly 370 farms in Britain are still restricted in the way they can use land and rear sheep because of radioactive fallout from the Chernobyl accident after 23 years!

Denmark legislated against building further nuclear power stations after Chernobyl.

Imagine the potential for disasters comparable to Chernobyl or terrorist outrages far greater than 9/11, if there are thousands of nuclear power stations all over the world, particularly in the poorest countries, where both safety and security standards may not be up to those of the most advanced countries. Imagine the health risks too.

Government argued that coal and nuclear power are needed to balance the fluctuations of wind, wave and tide. However, nuclear power makes a poor match with renewable sources.

Once a nuclear power station is up and running the best way to run it is to keep it producing at a constant rate until it develops faults and has to be shut down.

A dangerous culture of secrecy. There are reports of a secrecy culture has hindered safe operation, for example at Sellafield and Drigg where both the new owners are struggling to discover, respectively, what has been placed in storage ponds and what is in a waste dump.

Furthermore, it is increasingly obvious that nuclear power is an expensive option. Estimated costs of decommissioning old power stations are enormous, with estimates constantly increasing. According to the National Audit Office, the cost of decommissioning Britain's 19 ageing nuclear plants has jumped from £61bn to £73b in two years and could land the taxpayer with even higher bills in the future. These massive sums could be put into developing green alternatives. Estimates of construction cost are constantly rising too.

Below is my summary of these arguments.

The Case Against Nuclear Power

- Safety, made worse by a culture of secrecy, is still a big unresolved issue as frequent new reports of lapses confirm
- In 2008 the captains of nuclear industry acknowledged they cannot bring nuclear power on-stream for 10 years
- That is not fast enough and 2018 may be optimistic
- In 2018 new plants coming on-stream would replace only a bare minority of 429 plants in the world, many near or past their supposed decommissioning dates
- Costs are likely to run over budget as in Finland and France, whose first new plant in 15 years is currently 20 per cent over budget

- Even if they could make a substantial contribution in 20 years, the industry has found no way to deal with its wastes after many years
- To go ahead, despite this, is acting with total irresponsibility to future generations
- The French government tests have found groundwater radiation leaks under its 58 reactors after a spate of radiation leaks
- Channelling billions of dollars/pounds into nuclear plants will divert resources from energy conservation, energy efficiency and renewables which can produce more rapid results
- There is the problem of multiplying the risks from aggressive states, terrorist weapons, suitcase bombs and smuggling rings
- The Government's Low Carbon Buildings consultation identifies energy-efficient solar photovoltaics as the cheapest technology combination for reaching the first step towards zero carbon in all homes by 2016.
- Thanks to Jeremy Leggett, whose article, *A Nuclear Conversion*, *Ecologist*, April 2009, inspired this summary.

Is government subservient to interests of yesterday's Big Business? Or swayed by those who, wrongly in my opinion, think that despite the arguments above, climate change is so urgent that the nuclear option is essential? We need to be highly sceptical and get the best information we can from different sources to make wise decisions. David MacKay's book is a good starting point.

Nuclear Fusion To cap it all, nuclear fission, the current technology, may be completely replaced by nuclear fusion if the work of Dr Brian MacGowan at the National Ignition Technology Facility (NIF) in central California bears fruit in the form of Laser Inertial Fusion-Fission Energy (LIFE), and a prototype capability could be available in 2020.

What Governments must do

Governments worldwide

Governments need to create an international level playing field, global and regional frameworks, so that nations and corporations can act responsibly without severely disadvantaging themselves. Global action, to create a level playing field, is essential to enable national governments to take action that would otherwise jeopardise their national competitive position. Jonathan Porritt proposes this could be a new role for the World Trade Organisation, instead of fuelling unsustainable growth. USA and China together produce 40 per cent of global CO2 emissions. Barack Obama is seeking agreement with China on joint action to curb emissions. Countries like Denmark, Sweden and Norway are already taking action and it does not seem to be jeopardising their economic position. So, do governments really need to wait?

The global economic system is unsustainable and must be completely rethought. It is obvious that we need a total rethink about how we live and do business. An economic system based on rapid, continuous growth, high consumption, a throwaway society, free trade, global sourcing for lowest cost on a scale requiring massive transportation backwards and forwards across sea and sky, constant redevelopment and construction cannot continue. Complete reappraisal of world trade and European Economic Union policies is needed. Too few people, especially those in government at national, regional and global levels, think in terms of or recognise the extent of what needs to happen. Whole system thinking is required to get us out of the current economic crisis ***and*** the environmental crisis.

Rich countries bear the heaviest responsibility both currently and historically. We have the technological capability and the means. The "West", seen by other nations to have created the problem, needs to show the way, set an example and help poorer nations develop their own ways out of poverty and into sustainability. Ultimately the fairest solution may be a personal CO2 limit of 2 tonnes for every person on the planet. The technology to implement this exists. See Part Two.

UK Government

Government must provide a clear, consistent, joined up and comprehensive strategy that will inspire and enrol the nation as the government did in WWII. It needs to provide a clear framework within which business and local government can deliver the goods. It needs to reward the sustainable, penalise the unsustainable, make sustainability affordable for everyone, nurture nascent green technology, help make "going green" profitable and give local communities much more responsibility and say. Enabling measures are needed to remove obstacles. Government has ample scope to set an example: how it operates its buildings, investments in infrastructure, sourcing decisions and the influence it can bring to bear on suppliers.

Government spending on going green. Back in 2009, Lord Nicholas Stern recommended 20 per cent of all new spending should be devoted to green measures and warned delay will cost us much more. This is by far the highest and most urgent priority. It could lead us out of recession and, as proposed in Part Two, without creating more debt. Government must to face up to radical reform that incentivises the sustainable and penalises the unsustainable. Taxing energy at source is essential to provide funds for a green industrial revolution and to ease the transition. Will it happen under the coalition's big squeeze? We need to make sure it does.

Momentum is growing

Change comes about in two ways: Quantum leaps often initiated or led by extraordinary individuals; and millions of steps taken by people all over the world. Sometimes, inexplicably a tipping point is reached. Two small examples: suddenly people are using hessian carrier bags all over our town. Giving up carrier plastic bags and fitting eco light bulbs will not save us but it shows how changes can come about quite quickly. Collectively, individuals can make a difference but strong government initiatives are essential.

Daring to dream. It's important for us to see breakdowns as opportunities, full of exciting possibilities. For example, how the US can generate 90 per cent of its electricity from solar energy captured in an area of desert smaller than Nevada. Half of US States have acted to cut emissions and more than 800 cities have promised to meet or beat Kyoto Protocol targets. Once human beings fully understand the problem and are inspired by future possibilities their creativity is extraordinary.

A note before embarking on the next section: Everything is inter-connected in a complex living system. Thus, many of strategies and actions needed to resolve those described in Section A will also apply to the following sections of this chapter and vice versa. I hope this will not lead to undue repetition.

Section B: Peak Oil and Its Impact on Our Lives

World leaders are still calling for the continuation economic growth and of global trade free on a vast scale. Yet both are dependent on abundant fossil fuel and simply unsustainable. Peak Oil and climate change combine to create a dual crisis, an emergency requiring urgent action we are not taking. We are behaving as if we can restore the status quo. We are squandering a precious commodity. It's insanity!

The definition of insanity is doing the same thing over and over again and expecting different results.
Albert Einstein

Most experts say that oil supplies have peaked or will do so within a few years. The Association for the Study of Peak Oil and Gas (ASPO) says "regular" oil peaked in 2005 and oil and gas combined will peak in 2015. Three years ago the price was $55 per barrel. In June 2008, before the recession, Gazprom predicted $250 in 2009. In July 2008, it rose to $147. By 19 January, 2009, it was down to $35, the lowest price for many years! The recession is keeping consumption and prices down. Ultimately prices will escalate. The International Energy Agency (IEA) expects oil prices to return to $100 per barrel before 2015.

Oil from tar sands. As the best reserves are exhausted, oil companies are starting to extract oil from tar sand reserves beneath the boreal forest that stretches across Russia, Canada, Alaska and Scandinavia. The forests destroyed in the process are enormous carbon sinks that absorb large amounts of carbon. Extracting oil in this way will be harder, costlier and more polluting. Producing oil from tar sands unleashes two to three times more pollution than conventionally produced oil. This defeats our efforts to cut carbon emissions. The refining process requires large amounts of toxic chemicals. The current development of oil production from the oil sands of Alberta is the biggest construction project on the planet. Pristine forests and sensitive wetlands are being destroyed and toxic lakes are being created. Birds die on contact with the water and mutated fish are found downstream. Aboriginal people living downstream are reported to be suffering disproportionately high rates of cancer. Ultimately the toxic waste ends up in the Arctic Ocean, destroying ecosystems on its way.

Yet, oil companies are ruthlessly pursuing this for profit, perpetuating an unsustainable way of life, and acting as if we did not face a crisis. Such developments involve not only oil companies but many large corporations supplying them and banks providing capital. Your bank may be involved. For further information and action you can take, read *Ethical Consumer*, Stop the Oil Sands, July/August 2009.

George Monbiot says no one really knows when oil production will peak (gas will come later and coal much later) whether ten or thirty years hence, but warns that we may face simultaneously catastrophic climate change and an unprecedented global depression. Not only are we running out of oil and natural gas and, in the long-term, coal and uranium, we are running out of most major materials used in manufacturing. Although coal is likely to last much longer, it is extremely polluting. Carbon capture, not available on a large-scale, cannot be guaranteed to work and is likely to be expensive. Those who favour a nuclear solution argue that reserves of uranium will last a long time and the amounts required are small. If objections to its use are accepted, we shall have to find renewable alternatives.

A "global energy revolution" is needed yet there is no evidence of any Peak Oil contingency plans. George Monbiot's article Cross Your Fingers and Carry On, published in the *Guardian*, 14 April 2009, is extremely worrying. He reported his interview with the Chief Economist of the International Energy Agency (IEA), who said that global conventional oil would plateau in 2020 and a *"global energy revolution"* is needed. George Monbiot quoted the conclusions of Robert L Hirsch, commissioned by the US Department of Energy, who warned that, *"Without timely mitigation, the economic, social and political costs will be unprecedented,"* and that to avoid global economic collapse, we need to begin *"a mitigation crash program 20 years before peaking."* That makes us nearly ten years too late. From conversations with UK government officials, he could find no evidence of any contingency plans to avoid disaster.

Imagine the situation at the end of the 21st century when oil and natural gas supplies may be largely exhausted. Imagine the scale of the change needed in a world economy based on fossil fuel and non-renewable resources. Imagine the impact on construction and farming. There will have to be a complete change in the way we live. If we do not adapt soon enough, there is a real possibility of global collapse, widespread unemployment and starvation. The global economy, and our unsustainable lifestyles, based on abundant cheap oil, will be transformed. The recession, keeping down oil, gas consumption and CO2 emissions, is the calm before the storm.

We need to completely rethink the global economic system.

The case for "free trade" and global sourcing, the basis of the global economic system, must be rethought. Nations and regions will need to be free to work out their own policies and become far more self-sufficient. This will be a problem for countries like the UK who have lost most of their manufacturing capacity and a substantial percentage of their agriculture. Our whole global economic system, based on global sourcing for lowest cost, and on global and national distribution systems are dependent on cheap fossil fuel. Electric power for vehicles and trains will not offer a sustainable solution whilst electricity continues to be mainly generated by using fossil fuel. Oil is embedded in almost everything we consume: fuel, power, heating, transport, plastics, fabrics, packaging, food and utensils. Oil, especially, needs to be treated as a precious resource to be used sparingly and increasingly heavily taxed at source to discourage its unnecessary use and provide funding for the green revolution and measures to ease the transition.

Our supermarket and superstore system for distributing food, household essentials and other goods is unsustainable and may not survive. Local food production and distribution may supersede it for many reasons. Could we see supermarket buildings converted into market halls for small producers and traders and a resurgence of local shops and businesses?

Food: the implications of Peak Oil for food

Food security is at risk. As a result of this oil-based industrialised and globalised food production and distribution system, we are now a net importer of food, heavily dependent on other countries. Our self-sufficiency is estimated at 60 per cent. Other data gives a UK self-sufficiency figure of 49 per cent. That overall figure hides much larger gaps, such as 94 per cent of all fruit and over 50 per cent of vegetables consumed in the UK are imported. Seventy per cent of animal feed used in EU is imported. Another threat to food security is the domination of food production of by a few very large global corporations and the small number of food crop varieties that has resulted. One owns 23 per cent of global seed production. That makes us vulnerable to business collapse and exposes us to famine.

In UK, without cheap oil, we will have difficulty feeding ourselves. Oil is a major component of agriculture. Intensive agriculture is dependent on oil. Present-day methods of farming depend on large machines, including some absolutely enormous ones guided by satellite navigation systems, and on the use of oil-based pesticides and herbicides. Nitrogen fertilizer is made from natural gas which is not yet peaking but will do in time. Potash and phosphorus, coming from phosphate, are mined minerals in plentiful supply but their application and their distribution to farms depends on oil (nitrogen fertilizer releases nitrous oxide which is three times more damaging to the environment than CO2).

Clearly, we shall not be able to continue using machines on the current scale or herbicides and pesticides based on fossil fuels and we'll need to cut back on artificial fertilisers.

We'll need a lot more farmers, preferably with organic farms. Yet, only 150,000 farms are left in the UK; the average age of farmers is 60; hill farming is in danger of dying out within ten years; 95 per cent of our food is totally dependent on fossil fuel; we have lost much of our knowledge about how to farm without it and how to farm sustainably. Our 125,000 farm workers are amongst the lowest paid workers. Many young people, who might choose to be farmers, can no longer afford to live in the villages they were brought up in because of the unaffordable prices of homes, inflated by the influx of affluent people, many of whom are downshifting or choosing to retire to the countryside.

It would not take much to provide more houses for young people who wish to stay where they were brought up and contribute to the rural economy that we shall depend on more and more.

We need more food production to be locally or regionally based to save oil. Yet, of all Common Agricultural Policy (CAP) money, 80 per cent went to only 20 per cent of farmers and mainly to the biggest and wealthiest ones. It is likely that we'll need to grow far more in allotments, community allotments and our gardens.

Oil-based agriculture has degraded our soil and killed the microorganisms that create healthy soil. We have destroyed much of the living ecosystem including hedgerows and woodlands that are an important part of the wider ecosystem that provides fertility and controls pests. We need to return to old wisdom about agriculture, learn from permaculture and forest gardening, adapting it all to a vastly larger need. We have degraded our soil and microorganisms that create healthy soil. Again, we need to eat less meat because it requires much more oil than vegetable sources of nutrition.

Worldwide the problem is far more serious than in the UK and Europe. Latest estimates from the UN Food and Agriculture Organization (FAO) show that another 40 million people have already been pushed into hunger in 2008 as a result of higher food prices resulting from higher oil prices.

Growing cash crops for rich nations makes poor countries even more vulnerable. They too have been encouraged to industrialise their agriculture and use oil-based chemicals. The system of Western nations sourcing vegetables and flowers, whatever the season, from poor countries has resulted in their growing cash crops for us on a large scale. This has undermined their own local food production and their traditional wide range of crop species and their traditional expertise and methods adapted to their climate and soil conditions, making them even more vulnerable to malnutrition and starvation. The free market has put many local farmers and market traders out of business, unable to compete with imports from Western countries.

Further reading: *Ethical Consumer*, Stop the Oil Sands, July/August 2009

Section C: Destruction of the Earth
The effect of continuing economic growth on the planet

> *As the world struggles to recover from the most serious global economic crisis since the Great Depression, we have an unprecedented opportunity to turn away from consumerism. In the end, the human instinct for survival must triumph over the urge to consume at any cost.*
>
> **Christopher Flavin**, President, Worldwatch Institute

We are consuming and destroying the planet's resources at a rapidly growing rate that is unsustainable.

Since the early 1970s we humans have been steadily exceeding the Earth's bio-capacity by more and more. There's a limit to what "spaceship Earth" can provide. Currently we consume 30 per cent more than the Earth's capacity and both world population and their expectations are growing. We are spending our capital. Every year human beings consume 400 years' worth of ancient solar energy in the form of fossil fuels. We cannot go on like this.

Ecological footprint

Ecological footprint measures humanity's demand on the biosphere in terms of the area of biologically productive land and sea required to provide the resources we use and to absorb our waste. This needs to be in balance with the biosphere's capacity to provide what we need, cope with our waste and regenerate (ecological footprint). In 2005 the global Ecological Footprint was estimated at 17.5bn global hectares (gha), or 2.7gha per person (a global hectare is a hectare with world-average ability to produce resources and absorb wastes). Putting it another way, our footprint was 1.3 planet Earths and humanity used ecological services 1.3 times faster than Earth can renew them.

On the supply side, the total productive area, or bio-capacity, was 13.6bn gha, or 2.1gha per person. A country's footprint is the sum of all the cropland, grazing land, forest and fishing grounds required to produce the food, fibre and timber it consumes, to absorb the wastes emitted when it uses energy, and to provide space for its infrastructure. Since people consume resources and ecological services from all over the world, their footprint affects everywhere, regardless of where they are located on the planet.

Bio-Capacity is Divided into Six Main Land Types:

- **Cropland:** subdivided into primary and marginal land (e.g. wheat, olives), measured in tonnes per hectare per year of crop that you can harvest
- **Pasture:** tonnes per hectare per year of meat/dairy, thought the total footprint of the livestock will take into account the cropland and fisheries needed for animal feed
- **Forestry:** metres cubed per hectare per year, there is no difference between natural or managed land
- **Fisheries:** the maximum sustainably caught yield in

tonnes per hectare per year

- **Carbon:** the area of forestry required to sequester the tonnage of carbon dioxide, including nuclear, which is considered to be equivalent to fossil fuels
- **Built up land:** considered to be replacing primary cropland, though this assumption is obviously shaky e.g. think of Dubai or Tibet with their vast areas of land that cannot be cultivated!

Source: *Chance, T.* (http://tom.acrewoods.net)

Andrew Simms, Policy Director of the New Economics Foundation, calculated that the world overshot its biological capacity for the year on 23 September 2008, the earliest "ecological debt day" on record and that we are heading for ecological system collapse. Another indicator is the increasing proportion of the Earth's land prone to drought. UK Hadley Centre for Climate Prediction and Research says that area is likely to rise to nearly one third. Together with rising food prices, this is leading to increasing numbers of hungry people who are likely to migrate. In California, drought is having a devastating effect on people, the economy and agriculture in the state that is the largest producer of food and agricultural products in the USA. Governor Arnold Schwarzenegger has declared a state of emergency.

Wealthy nations like us take far more than our fair share of world resources, as I show in the chart below. Putting it bluntly, it's greed. Citizens in Europe and other rich countries generally consume far more resources than people anywhere else. London's "footprint" is huge. London requires 125 times its surface area to provide its needs. If everyone consumed like Londoners, we would need three planets; five at the Los Angeles rate! Yet most countries aspire to this unsustainable "Western" way of life. The UK's food and farming footprint is up to six times the food growing area of the UK. In the UK we are taking very much more than our fair share and we must substantially reduce it. We need to take this seriously and reduce our consumption of resources, make better and more efficient use of them and, in particular, avoid new construction unless there is a powerful justification.

Eco-Footprints per Country

Average hectares* per person

1	United Arab Emirates:	15.99
2	United States:	12.22
3	Kuwait:	10.31
4	Denmark:	9.88
5	New Zealand:	9.54
6	Ireland:	9.43
7	Australia:	8.49
8	Finland:	8.45
9	Canada:	7.66
10	Sweden:	7.53
11	France:	7.27
12	Estonia:	7.12
13	Switzerland:	6.63
14	Germany:	6.31
15	Czech Republic:	6.3
16	United Kingdom:	6.29
17	Saudi Arabia:	6.15
77	China:	1.84
108	India:	1.06
141	Bangladesh:	0.6
	Weighted average:	**3.1**

*hectare = 11 959.9005 square yards

Sources: World Wide Fund for Nature (WWF), *Living Planet Report 2000*, Gland, Switzerland.

The inconvenient truth. As populations and their aspirations increase, we face an even greater problem. A fair share would be approximately 1.8 global hectares per person. The inconvenient truth is that ultimately, people in the USA, Denmark, Germany, France and the UK for example will need to reduce their average ecological footprint per person from 12.22, 9.88, 6.31, 7.27 and 6.29 respectively to 1.8 global hectares. This is a major adjustment!

I asked Tom Chance to help me make sense of how we can meet this challenge. He referred me to "tom's blog" (at that time):

> *Most people including BioRegional and WWF calculate our fair share according to the projected global population in 2050. That works out at 1.8gha rather than the figure based on current population – which works out at 2.1gha – because most targets relate to our average footprint in 2050. That also doesn't leave any land totally protected for other species, for example wilderness reserves and national parks. There is no agreement on the total proportion of land that we should leave – estimates range from 10 per cent to 40 per cent – but we can say that 1.8gha is definitely too generous if you care about biodiversity. You might think it's important to protect other species; you might agree with James Lovelock that biodiversity is necessary for a healthy biosphere and atmosphere that can support us … or you might just be cautious about overexploiting every last bit of land!*

So, clearly, even 1.8gha is too much if we take account of other creatures. Even if our only reason for caring about their fate is that our lives actually do depend on them as they are part of a complex ecosystem.

However, in his blog *Why I am not an eco-angel,* Tom also says:

> *If you (or we!) do everything much more efficiently, you don't need*

to cut everything out. What I mean by that is that, if you produce food twice as efficiently (for example) you don't need to go on a severe diet! The way we make stuff at the moment makes it basically impossible for a UK citizen to lead a reasonable life within their fair share, but it is possible if we really reinvent our economy.

He continues:

I've gone past the suggestion that it's our individual responsibility to somehow reduce our impacts down to a sustainable level on our own. Not only is this message impossible to sell to anyone outside the "keen green" demographic (because it's too hard); it's also fundamentally wrong! Here are 3 reasons why:

- ***We won't change people's values by being angelic.*** *We merely reinforce how different we are to the norm, which is heavily marketed by government and business. It's good to avoid charges of hypocrisy, but it's also important to explain with humility why you – like most other people – find it hard. That takes the conversation to the more important changes we need to enable and facilitate sustainable lifestyles in the mainstream.*
- ***We lack the infrastructure and services*** *to make many sustainable lifestyle choices. Our towns and cities embed the car as the most convenient mode of travel; moving to living streets, car and bicycle clubs, better public transport and so on enables people to make a shift. Without the infrastructure and services those choices remain very unlikely outside of the keen green demographic. So long as this remains the case, our super-sustainable choices will be of little consequence because they won't spread out to the majority of the population. Better to work on the underlying causes, and make your own life easier as a result.*
- ***Upstream efficiency*** *in the supply chain reduces the impact of your lifestyle choices. Eating less meat and dairy is definitely*

> *necessary; but if farming, your cooking and every process in between are made more efficient, you need to make less of a reduction through your food choices. If you want to reduce your transport emissions to a sustainable level today you get a budget with zero flying miles, zero foreign train holidays and a few train holidays around the UK, with the majority of commuting by bicycle or foot. If you model resource efficiencies throughout the economy, you suddenly get to travel quite a lot more.*

> *The changes we need in the economy, political systems, civil society institutions, neighbourhoods and personal values are complex and profound. Insisting that we all "walk the talk" not only backfires as a strategy, it's also a self-deception.*

This means we have to lobby for system change if we are serious about "saving the planet" or more accurately, saving ourselves, our children and grandchildren, the whole of humanity and all the other creatures on the planet.

We are the most destructive creatures on the planet. Many scientists believe the rate of species loss is greater now than at any time in history. We have already lost 30 per cent of species and three quarters of the genetic diversity of agricultural crops. That endangers food security. Today's forest contains around 70 per cent to 90 per cent of the Earth's species. We are dependent on forests for many of our pharmaceutical remedies. Yet we are rapidly destroying forests. We have already lost half. We do not appreciate that we are dependent on ***all*** species for our well-being.

Homo sapiens? Do we deserve that name? In the next 30 years, half of the species on the Earth could die in one of the fastest mass extinctions in the planet's 4.5 billion years' history. Nearly 4700 species are now in danger of extinction, according to David Attenborough. Dr Leakey, author of *The Sixth Extinction,* believes that 50 per cent of the Earth's species will vanish within 100 years. Such a dramatic mass extinction threatens the complex fabric of life, including homo sapiens. The problem is not just the loss of species. There is the loss of the genetic diversity ***within*** species, and the loss of diversity of different types of *ecosystems,* which can contribute to whole species extinction. Preserving the wider gene pool's diversity provides the raw material for the evolution of new species in the future. According to National Wildlife Federation's estimates in *Web of Creation,* every day, 100 plant and animal species are lost to deforestation and the about 27,000 species a year are lost.

Take the example of fish. Eating fish is good for health. Fish used to form 25 per cent of our diet. Now it is a fraction of that. Some of us take supplements to compensate for this loss. Yet, we throw vast quantities of dead or dying fish back into the sea: nearly a third by weight in the North Sea, 1.3 million tonnes annually or 13 per cent catch in the North Atlantic and 75 per cent of red fish worldwide. Of those thrown back live, only about 1 per cent survive. 75 per cent of remaining fish are under severe threat.

Under EU rules, some 40 per cent to 60 per cent of the fish caught are thrown back dead into the sea – think about how fishermen feel about that! Norway, not a member of the EU, has a sane, strictly enforced policy. Fishermen throw nothing back; they are forced to land all fish for sale; but they are severely fined if they exceed the limits. Now the EU is considering adopting the same policy. There is a lesson here: remote, unaccountable bureaucracies get it wrong; work out policies with those on the ground or, in this case, on the sea!

Earlier this year I was on holiday in Aldeburgh, Suffolk. I regularly went down to the beach early in the morning to buy fish, caught a few hours before. We cooked it in the evening. It was so different from the fish we have grown used to in supermarkets, no unpleasant smell and delicious. I chatted to the elderly fisherman who sells fish for his younger colleagues. He told me they fish just off the coast, mainly using lines. There is only one trawler left now as a result of the EU policy. He said there are plenty of fish and small scale fishing does no harm to fish stocks. It is the big vessels with huge nets that have caused the problems. He said the policy of throwing back good fish makes no sense. Fishermen had the backing of local MPs, judges and other influential people who made representations; but it made no difference. The committees don't include fishermen. Brussels and Westminster don't listen to fishermen. Nor do the inspectors who enforce the policy or the authorities. Soon, only the big fleets will be left. As for MPs, *"you might as well have fish crates sitting in their seats for all the difference they make!"*

Humans, to survive, need all diverse species – the web of life! We are part of intricate, interconnected relationships between Planet Earth and all living things. For a sustainable future, we need to treasure and cherish this ecological diversity of which we are a part. Surely we must recognise that other creatures have rights too, as has been acknowledged recently in Ecuador. Satish Kumar, like Gandhi, says all nature is holy; all life has intrinsic value. Everything is interconnected. We are who we are in relationship to others. We need to respect different peoples, cultures and religions, and abandon violence in every form: thought, word and deed, including violence towards other animals and the planet of which we are a part. Ecuador has recently legislated to grant constitutional rights to nature.

We face degradation of the Earth, increasing pollution, growing shortages, not only of fossil fuels, but food, agricultural land and water and a colossal waste problem. Already scarcity is leading to conflicts. We need to abandon the idea that we are the masters: everything is there for us to exploit and the fate of other peoples and species is relatively unimportant.

> *We have to make people realize we're destroying the basis of all our lives.*
> **Winfried Blum**, secretary-general of the International Union of Soil Science (IUSS).

Scientists say impoverishment of the soil is a major threat to the global population's ability to feed itself. They have found that nearly 40 per cent of the world's agricultural land is seriously degraded. The damage has already had "a significant impact" on the productivity of about 16 per cent of the planet's farmland.

> *Soil is not well understood but it is the basis of our lives. It also provides a sink for carbon emissions. Desertification is likely to spread as a result of human activity.*
> **Sophie Boukhari**

Food

The system of global sourcing and industrialising food production is harmful. Apart from producing huge amounts of CO_2 through transportation (e.g. "food miles"), it damages the provision of good, fresh food on which human life and health depends. It puts our food in the hands of too few large corporations and destroys variety. This is unsafe.

In the UK we are steadily destroying our farming and local food production. Thirty-seven per cent of the UK's food is now imported compared with 27 per cent in 1995. We were virtually self-sufficient in WWII. The effects on farmers everywhere are devastating. For food to be fresh and sustainable, production needs to be largely local. People have become separated from the sources of food and from cooking. We are endangering food security which requires diversity and an understanding of local soil and climate conditions. We are destroying indigenous ancient knowledge about ecology, cultivation, nutrition and healing. Industrialised farming methods destroy the millions of tiny organisms that are an essential part of healthy fertile soil. We are making food more, not less, expensive. As we buy our out-of-season vegetables and flowers from places like Kenya, we use precious water needed for local food crops. Embedded water is as important a measure of sustainability as food miles or CO2 emissions.

We are over fed but undernourished. In the UK we suffer a major obesity epidemic because of poor diet and lifestyle. There is an explosion of diabetes linked to growing obesity (46 per cent of men and 32 per cent of women are overweight). Obesity is growing at a faster rate than in Canada and the USA. In the UK, 33 per cent of men, 28 per cent of women and 20 per cent of children will be obese by 2010. Obesity rates have trebled since the 1980s. The £20bn cost of diet-related diseases to the NHS is unsustainable and could reach £50bn by 2050. But in countries like the USA, where until recently 40 million had no health care insurance, or worse still India, where there is no NHS, the consequences are even worse. Unhealthy Western diets, including soft drinks instead of water, lifestyles and methods of producing food are spread throughout the world.

The effects on our food and health of industrialised worldwide agribusiness

Because of large-scale mono-cultures there has been a major loss in biodiversity. Seventy-five per cent of the world's food is dependent on 12 plant types and 5 animal species. This exposes the world to great risk. Multiple varieties are important to food security. In 1971 it became illegal to sell seed varieties in the EU unless they were registered, a process that is too expensive for small varieties. So only a basic range of seeds, convenient to grow in large quantities, is available. Garden Organic warn that because of the industrialisation of food production, distribution through supermarkets and the domination of seed production by huge companies, we have lost thousands of vegetable species.

In Victorian times there were 120 different varieties of tall garden pea. Now there are only two and a few varieties of dwarf pea dominate.

During the past half century vegetables, fruit, meat and milk have lost considerable percentages of mineral content that is important to health. This is because of artificial methods of fertilising soil which destroy the microorganisms that release these minerals, as opposed to using crop rotation and manure. Nitrogen fertiliser actually depresses the biological activity in soil. Organic food contains higher levels of essential nutrients than non-organic including minerals and 40 per cent more antioxidants.

Some Food Facts

Pesticides 311 pesticides are available to non-organic farmers. There is little control over how they are used; for example, crops of Cox's apples can be spayed 16 times. There are concerns about links between pesticides and cancers, damage to the nervous system, decreasing male fertility, foetal abnormalities and chronic fatigue syndrome. Organic farmers are allowed to use only four pesticides and if all farmland switched to organic, a 98% reduction would be achieved.

Antibiotics are used as growth promoters and to prevent diseases that would otherwise make it impossible to rear animals in cruel conditions. Overuse of antibiotics is thought to be contributing to increasing cases of superbugs and the WHO has called for a reduction in their use as a risk to human health. Organic farmers are limited to their use only for essential veterinary applications. Disease is avoided by good husbandry and lower density.

Additives Over 300 additives are allowed for non-organic processed foods. Many have been found unsafe and some have not been tested. Allergies, child hyperactivity and osteoporosis have been linked to some which are in continued use. Only those required by law are allowed under Soil Association standards.

BSE There have been over 100 deaths probable or confirmed in UK from CJD since 1996 as a result of eating beef contaminated by BSE as a result of cattle fed with animal protein. Organic standards demand that cows are only fed a natural diet predominantly of grass, hay and other roughage. No case of BSE has been recorded in any animal born or reared organically in UK.

Source: *The Soil Association*

Epidemics and pandemics amongst farm animals and poultry are growing and having devastating effects on farming. Cheap meat production involves a high degree of cruelty, animals enduring appalling conditions that must desensitise the workers and owners involved. The scale of pandemics with animal origins that may wipe out vast numbers of humans is being attributed to the industrialisation and inhumane conditions involved in animal food production.

Some scientists believe pandemics like avian flu and the current swine flu are a consequence of grossly cruel and unethical animal husbandry, previously hidden from the public. We are becoming aware of the terrible conditions in which chickens, turkeys, pigs and cows are being kept to provide cheap meat and milk. As Professor Mark Woolhouse, an epidemiologist at the University of Edinburgh, reminds us, the transfer of illnesses from animals is not new, but globalisation creates "happy days" for many diseases.

A recent BBC1 *Country File* programme showed Holstein cows kept inside, fed a mixture of cattle feed, never seeing a field of grass. Weighing three quarters of a ton, standing up to five feet high, they were specially bred to produce massive amounts of milk. Lameness and udder disease in UK dairy herds are amongst the highest in the world. Our dairy industry has one of the worst animal welfare records in Europe. The RSPCA says that we are in danger of "milking our cows to death". Another farmer showed how she ran a successful dairy farm using smaller Friesian cows in green pasture to produce her milk. A scientific study into the welfare of dairy cows in Europe may result in new directives for standards of welfare.

Would you knowingly buy milk, yoghurt or cheese produced in this way, because it's cheaper?

Bee colony collapse: another threat to food security. The British Beekeepers Association warns that colony collapse could wipe out bees in Britain by 2018. Bees are essential for pollinating crops. The causes are complex and may include toxic pesticides and bees being under stress. One thing people can do to help is to plant more flowers and shrubs that attract bees in their gardens. The same thing needs to be done in public spaces like parks, verges and roundabouts. There is also a campaign by the British Beekeepers Association to encourage more people to keep bees.

World Poisoning from Pesticides

- Each year, around 2.5 million tons (2,500,000 tons = 5 billion pounds) of pesticide are dumped on the planet's crops.
- In 2002, an estimated 69,000 children were poisoned by pesticides in the US.
- The World Health Organization reports 220,000 people

die every year worldwide because of pesticide poisoning.

- In 2001, the world pesticide market was valued at $32bn ($32,000,000,000).
- Although most pesticides (80%) are used in rich countries, most poisonings are in poor countries. This is because safety standards are poor; there may be no protective clothing or washing facilities, insufficient enforcement, poor labelling of pesticides which are used by farm workers who can't read anyway. Few people know much about pesticide hazards.
- Pesticide residues in food are often higher in poor countries.
- Farmers who use pesticides have a 'significantly higher rate of cancer incidence' than non-farmers.
- In the US, nearly one in ten of about 3bn kilograms (6,613,800,000 pounds) of toxic chemicals released per year is known to be capable of causing cancer (in other animals as well as people).

Source: *One World Net*

Cash crops produced by poor countries for wealthy Northerners are a major contributor to water scarcity, desertification and salinisation caused by excessive irrigation in dry areas. Salinisation is one of our biggest environmental problems, a major cause of desertification and soil degradation. Salinisation and sodification are among the major degradation processes endangering the potential use of soils in Europe and elsewhere in the world. Furthermore, to produce these exports, peasants are ***deprived*** of the land that gives them independence; local food production is damaged and forests destroyed to make way for meat, grain and now biofuel exports. These are of little benefit to poor, dispossessed people or local economies.

Dietary diversity is vital to health and disease prevention. A healthy diet requires a complex mixture of nutrients, not just protein, energy, fats, carbohydrates and vitamins. We need complex diets rich in micronutrients. We are learning that traditional food, made from a variety of crops, grown for centuries from seeds saved over generations, unique to the environment in which people live, are full of important micronutrients that are vital to health and preventing diseases. As Westernisation took hold, these were often discarded as "poor peoples' food" and replaced by imports or new crops. In places like Kenya there are now efforts to publicise this information and reintroduce such indigenous crops, as well as how to cook them to make them delicious.

Globalisation is undermining the production and use of indigenous foods, so important to our health, all over the world, including in Western countries.

Crop diversity is vitally important. Many of old species have drought resistance or other qualities valuable in growing crops in adverse conditions. The reduction in varieties to a very small number for industrialised agriculture thus damages food security as well as nutrition and health.

We are degrading our built environment too.

Not only are we degrading the Earth. By putting power and profit before people, we are creating more and more ugliness. We are destroying those aspects of our built environment that have historic and cultural meaning and beauty. People thrive in beautiful places and become depressed in ugliness. The human spirit suffers in ugliness and dereliction.

Older buildings of a more human scale, often built lovingly by craftsmen using natural and local materials, are being replaced by monster developments, symbolic of the false values of many big corporations and government. These are expressions of masculine domination and power. Institutions shape our mindset. Business without soul creates ugliness; ugliness is bad for our spirit and energy.

The process of massive redevelopment: demolition, new building and construction, greatly adds to our Carbon and Eco impacts. It creates enormous externalised environmental and social costs. There has to be a careful assessment of the balance of gains and harms.

Section D: Poverty and Economic Injustice

In writing this part, I am much indebted to David Woodward and his report for the New Economics Foundation report, *Growth isn't working*, January 2006.

Global poverty

Vandana Shiva calls the current credo of global institutions, national and regional governments and big business: *mono-thinking and mono-culture.* It is mono-everything. This one size fits all policy requires continuous economic growth, measured by Gross Domestic Product (GDP), a misnomer, as really it is Gross Domestic Cost (GDC). It also demands unfettered free trade. That flies in the face of economic history. Nascent economies require protection. Trade liberalisation has not brought the benefits we were given to expect. Growing wealth is concentrated in fewer people.

Rapid economic growth is far too slow in reducing poverty. If global GDP per capita continued to grow at around 2 per cent per annum, it would take more than a century to reduce poverty below the $1 a day level. Between 1990 and 2001 the incomes of those below $1 a day grew only half as fast as global GDP. If this trend were to continue, their incomes would rise by only 1 per cent per year, and the process to reduce poverty below the $1 a day level would take more than 200 years, and require the global economy to expand to more than 60 times its current size even without population growth .

Continuous Economic Growth Isn't Working

- Until the eighties the poverty gap was closing
- Between 1990 and 2001, for every $100 of growth in the World's per person income, only $0.60 contributed to reducing poverty below the $1 a day level
- UK growth benefits the richest 10 % 10 times as much as the poorest 10 %
- UK top executives earn nearly 100 times more than a typical employee. Ten years ago the differential was 39
- US CEOs were paid 344 times more than workers in 2008, up from 104 in 1991
- The wealth of the world's 475 billionaires is now more than the combined income of the bottom half of humanity
- The richest 1% of adults in the world own 40% of the planet's wealth
- More wealth does not = more happiness – beyond a certain point
- Where the income gap is highest so are all the measures of unhappiness

A recent UN-Habitat report said the wealth gap is creating a social time bomb of unrest and increased mortality.

India has dramatic poverty after sixty years of independence. It is not being helped by large corporations or the industrialisation of agriculture. Well over 100,000 farmers have committed suicide since 1993, largely as a result of debt and failed GM crops. Globalisation is certainly not working for the 73 per cent of Indians dependant on agriculture or the 280 million poor living in India's 600,000 villages or the slums of Mumbai. Often, the process of rapid economic development deprives poor people off the land – the only thing they can depend on for their living. Compensation for the loss of land is useless.

New Delhi authorities, in their attempts to Westernise their city by sweeping food stalls off the streets, are destroying a source of cheap, nourishing food and putting poor people out of work. What replaces street food will be more expensive and less healthy "fast food". There is also a battle going on between those who value the current system in which poor people earn a living by reclaiming waste and those who want to use incineration which, amongst other toxins, produces harmful dioxins.

Instead of reducing worldwide poverty, rapid economic development in developing and wealthier nations makes a growing elite of super-rich people vastly richer. Of course relatively small numbers are rising out of poverty to become middle class. We see this most graphically in Mumbai where, despite rapidly growing prosperity, 62 per cent of the population live in slums. This pattern of economic development creates problems everywhere, most of all in poor countries and poor areas of rich ones. Certainly some countries, like Singapore, have been lifted out of poverty, but in many cases, ***not through free trade***. Like us, they enjoyed protection whilst developing their economies. Adam Smith (1776), misquoted by advocates of unrestrained free-market capitalism, had a much more complex view.

International efforts to eradicate poverty, over the years, have failed. They create huge debt; destroy livelihoods and local food production, further undermine self-reliance and pride and create dependency. The conditions of aid, restructuring meaning privatising public services and reducing expenditure on education and health services, have been very damaging. Livelihoods of local farmers and peasants are being ruined in many poor countries by land grabbing and the incursions of large national and global corporations. The rush to produce biofuels is a disaster for people and the environment.

The fundamental obstacle to overcoming poverty is a global trade system. The following figure summarises the policies that do most harm. These are enforced by unrepresentative bodies pursuing the interests of big business and wealthy countries, General Agreement on Tariffs and Trade (GATT), World Trade Organisation (WTO), World Bank, International Monetary Fund (IMF) and European Union (EU).

Rich Countries' Unfair Trade System

Trade policies

- International organisations (WTO), World Bank, International Monetary Fund (IMF) and European Union (EU) and negotiations are dominated by the countries with the highest GDP who set the agenda
- Imposition, by such institutions together with big corporations, of Western ways of doing things, which are frequently inappropriate, shows disrespect for local populations and disempowers them – the reverse of what is needed
- Loans and aid are conditional on "Structural Adjustment Programs" (SAPs) that privatise or reduce public spending on health, education and social services, falling hardest on the poor
- Privatisation enables rich countries to take over public services, like water, often at much higher cost to poor people
- Loans instead of aid create enormous debt and interest burden
- Many poor countries have to allocate the majority of revenues to debt repayment instead of health care and education
- Western countries impose free trade and do not allow

the protection needed for local enterprise to grow
- Removal of tariff barriers to imports from rich countries is not reciprocated
- Heavily subsidised Western products are dumped on poor countries, thus undermining or destroying the capacity of local producers and traders and the capacity of poor countries to build their own economies
- Food aid frequently has the same effect
- Basically these policies exploit poor nations' resources without proper benefit to them

Irresponsible corporate practices
- The high cost of Western drugs and copyrights obstructing generic drugs (Agreement on Trade Related Aspects of Intellectual Property Rights (TRIPS).
- Imposing GM seeds linked to expensive pesticides that require extra cost and do not live up to yield expectations
- Attempts to copyright indigenous plants and trees used for traditional pesticides harm local farmers and peasants
- Western companies show lack of concern for environmental impacts and low employment standards
- The health, well-being and civil rights of indigenous peoples and forest dwellers are frequently disregarded

Damage to local economies, livelihoods and food production
- Opening up local markets to rich country financial services suppliers undermines development of local financial services which may be more appropriate

- Encouraging cash crops for export takes away scarce resources, including water, needed for local food production
- Western factories have the same effect – local people are persuaded to sell their lands which provide a living and become factory workers
- Mega projects financed by World Bank displace millions from their lands
- Use of so-called marginal lands for crops like biofuel destroys an important part of the ecology
- The food supply is endangered by damaging local small farmers
- and ancient knowledge of farming in local conditions

NGOs such as Christian Aid, World Development Movement, the Jubilee Debt Coalition Campaign and many others fighting these policies for a long time are succeeding. However, it is a continuing battle against the vested interests of the wealthiest countries.

Poor countries need support in finding their own unique solutions, not exploitation. Africa need not be poor; it contains 40% of the world's resources. An attitude of respectful partnership and seeking to understand, giving up the mentality of colonialism, exploitation and "we know best" is needed. Handouts and charity, however much needed, offer only temporary solutions and undermine local suppliers. More loans with interest worsen the situation. Instead, the emphasis needs to be on capacity building, infrastructure and technical assistance in greening their economies and well targeted grants.

Tax avoidance and evasion. Christian Aid reckons that through corporate tax evasion by transfer, mispricing and false invoicing, poorer countries lose some $160bn in lost tax revenues, roughly one-and-a half times the aid given by rich to poor countries each year. This would be enough to achieve the UN Millennium Development goals several times over. It could save the lives of 350,000 children per year. Because Western multinationals do not disclose where their profits are being made, Christian Aid is campaigning to get country-by-country reporting of where companies make their profits and how much tax they pay. However, this is only a small part of the colossal tax evasion by corporations and "High Net Worth Individuals", disclosed in Tax Justice Network's website. So Christian Aid and Oxfam are campaigning for all tax havens to be closed.

> *Developing countries are estimated to lose to tax havens almost three times what they get from developed countries in aid.*
> **Angel Gurría**, OECD Secretary-General

Tax evasion by multinational corporations

Climate change aid. Whilst under the Kyoto agreement, rich countries are under a legal obligation to help poor countries adapt to climate change, little has been delivered. Of the $18bn (£12.5bn) pledged by rich countries over the past seven years, less than $900m or 5-10% has been delivered. The very small proportion that has been delivered has gone to the poorest countries like those in Africa. Much of this aid comes from other aid budgets leaving less for health, education and poverty action. Britain has pledged $1.5bn but delivered less than $300m.

Vulture Funds based in New York and London are the latest example of ruthless greed. It is reported that these funds are buying up the debt of extremely poor countries and then suing them. At least 54 companies are known to have taken legal action against 12 of the world`s poorest countries in recent years, for claims amounting to over $1.8bn (£1.2bn). For example the government of the war-torn Democratic Republic of Congo is incurring fines of $20,000 a week in a case brought by a New

York-based vulture fund over a debt incurred from Tito's Yugoslavia in the 1980s. Another example is a London law firm seeking a $40m payment from Zambia on a $40m debt.

Poverty and the growing income gap in UK

Ours is a very unequal country. There is an escalating gap between rich and poor in the UK and between North and South.

Until thirty years ago, real incomes were rising and the poverty gap was reducing. I do not want to paint a rosy picture of that time. There were profound problems that had to be resolved, especially in the UK economy. The world had changed; we were not adapting. Mrs Thatcher was confronted with a major crisis. Unions were abusing their power. British business leadership and entrepreneurialism were in deep decline. However, the "trickle-down" she promised did not deliver.

In the UK, growth benefits the richest 10 per cent of the population 10 times more than the poorest 10 per cent. The ratio between bosses' rewards and employees' pay has risen to 98:1 from 39:1 ten years ago. Before the current crisis, average total pay for a UK chief executive was £2,875,000; more than 11 times the increase in average earnings and nearly 20 times the rate of inflation as measured by the consumer price index. Basic salary increases were more than three times the 3.1% average pay rise for ordinary workers in the private sector. Directors' basic pay rise, over double the rate of inflation, came whilst many of their companies were imposing pay freezes on staff and starting huge redundancy programmes to slash costs. The 10 most highly paid executives earned a combined £170m in 2008 – up from £140m in 2007. Five years before, the top 10 banked some £70m. Women bosses are still left behind. These figures do not include all the "perks".

There is a sharp contrast between the pension schemes of top directors and employees, many of whom face uncertainty.

Pension schemes for ordinary workers have been steadily diminished, in some cases raided, over the past twenty years. Yet 26 top directors will retire on annual incomes between £500,000 and £1m plus; over 100 more can look forward to retiring on at least £200,000 a year and 80 FTSE firms retain final salary schemes for all or some of their directors whilst axing them for staff.

Disproportionate wealth contributes to the problem of unaffordable housing in London and the South East. Similar problems are created in the countryside with the growth of second homes or homes for wealthy retired.

Tax evasion and avoidance is a highly controversial subject. Many conflicting figures are quoted. I suggest you do your own research. My conclusion is that evasion and avoidance by wealthy individuals and large corporations runs into billions if not trillions. In contrast benefit fraud, though intolerable, pales in to insignificance, yet that is what is emphasised.

Poverty in UK. A survey published by the anti-poverty charity Elizabeth Finn Care (EFC) claimed that 12.5 million people or 20 per cent of the UK's population live in poverty. EFC claimed that 3.9 million single people lived in poverty. This number had risen by around 300,000 since 1997. There are more and more single-person households in the UK today, and there is considerable evidence to show that many singletons live far away from and even lose touch with their social and family circles. Many people living alone are divorced, widowed and separated women, a group particularly liable to poverty. And precisely because many single people are outside firm social structures, it can be hard to keep track of them. Adults with children make up 22 per cent of Britain's poor; 900,000 of their number are single parents.

Since 2005, incomes for the poorest 10% of households have fallen by £9.00 to £147 in real terms per week and the richest 10% have risen by £45 to £1,033. This is a higher growth in the gap than at any time since the Thatcher era. The number of working adults living below the official breadline rose by 300,000 to 11m. One in seven adults of working age without dependent children are now living in poverty. The low skilled, with low education, and young workers will suffer most in the depression.

Child poverty. In the UK, 3.9 million, one third of our children, live in poverty. End Child Poverty argued that progress on child poverty is at risk. Tony Blair's promise in 1999, when 3.4 million children were living in poverty i.e. in families with 60% less than the median average income, was to halve child poverty by 2010 and be abolished by 2020. By 2005, this had fallen by 16% to 2.7m but it rose again to 3.9 million.

The UK wealth gap is the widest in over 40 years. A report in May 2009 by the Institute of Fiscal Studies (IFS) shows the gap between rich and poor to be the widest since the 60s. The British inequality index, called the Gini co-efficient, with a base line of 100 in 1961, shows that the poverty gap was declining until Margaret Thatcher came to power. A de-unionised economy, with pressure bearing down on the low paid, reversed this trend and made it inevitable that the gulf would widen. So under her premiership the index increased from 92 to a peak of 131 before finally declining to 128 at the end of her term. From 1987 under New Labour it rose to 138, the highest gap ever.

Margaret Thatcher's housing policies gave many people on moderate incomes the chance to buy their homes. However, her policy of preventing local authorities from building affordable housing, continued by New Labour, greatly contributed to poverty and homelessness. Now there are over 1.67m households on the waiting list for affordable housing, an increase of 64 per cent since 1997. Over 600,000 of these households are living in temporary, unsuitable accommodation. Around 150,000 private sector homes have been turned out every year, about 62 per cent of what is needed, but the amount of social housing has "plummeted" (Minton, A, 2009).

Whilst a third of the food we buy goes into waste, five per

cent of those on low incomes in the UK skip meals for a whole day. There is a polarisation between the wealthy in southern suburbs and the poor elsewhere, particularly in the North and former industrial areas. In the seventies, incomes were getting more equal; now the reverse is happening. There is growing poverty in the countryside: rural services are declining; the rural population is ageing, as the young people cannot afford to stay and migrate to cities.

As sources for the above paragraphs, I am grateful to articles from the *Guardian* by Larry Elliot and Polly Curtis, *UK's income gap widest since 60s*, 8 May 2009, and Larry Elliot, *Labour's poverty of progress laid bare*, 7 May 2009.

Low social mobility leads to wasted lives in UK. Social mobility in Britain is worse than in other advanced countries and is declining. Educational attainment is strongly related to family income according to the London School of Economics and Sutton Trust and the cross-party report on social mobility in the UK, July 2009. A huge amount of potential talent is wasted and massive social problems result. In his article in *The Observer*, 10 January 2010, *Of course class still matters*, Will Hutton points out class still matters in the UK and it has a pervasive influence.

Ten million men and women earn less than £10,000 a year. Most of their parents were in a similar position. The family you are born into has a powerful influence, for example, on the size of your vocabulary. This affects the cognitive development of children. Diet affects physical development and lifetime health. Our education system, in which money buys advantage, results in the 7% of children who are privately educated becoming 75% of judges, 70% of finance directors, 45% of top civil servants and 32% of MPs. If this trend continues, professionals will continue to come from the better-off families. Is it right that private schools enjoy the advantages of charitable status?

The Fabian Society report, *In the mix,* argues that by splitting up those living in public and private housing, successive governments have fostered suspicion towards those who live on council estates. It concludes that segregated estates have had a devastating effect on social mobility and that much of the problem has been caused by political and institutional processes.

Symptoms of social distress. The UK ranks low amongst advanced economies on many measures of well-being and happiness: prison population, crime, child poverty, teenage pregnancy (the UK has the highest rate in Europe). After Bush took power, every social indicator in the USA worsened. Between 2000 and 2008, household income declined 1% whilst corporate profits rose 70% and the gap between rich and poor is higher than at any time since 1929; families living in poverty and those without health insurance have increased by 20%. USA has amongst the highest levels of alcohol and drug abuse, literacy, political alienation and upward social mobility in industrialised nations. England and Wales have the highest per capita prison population in Western Europe. At last, Ken Clarke is saying this should be cut and the money saved spent on rehabilitation. These conditions appear to be in part the result of pursuing economic policies that enable a few to become immensely rich at the expense of the majority.

Where the Income Gap is Highest so is Unhappiness

- In wealthy nations US, Portugal and UK the richest fifth are respectively 8.5, 8.0 and 7.2 times richer than the poorest.
- Japan, Finland, Norway, Sweden, Denmark have the lowest gaps – 3.4, 3.7, 3.9, 4.0 and 4.3.
- Combined social problem scores are highest in US, Portugal and UK and amongst the lowest in Japan, Sweden, Norway, Finland, Netherlands and

Switzerland.

- The British inequality index, starting at 100 in 1974, rose to 140 by 2006, more rapidly than elsewhere in Europe or the developed world.
- The gap, measured by this index, fell in UK during the seventies, rose most in Thatcher's time from 1979 up to a peak of 136 in 1991 under Major; under New Labour it rose to 140.
- Mental illness is about 3 times higher in the most unequal societies; 8 times more prisoners; the percentage of obesity is over twice as high in unequal countries; teen pregnancies are up to 10 times higher in more polarised countries, USA by far the highest, then UK; death rates for working men of all classes are higher.
- Literacy scores are higher for everyone in more equal countries

Sources: The *Guardian*, Friday 13th March 2009 pp 20-21 and *The Spirit Level – Why More Equal Societies Almost Always Do Better*, Richard Wilkinson and Kate Pickett, Allen Lane, 2009.

Around the world, people have grown happier during the past 25 years, according to the most recent World Values Survey, an assessment of happiness in 97 nations. On average, people describing themselves as "very happy" have increased by nearly 7 per cent. However, Americans, now twice as rich as they were in 1950, are no happier according to the survey. Other rich countries, the United Kingdom and western Germany among them, show downward happiness trends. Happiness appears to be associated with improved economies, greater democratisation and increased social tolerance. Material stability and freedom to live as one pleases are major factors in subjective well-being. It is not associated with high consumption or materialistic values.

It is well-being that counts. According to the New Economics Foundation (NEF) Happy Planet Index, the G8 countries generally score badly in the Happy Planet Index: The UK comes 108. Italy is 66, Germany 81, Japan 95, Canada 111, France 129, United States 150 and Russia 172. El Salvador ranks in the top 10 countries in the world in this index. Central America is the region with the highest scores. Amongst European nations, the UK is 13 out of 22.

UK Well-Being

- 87% think today is "too materialistic, with too much emphasis on money and not enough on things that really matter"
- UK is hugely inefficient in converting planetary resources into well-being
- 62% in UK have jobs they find too stressful or uninteresting
- Levels of trust have halved since the Fifties
- Mental illness, particularly anxiety and depression, causes about 40% of incapacity claims
- Someone consuming at the rate of one-planet living is just as likely to have high life satisfaction as someone over-consuming at seven-planet living rate

Source: *Happy Planet Index,* New Economics Foundation (NEF)

These findings demonstrate that system blindness is the problem. New Labour was unlikely to achieve their aims. Throwing billions at social problems in an unequal society does not address the root cause – see Chapter 6.

Further reading:

- Institute for Policy Studies (IPS) USA, linking peace, justice, and the environment
- Shiva, V, 2005, *Earth Democracy*, Zed Books, London.

Section E: Violence, War and the Threat of Nuclear Annihilation

It is impossible to conceive of a world at peace when the poorest 60 per cent of humans live on just 6 per cent of the world's income.
Mohammed Yonis, winner of 2006 Nobel Peace Prize

The 21st century is the time for us to give up war and learn non-violent ways of resolving conflict. War diverts us from the urgent need to focus all our collective efforts on tackling climate change and other threats to the future of humanity. The dire consequences of war are greater than ever. Waging war increases the risk of unleashing worldwide nuclear devastation and nuclear terrorism. A leaked Pentagon report spoke of the dangers of nuclear conflict arising from climate change and pressures on dwindling resources. The Bulletin of Atomic Scientists expressed the same view.

The costs of war: lives

The 20th century accounted for 95 per cent of over 120,000,000 war deaths since 1700, 40 million from 1945 to year 2000. State violence far exceeds that committed by individuals. Nearly 20 million died in WWI. Total WWII deaths are estimated at 52 million. The Atomic bombs killed 140,000 people in Hiroshima and 80,000 in Nagasaki by the end of 1945 but many more died later. There are indications that this outrage was unnecessary. Japan was ready for peace. Mark Curtis estimates British foreign policy from the end of WWII has been directly or indirectly responsible for around 10 million deaths worldwide. He adds that New Labour continued to make claims about the morality of its foreign policies, wishing to be a "force for good in the world." Yet never in British history had there been such a gap between government claims and reality.

In today's wars over 80 per cent of deaths are civilians. At the end of the century, despite *"precision weapons"* demonstrated on TV, over 95 per cent of these deaths were civilian compared with 52 per cent in the 1960s. The Iraq and Afghanistan wars created almost half of the world's 11 million refugees by the end of 2007. In Iraq, in addition to over 4,000 US military deaths, 100,000 to 650,000 civilians have died. Four million people have been uprooted from their homes, 2 million displaced inside their country and 2 million have fled to other countries. A relatively advanced society has been reduced to poverty. Iraq's infrastructure was partly destroyed. A third of Iraqis are said to be in urgent need of aid. The children have been described as a stunted generation. The more troops there are in Afghanistan, the more aerial attacks in Afghanistan and Pakistan, the more civilians are killed and the more people are pushed into grief and anger, the more are driven into the hands of extremists.

What if such so-called surgical strikes had been inflicted on London, Paris or New York or your home town, destroying the infrastructure, leaving people without water, heat or power and destroying their livings? Imagine British people fleeing their homes, migrating to the North or across the Channel, Irish or North Seas. Is it that we regard people in other lands, or of other races, as less important, less human than ourselves? Do we fail to identify with others who are further away?

Many believe the Iraq war was illegal, its initiators guilty of a war crime.

The loss of over three hundred British soldiers in Afghanistan is tiny compared with the large numbers of Afghan, Iraqi and Pakistani civilians killed, wounded, displaced from their homes or driven into exile. In Afghanistan many thousands of civilians have been killed as a result of the US led invasion, many as a result of US air attacks. There are no official figures for civilian deaths but upper and lower estimates of 8000 to over 30,000 are given on Wikipedia, though caution about these numbers is advised. The UN News centre reports some 2 million people displaced in Pakistan by the fighting between government forces and militants in the northwest of the country.

In Afghanistan, nearly three hundred British soldiers have died since 2001. Earlier this year, the media showed pictures of British soldiers, women and men, killed in Afghanistan. Many more have been severely injured and there have been 51 amputations. Wounded and maimed have soared by 300 per cent in the past three years. We now know that injured soldiers often need considerable support. Large numbers of returning soldiers suffer combat stress or post-traumatic stress disorder (PTSD) and depression. The MoD reported 3181 new cases of "mental disorder" in 2008. Some fall into alcoholism and drug addiction, and marital difficulties are common. The NHS is ill-equipped to deal with this.

Pictures and accounts of these gallant soldiers and their grieving families and friends and scenes of funeral processions on the streets of Wootton Bassett bring home to us the full personal tragedy of war. Probably the worst thing that can befall a family is the loss of a child, parent or sibling. It is especially tragic when a young person in his/her teens or early twenties, at the beginning of adult life, nurtured for years by loving, proud parents, is killed in war. It takes years to come to terms with such avoidable tragedies. Many families never completely recover.

These accounts give meaning to the otherwise incomprehensible numbers affected by war in other countries. In total, there are millions of deaths and injuries, not to mention the destruction of homes, communities, towns, cities and livelihoods, the mass displacements of people within their own countries or to other countries. What will be the effect of generations of children growing up surrounded by violence, loss, destruction and insecurity?

Deaths in civil wars are equally appalling. For example, 5 million people died in civil war in the Democratic Republic of the Congo. Dreadful atrocities were committed. In Kenya, following a disputed poll in December 2007, at least 500 people are dead; over 200,000, mainly extremely poor women and children, were forced to flee their homes. Livelihoods and food growing in a continent where so many people go hungry were destroyed. The economic consequences are dire.

The costs of war: financial

World spending on war. Global military spending, now over $1trn per annum, is approaching the highest level reached in the depths of the Cold War. G8 countries spending on arms exceeded $1tn in 2004. Only $79bn was spent on development aid by the 22 biggest donor nations in 2004. According to the OECD Departmental Assistance Committee, the USA spends $455.3bn on arms and $19bn on aid; the UK $47.4bn and $7.8bn.

The cost of the Iraq war is now estimated at over $3trn including compensation for deaths and injuries and debt repayment and interest. That is nearly $8,000 per man, woman and child in the USA. Ray Anderson, founder of Interface, once said the true cost of oil, including wars and subsidies, was $200 per gallon!

The cost of the Afghan conflict. The *Independent* summarised the cost of the Afghan conflict:

The Cost of the Afghan conflict

- Overall cost – £12bn that arguably could have been far better spent
- Increase in Ministry of Defence spending 2006/7 to 2009/10 – 400%
- Estimated 30,000 Afghan civilians killed as a result of conflict
- Over 200 UK service personnel killed since 2001
- Increase in Afghan opium production 150%

Source: *Independent on Sunday,* 26 July 2009

Why are we so blind to the fundamental threats to our survival? They are much greater than terrorism, which is not to say that we should not do everything to prevent it. Is what we doing likely to achieve that? Unjust USA and UK foreign policies are a major cause of hostility to the West, violence and terrorism. Global justice, conflict resolution and non-violence would have a more positive impact.

Militarism and military economy. Militarism and arms production are a major part of the global economy. Militarism and war are externalised costs of our lifestyle. Over $1,470,000,000,000, spent annually on the military,compared with only $79bn spent on development aid, and the arms trade is the largest single item of world spending. In comparison, the UN and all its agencies spend only $20bn annually or about $3 for each inhabitant.

When the world needs co-operative solutions to global problems, the thriving international arms market points to a squandering of resources which the international institutions can ill afford.
Paul Holtom, head of SIPRI's arms transfer programme

The biggest arms suppliers are the USA, accounting for 31 per cent, Russia, Germany, France and the UK. The world arms trade has expanded over 20 per cent in the past five years according to the Stockholm International Peace Research Institute – (SIPRI). Arms sales to Middle Eastern countries rose 38 per cent. Other key markets include China, India, Pakistan and Sri Lanka.

The US war machine is by far the largest in the world and its spending almost matches that for the rest of the world. Their 2009 budget $636,292,979,000 is 4 per cent of its economy and exceeds Australia's whole GDP. Next are: France, $70,613,746,423; China, $70,308,600,000; UK $65,149,500,000, all more than Russia's $39,600,000,000 (see Wiki's list of military spending). There is an unholy alliance between the Pentagon, arms manufacturers like Lockheed Martin and Boeing and Congress, because of jobs, lobbying and the cost of electioneering. That is how US democracy is corrupted. Rupert Cornwall calls this an *"Iron Triangle."* Hence, there is a substantial interest in keeping the US public terrified. General Eisenhower described this as a *"military-industrial complex"* and prophetically spoke of *"defending ourselves against one disaster by inviting another."*

These figures do not include the environmental costs of war. Apart from the greenhouse gases and **pollution** released in warfare, there is a huge diversion of attention and resources. Human and financial resources could be employed in so much better ways at a time when the greatest threats to humanity are the environmental catastrophe and starvation that will result from climate change and overconsumption unless we take urgent and decisive action.

Do we really want our governments to spend our money like this? Many military veterans who, unlike most politicians, have experienced battle are firmly against war. Many also oppose nuclear weapons. When the Government announced that it was prepared to spend up to £20 billion on replacing the four submarines that carry the Trident ballistic nuclear missile deterrent, three retired military commanders urged that the plan be scrapped. In a letter in *The Times,* they said that Britain's independent nuclear deterrent had become *"virtually irrelevant"*. They called on Gordon Brown to spend the money saved by cancelling the Trident replacement on providing more funds for the Armed Forces to meet their current operational commitments. They said:

> *Should this country ever become subject to some sort of nuclear blackmail — from a terrorist group for example — it must be asked in what way, and against whom, our nuclear weapons could be used, or even threatened, to deter or punish.*

Surely all this money and human effort would be far better spent educating people, alleviating poverty, combating climate change and degradation of the planet. In their 2005 State of the World report, World Watch estimated $50 billion additional annual funding could achieve the Millennium Development Goals.

Joss Garman believes that spending £100bn on hitting our renewable energy targets, thus reducing our dependence on foreign oil and gas and tackling climate change, is far more relevant to our security than spending money on nuclear. Unilateral renunciation of nuclear weapons would send an even stronger message. That, together with an even-handed, *truly* ethical foreign policy and fulfilling promises of aid to poor countries, would send out messages to the world that would reduce the risk of terrorism and enhance the chances of peace and nuclear disarmament.

Reflections of wise elders

"War is organised murder, and nothing else." We have remembered and honoured the recent deaths of two veterans of First

World War. Harry Patch, who died aged 111, said:

> *"War is organised murder, and nothing else." "If you declare war, it's simply the government given license to go to a foreign country and commit murder. That's all war is – murder." "I didn't want to go and fight anyone, but it was a case of having to." "At the end, the peace was settled round a table, so why the hell couldn't they do that from the start without losing millions of men?"*

He decided to shoot to maim, not kill his opponents.

Henry Allingham, who died aged 113, said of war:

> *War is stupid. Nobody wins. You might as well talk first: you have to talk last anyway.*

Soldiers have been led to believe they were fighting for their country when in truth they were laying down their lives to fulfil the unwise decisions of politicians, not the wishes or interests of citizens.

How wars come about

The causes of war and violence are multi-faceted. Amongst these are religious intolerance, attempts to impose religions or political systems on other nations, or the ambitions of national leaders, some with flawed personalities.

The roots of conflict lie in history. The insult of the Crusades had a deep effect on Islamic consciousness that continues today. The creation of empires by European countries, to secure wealth and resources, inflicted injustices on peoples who ultimately rebelled. The creation of artificial nations, as the Colonial powers did in Africa, sowed the seeds of today's conflicts in countries like Nigeria and Kenya. A major factor in WWI was German aspiration for empire and markets to rival the British Empire. George Monbiot, examining the causes of WWI, concluded that the British government lied to its people about a secret treaty and war might have been averted if the British government had sought to broker reconciliation between France and Germany over Morocco in 1911.

The major factors in bringing about WWII were an unfair and humiliating settlement at Versailles after WWI and the failure to take early action against growing Nazi militarism and breaches of the treaty that could have been nipped in the bud. The invasion of Iraq clearly made no sense. But it could have predicted that Blair would support Bush. That has been the pattern of British foreign policy since WWII ended. Only once did Britain depart from this when Harold Wilson stood up to President Kennedy, saying "no" to the Vietnam War. Generally the USA has not reciprocated. Europeans have been wiser.

European and USA political and military interventions cast long shadows. Oil and other commercial interests are at the root of Western wars, political interference, the overthrow of democratically elected governments and support for evil regimes in the Middle East, North Africa, West Africa and Latin America. There is a legacy of distrust and hostility. Iran's hostility today is hardly surprising.

The betrayal of the Arabs after World War I. Today's attitudes of the Arab world have their origins in the interventions of Western powers over many decades, including the betrayal by the French and British of the Arab League shortly after World War I. During World War I, TE Lawrence gained the support of the Arab League, led by charismatic King Faisal, in defeating the Turkish Ottomans, rulers of Arabia at that time. TE Lawrence saw the chance for an Arab Nation under the leadership of King Faisal and persuaded him this was his opportunity to bring it about. But Britain and France betrayed this agreement. They divided up the area in ways unfavourable to the Arabs under a secret deal that became known as the 1916 Sykes-Picot Agreement, named after its two negotiators. To add insult to injury, the Balfour Declaration of 1917 promised support for a Jewish national home in Palestine. Humiliating betrayal lies at the root of Arab hostility and distrust to this day. The interventions of the West are deeply resented. Rory Stewart in his two BBC2 television programmes, *The Legacy of TE Lawrence,* concluded that foreign military interventions in the Middle East are fundamentally unworkable. On both the Iraq and Afghanistan wars, Lawrence's advice would have been: *Don't do it!*

Some wars are defensive, i.e. caused by attack or fear of attack. That is the case in the Israel/Palestine conflict and Iran's alleged pursuit of nuclear weapons. It may be argued that North Korea's build up of nuclear armaments is rooted in the fear of being attacked again. Are North Korean attitudes affected by memories of atrocities and aerial destruction committed by the Americans in South Korea (Task Force Oregon), Laos, Cambodia as well as the use of Agent Orange, the massive aerial destruction of North Vietnam under Rolling Thunder, Operation Linebacker and the Mai Lai Massacre? President Richard Nixon is recorded as saying of North Vietnam in 1971, *"We're gonna level that goddam country."*

Clearly past and present injustices, hypocritical foreign policies, continuing Western abuses of power and unethical activities play a major part in hostility to the West and aid the recruitment of terrorists. The emergence of Al-Qaeda, however unjustifiable its acts of carnage are, partly results from unscrupulous and inhumane Western strategies affecting larger numbers. Are Al-Qaeda's attacks on Western cities in effect war against powerful nations against whom they otherwise feel completely powerless?

Vested interests are a major factor in the perpetuation of war and violence. No money is to be made out of prevention and conflict resolution. Africa is awash with weapons. The arms trade, legal and illegal, is enormous. Military spending is now well over $1 trillion. It is approaching the highest level reached in the depths of the Cold War. The unholy alliance between the Pentagon, arms manufacturers and Congress has been described above. Thus there has been continuing use of lethal chemicals produced by large corporations e.g. lethal gas in WWI and in concentration camps in WWII; Agent Orange in Vietnam and gas and chemicals in the Middle East throughout the twentieth century (e.g. by the British in the twenties and by Saddam Hussein against the Kurds). Jobs are at stake; a rapid transition to peaceful purposes is needed. A New Green Deal presents abundant opportunities for a far more constructive use of human skills and manufacturing resources.

Throughout history war has made money lenders, armaments manufacturers and suppliers of provisions for the military wealthy. Banking has been deeply involved in empire building and war. Bankers financed the merchants who travelled to the East to bring back merchandise. They financed the East India Company and the British Empire. Great wars were underwritten by bankers like the Rothschilds who grew enormously rich through debt creation and interest that had to be repaid through taxation. Without the bankers, wars on the scale of Napoleonic wars would have been impossible.

Most wars in human history have been resource wars, like those fought by the remarkably successful English in building their Empire. Now resource wars will be caused by shortages of food and resources such as oil, gas, minerals, land and water. In his British Humanist Association's Darwin Day lecture, Sir David King argued that the war against Iraq in 2001 is likely to be just the first of many resource wars in the 21st century. His predictions may come true unless we find ways of distributing the world's resources fairly between all peoples. That is one of biggest issues confronting the world in the 21st century. Up to now, rich nations, with powerful military machines, have systematically robbed less powerful nations, lacking technological expertise and too weak to challenge them, to make themselves rich without questioning their right to do so. Clearly that process will be challenged more and more. Global institutions need to tackle these issues.

What is best for security?

Frequently violence and war could have been prevented if those in power were more sensitive to peoples who felt injustices, threats to their safety, or wanted greater autonomy or independence. That is my interpretation of conflicts in India after Independence and the violent history of the Tamils in Sri Lanka.

Often the cause of violence is poverty, injustice and lack of opportunity. This applies in countries like Jamaica which has one of the highest records of shootings in the world and deprived areas in countries like the UK. As we learn from the media and travel more, we become more aware of how privileged we are here in the UK. It is very different for the majority of people in the world. Our prosperity is still built on the work of poor people and slaves and the resources of poor countries. Rich people stole poor people's land here through clearances and enclosures and in the colonies overseas. That was how our Empire worked. It continues today in another form of imperialism legitimised and enforced by the global trade organisations. We know the majority of human beings are relatively or very poor. Millions face starvation; many are afflicted with disease that could easily be prevented or cured. Millions of children die unnecessarily. If they survive, their lives are stunted by lack of education and opportunity. Many live in fear and insecurity generated by violence, fuelled by weapons supplied by us.

> *The world will not be peaceful or safe unless we attend to the poorest places.*
> **Clare Short**, former Minister for Overseas Development

Sustainability must include global economic justice. There can be no peace or security without global economic justice and respect for difference. The big powers are in denial about their corruption, greed, violence, militarism and the extent and effects of their huge military economies. They have spread weapons around the world. They created nuclear weapons, inevitably leading to proliferation and the threat of nuclear annihilation. Unprincipled colonialist foreign policies, compounded by a long historical record, create hostility and encourage international "terrorism".

George Bush and Osama bin Laden mirrored each other. The contradictions between rhetoric and actions are clear. Imposing our way, force, threats, bargaining and bullying are not the way to find enduring conflict resolution. Honest brokering, involving the UN, can be. Nations should no longer get away with taking unilateral action. Interventions like the Iraq war should only be made, if at all, through the United Nations.

Congruence If we want a more peaceful world, does it make sense to use violence to defeat violence and suspend civil rights and liberty in their cause? We need to use methods that are congruent with our aims, i.e. non-violent ones, and as Mahatma Gandhi says, walk the talk. The underlying injustices, lack of respect and humiliations, past and present, need to be acknowledged and addressed. We need to apply conflict resolution in our dealings with nations like Iran. The West must provide impartial support to resolve the conflict between Israel and Palestine if there is to be an end to the violence.

The time has come to end war and threats of war and unilateral action as a means of resolving conflicts. If we are to have peace, nations need to admit past injustices. Perhaps it would be a good idea to acknowledge, apologise for past policies and give them up. It is certainly worth trying.

General conclusions

Recently I gave a talk to bright young people at a North London Sixth Form College. One of them said with feeling:

> *It's OK for you. We and our children will have to face the consequences of your generation's irresponsibility, way beyond 2050.*

How will we be judged by future generations who face the full consequences of our inaction? Are we simply standing by and letting it happen? I ask myself, am I a criminal, "innocently" carrying on my comfortable way of life, allowing millions to die elsewhere, doing little or nothing to prevent it when I could do so much more? We are all responsible: individuals, organisations and governments. We are drifting.

We need whole systems solutions. We need the clarity to see that all the issues described in this chapter are linked. For example, many people now realise that current war on drugs policy, like the war on terror, is not working. It fosters violence, political corruption, further poverty, and crime in stricken communities. Legalising and regulating drugs might work. Wars that don't work, the credit crunch and recession caused by breathtaking greed and irresponsibility, divert us from addressing the biggest issues, namely the environment, injustice, poverty and the survival of our own and future generations. We need to stop living in denial or believing we are powerless. Technology and science will solve some of our problems, but not if the underlying intention is to continue a greedy life, make huge profits and exercise excessive power. Technology can be an excuse for continuing "business as usual" and an essentially perverse way of life that denies us what really matters.

How self-aware are 'good guys' like Sir Richard Branson, promoting biofuel for aircraft and holidays in space that will use masses of fuel? All very exciting but where are his values?

That's the problem with so many leaders: split minds. Peter Mandelson declared himself *"intensely relaxed about people becoming filthy rich, as long as they pay their taxes."* He may be relaxed; the majority of the world is not.

> *The world has enough for everyone's need, but not enough for anyone's greed.*
> **Mahatma Gandhi**

Above all we need a change of consciousness, a spiritual awakening, compassion for others, deep reverence for all life. Then we would see everything differently and be far happier.

> *Problems cannot be solved at the same level of consciousness that created them.*
> **Albert Einstein.**

Do things have to get much worse before we wake up? That would be a terrible tragedy.

Further reading:

- Curtis, M, 2004, *Unpeople – Britain's Secret Human Rights Abuses,* and 2003, *Web of Deceit – Britain's Real Role in the World,* Vintage, UK.
- Guha, R, 2007, *India after Gandhi, The History of the World's Largest Democracy*, Pan Macmillan, London.

Chapter 5

About the Corporation and Other Things You Need to Know

February 2009

Business is there to serve people and meet their needs. This is far from what actually happens.

> *Corporate social responsibility is an oxymoron.*
> **Mary Zepernick**, Director of Program on Corporations, Law and Democracy (POCLAD).

> *Corporations are designed to externalise their costs.*
> **Joel Bakan**, Professor of law at the University of British Columbia

I was reminded of these insights when I read *The Corporation* and viewed the two companion DVDs. They do not make comfortable reading or viewing but will deepen your understanding and, alas, confirm what you already know. Many other books have exposed corporate abuse of power and unhealthy relationships with politicians. But this book and these DVDs are amongst the most powerful. I thoroughly recommend them.

This chapter summarises some of the sharpest insights into the behaviour of big corporations and political and corporate leaders throughout the world. Although there are exceptions, in general, it is unrealistic to have too optimistic expectations of large corporations, given the current system and prevailing leadership culture.

Governments are slow to grasp systemic realities. The social and environmental problems they spend vast sums of our money trying to address, often without success, are caused by the Big Co practice of externalising costs to achieve greater market share, lower costs, and greater profit and share value. These practices destroy good food, meaningful work, livelihood, security and communities, the very things that provide well-being and mental health. The economy Big Co and government create is extremely hostile for local, small businesses. That said, Big Co also offer amazing opportunities for the fortunate few who can ride the wave.

The best we can all do is understand the system and help transform it. Most businesses have to comply with the rules of the global game in order to survive. Within that system it is almost impossible for good leaders to *"do well by doing the right thing"*. Too often that would jeopardise the business, the jobs of employees, the interests of shareholders and their own jobs. I am not anti-business. I worked in or consulted to businesses for some 45 years. I am against the abuse of corporate power and a system that encourages it. Corporate Social Responsibility is not all *"Green washing"*. What the best corporations are doing is extremely important but simply not enough. Some of it can be trusted but most people rightly view it with a sceptical eye. We have been misled, lied to and the truth withheld far too often. Think of the tortuous histories of all those "harms", such as unhealthy food and drink, fast food, tobacco, alcohol, asbestos, all that denial, resistance and obfuscation over the past sixty and more years. Whistle-blowers have been threatened and expelled.

We need to be fully aware of the harms done by large corporations, especially in poor countries: the theft of "commons", buying of land from innocent peasants which they need for their survival, reducing diversity by buying up hundreds of small companies to achieve dominance in markets like seeds, hiding their dominance by using nice homely names, their treatment of indigenous peoples in oil field areas in Nigeria and Latin America, the human rights violations and poisons these people suffer, prosecuting farmers for "stealing" GM seeds when their crops have become contaminated after pollen from modified plants had blown on to their property from nearby farms, controlling the sale of seeds, previously saved by peasant farmers for generations and attempting to patent plants like the Neem tree. Read about the Neem tree on the Third World Network (TWN).

The ruthlessness is staggering.

I urge you to do your own research. Here I make some suggestions as to what you might investigate by using your search engine.

Read about small farmers and peasant people in India. A source of information about the harms done by big corporations to farming and food security in India is Vandana Shiva's website Navdanya. She provides profound insights into the workings of the global economic system. Her work is equally relevant to the production of good food and farming in rich and poor countries. She defends and supports small farmers in India, many of them women, demonstrating how they can be successful using organic farming methods and training them. She has a huge seed library of diverse grains and her farm is a demonstration of how completely degraded land can be restored to high fertility by composting. At her international conference centre on her beautiful farm, she offers courses about farming, food, and the relevance of Gandhi to our 21st century world.

Vandana exposes the effects of transnational GM seed corporations linked with chemical fertilizers, herbicides and pesticides. Often farmers became heavily indebted. Thousands committed suicide as a result of the failure of their farming businesses. She campaigns against the acquisition of the lands of poor farmers, who thus lose their livelihoods, for factories and huge development schemes like dams, created to provide hydroelectric power and irrigation, and the exploitation of wilderness and forests that provide a living and way of life for tribal peoples.

After the end of the British Raj the Indian government was faced with the huge problems of poverty and the desperate need to feed millions of poor people in danger of starving. They sought to feed the population and overcome poverty through a Green Revolution, modernising agriculture, bringing electricity and roads to rural areas, developing the economy and building factories. As in other places, these developments had unintended consequences.

Read the story of the attempt to patent use of Neem tree seeds for pesticide purposes. The Neem tree had been used for centuries by Indian farmers to provide insecticides. A corporation attempted to patent the use of seeds from this tree for pesticide purposes. Two hundred organisations from 35 nations mounted a legal challenge in the US Patent and Trademark office against a patent granting the multinational chemical corporation, the W R Grace Company, the exclusive use of a pesticide extract from Neem seeds. The corporation eventually lost its case.

Read about the Bhopal disaster in which at least 8,000 people died immediately and more than 23,000 died later from their injuries, and the subsequent avoidance of responsibility for compensation and help for 30,000 victims who continue to suffer.

Read the story of Dr Árpád Pusztai, the Aberdeen-based scientist who first raised concerns about the safety of eating genetically modified potatoes, now turning his attention to GM maize. Dr Árpád Pusztai, a world-renowned biochemist lost his job at Aberdeen's Rowett Institute after he announced the findings of animal experiments in a television documentary about his laboratory-based work on rats, conducted where he had been employed for 36 years. His research indicated that eating GM potatoes had an effect on the animals' organ development, causing brain shrinkage and gut problems. After he went public Pusztai was attacked by the British scientific establishment which attempted to discredit his work. His laboratory was disbanded and his scientific team broken up.

Read the story of Percy Schmeiser. This brave seventy year old canola farmer, from Saskatchewan, was accused of patent infringement by Monsanto who demanded restitution for its seeds when his crops became contaminated by GM crops on a neighbouring farm. Supported by his wife of 55 years, he decided to fight the company. Genetically engineered corn, soybeans, cotton and canola have become widely used in the United States, Canada, Latin America and India. It was claimed that their pollen spread to conventional crops. The Monsanto canola contains a gene that protects the crop from the herbicide Roundup. With Roundup Ready canola, farmers can spray the herbicide widely and control weeds. Hence there is a clever linked market for the herbicide too. Seed companies representing Monsanto, and similar biotechnology companies, sell their genetically modified seeds to farmers under an agreement that they use them for only one season.

Traditionally, farmers saved their best seeds and replanted them. Margaret Mellon, director of the agriculture and biotechnology program of the Union of Concerned Scientists says people who are in the neighbourhood of genetically modified crops may have to pay royalties to the companies for products they never purchased and got no benefits from. A spokeswoman with the National Farmers Union, which represents 300,000 small farmers and ranchers in the United States says, *"We're extremely concerned by what liabilities may unfold for the farmer, particularly with cross-pollination of genetically modified plants."* Some 82 per cent of customers *"tell us they will not buy GM wheat,"* says Louise Waldman, Media Relations manager for the Canadian Wheat Board. Currently, over three quarters of Canadian wheat is exported to 70 countries, generating $4 billion (Can.) in annual sales. *"Our position is not ethical or moral or scientific; it's purely economic. Our customers are telling us they don't want to buy GM wheat, the market is telling us they don't want it, and we certainly haven't seen evidence that people want it."* Basically the threat is that Canadian farmers will be unable to grow or export organic crops to countries where people want organic or GM free soya, corn and canola.

GM: The position of the UK government and many MPs on GM is worrying. This is a key area in which most are uninformed and appear to accept the GM line uncritically. They appear not to understand the importance of the precautionary principle. Of course they have to take account of diverse views and interests. But whose interests are they serving, citizens' or corporate interests?

Nanotechnology. GM and Nanotechnology were being advocated by Sir John Beddington, the UK government's chief scientific adviser, supported by Hilary Benn, the secretary of state for environment, food and rural affairs, as part of a hi-tech "new greener revolution", a 20-year plan to feed Britain as our population rises and our self-sufficiency in food declines as a result of our policies. Again, government is serving the interests of scientists and corporations rather than protecting citizens from the unknown risks. Many farming experts have expressed concerns about Nanotechnology. Ethical Consumer provides a comprehensive report, listing the widespread applications, potential health effects, and express concerns about the lack of a public mandate to develop them, lack of resources for research into the potential harms compared with the sums provided by government for their development and the lack of public debate and transparency. Typically an average of £600,000 pa was spent over the last five years on research into the toxicology, environmental and health effects of nanomaterials compared with government spending of £90m in 2004 on nanoscience research and commercial promotion. This is something else you may wish to investigate through the Soil Association, Which and the

Ethical Consumer.

Now there is another danger, creating new life. Craig Venter Institute has successfully genetically engineered an entirely artificial organism that can replicate itself. This raises many ethical, scientific, economic and safety issues. GM Freeze believes the general public should be fully involved in debating them. Creating a new life without adequate regulation or public oversight is highly irresponsible.

A case of exceptional importance. I suggest you read *Burying The Truth*, by Jon Hughes & Pat Thomas, *Ecologist*, 11th October, 2007, the 40 year story of *"one of the biggest environmental crimes ever to have occurred in the UK,"* how a dangerous mix of chemicals including now banned PCBs were buried in a Brofiscin Quarry in Wales, the alleged effects this had on local cattle and people, alleged suppression of what was known about these chemicals back in the thirties, alleged intimidation and attacks on the chief surviving witness, Douglas Brown.

The record of oil companies is disturbing, despite their "green washing" and denial. I have yet to find an exception. Read the account of alleged activities by oil companies in *New Frontiers of the Carbon Web,* by Mika Minio-Paluello of campaign group PLATFORM.

Read Amnesty International's reports about Chevron's alleged harmful activities in Ecuador, where they are accused of dumping toxic waste, poisoning the water, destroying ecosystems, causing serious health issues for thousands of people and other creatures. Amnesty International claims that independent studies of the contamination's health impacts on neighbouring communities have found that exposure to and consumption of the contaminated waters has led to numerous types of infections and cancers, far exceeding historical incidence rates, and that children under 15 are three times more likely to contract leukaemia in the area where Texaco operated than in other Amazonian provinces.

There are similar reports of the activities of other oil and mining companies in Africa, for example in the Niger Delta. Nigeria is the largest oil producer in Africa and the eleventh largest producer of crude oil in the world. They have extracted hundreds of millions of barrels of oil, sold on the international market for hundreds of billions of dollars. Yet the people of the Niger Delta, many of whom live in squalor, have seen little benefit.

Remember Ken Saro-Wiwa. On November 10th 1995, Ken Saro-Wiwa and eight Ogoni colleagues were executed by the Nigerian state for campaigning against the devastation of the Niger Delta by oil companies, especially Shell and Chevron. He was Vice-President of the Unrepresented Nations and Peoples Organization (UNPO) General Assembly from 1993 until his death in 1995. The trial was widely criticised by human rights organisations, and later, Ken Saro-Wiwa received the Right Livelihood Award for his courage as well as the Goldman Environmental Prize. He was executed by the Nigerian military in 1995. His death provoked international outrage. Shell has been extensively criticised for its activities, involvement and misleading public relations and advertising.

> *Human life does not mean much to those who have benefited from the oil.*
> **Ken Saro-Wiwa**

By proxy, that includes any of us who benefitted from Shell oil, however innocently!

Investigate for yourself corporate campaigns against complementary medicine, alternative medicine and supplements using the Codex Alimentarius. Few people are aware of these campaigns, perhaps because it is a complicated and almost unbelievable subject. A key US campaigning organisation is the Natural Solutions Foundation founded by Dr Rima E Laibow,

MD and Major General Albert Stubblebine. Such pioneering, brave people are often dismissed as alarmists or peddlers of conspiracy theories. This is how deception prevails. Look up Wiki, Natural Health Information Centre, *Codex Alimentarius: The Sinister Truth Behind Operation Cure-All*, by Ruth James, Alliance for Natural Health and Natural Solutions Foundation.

Here are some simple truths that most people instinctively understand:

Simple Truths

- **Big Business is about** maximising short-term profit and share value. It is about gaining increasing market share, pursuing cheapest sourcing, a "chase to the bottom", and achieving global dominance. CSR is indeed an oxymoron.
- **Politics is about** power, staying in power and winning elections, responding to popular prejudices and sensational stories in the media.
- **The media is about** selling papers and advertising. Sensational stories, gossip, conspiracy, unbalanced, extreme opinions not based on proper research; crime and bad news sells. Most of the media is owned by rich and powerful businessmen. There is an unhealthy concentration of global media ownership. They can determine the outcome of elections.
- **There are unhealthy relationships between all of the above.**
- **Much of the activities of government and corporations are covert.** The truth has to be extracted painfully. They don't want us to know.

Basically, once a business ceases to be privately owned it is at the mercy of the stock market. The ideals of the founders are in jeopardy. Once a public service is privatised the same applies. Acting responsibly, sustainably or in the public interest becomes secondary to profit and share value maximisation. It is naïve to expect otherwise.

Corporations are out of control. They are unaccountable and undermine democracy. The economies of transnational corporations exceed the wealth of many countries. They dominate equally unaccountable, unrepresentative global institutions such as the World Bank, World Trade Organisation, International Monetary Fund and NAFTA who create unfair rules for international trade. These organisations set conditions for aid and loans to poor countries, such as insisting on privatisation and unlimited access to their markets for large corporations, whose products are often subsidised. Their policies have contributed to huge indebtedness. By means of globalisation, corporations are able to shift their investment or sourcing to countries where labour is cheapest and least regulated. This will have to change as oil becomes scarce, more expensive and the climate change becomes increasingly serious.

The sovereignty of national governments, to manage their societies, cultures and economies in their own unique way, is being taken away. Electorates have very little choice as all political parties converge. Political parties are beholden to media giants. They face the power of newspapers and media controlled by big business. Political parties fear becoming unelectable if their policies result in their countries losing out in competing for investment in their economies. First past the post voting systems, such as ours, mean more liberal parties like the Greens have little chance of gaining influence let alone power. Nations like ours compete to be the best places for doing business.

Corporations exert far too much influence on the political process everywhere, especially in the USA. They have the money, far more than organisations representing people. They spend vast sums of customers' and share holders' money on lobbying and funding political campaigns. Hence, despite informed opposition, our previous government supported airport expansion, investment in roads rather than railways, coal fired power stations, biofuel, nuclear power and the flawed car scrappage scheme. They gain access to vast quantities of taxpayers' money for highly dubious subsidies e.g. for oil corporations.

> *Most American politicians fear to challenge corporate power not only because they need the financial support during elections, but for a deeper and more reasonable reason as well: they fear that corporations can always threaten to move their base of operations, leaving joblessness and economic devastation in their wake*
> **Rabbi Michael Lerner**, Beyt Tikkun

Corporate harms and corporate crimes. Over the years we have become increasingly aware of how much harm large corporations do and how economical they are with the truth. Long ago, they knew that certain products were harmful to health or new drugs carried huge risks. Tobacco is a prime example but there are many more. It often requires years of campaigning to extract the truth, stop the harm or get compensation. Corporate crime is pervasive, probably massively undocumented, often not defined as crime, insufficiently policed, with weak regulation and insufficient penalties. Blue suited criminality is taken less seriously than "low class" criminality. Penalties for corporate "crime" are insignificant compared with the sums to be gained, just treated as part of the cost of doing business.

Theft of the "commons" such as human genes and resources like oil, minerals, land, air and water; and the patenting of life, seeds and trees like the Neem are abuses of power. Noam Chomsky in the USA and Vandana Shiva in India are amongst those who expose and fight these excesses. She uses the term, bio-piracy. Noam Chomsky argues that for the most fundamental commons that the world community will need over coming years, and over which conflict and war could arise, a Trust is needed like that set up for Antarctica.

The world needs a transformation *from* pursuing selfish national interests, by war if necessary, *to* global collaboration and fairness.

Independent scientists have been fully aware of the harm being done and the risks to health. But it was decades before they were listened to. Senior people knew the risks yet took them nonetheless. New exposures constantly emerge. Today many of us are well aware of the damage our current way of life is doing to us and the ecosystem. A recent revelation is the damage to sea creatures resulting from plastic waste in the oceans and how that will affect humans as the toxic chemicals released pass up the food chain.

Epidemics. Amongst the great epidemics in developed nations, and developing nations as they follow Western patterns, are:

- Alcohol abuse
- Alzheimer's disease
- Asthma
- Cancer – one in 2 men will get cancer and one in 3 women
- Child obesity on a massive scale
- Diabetes
- Heart disease
- Infertility and birth defects
- Mental illness including anxiety and depression
- Obesity

Are these conditions caused by our genes and simply our living longer? Clearly our genes play a major part. There is evidence that greater genetic diversity or *"heterozygosity"* confers advantages making some humans less likely to succumb to major diseases such as dementia, skin cancer and multiple sclerosis, diseases which are more common amongst Europeans who are more inbred than other populations with greater genetic diversity.

We don't know the extent to which many of these conditions are caused by polluted air, land and water; harmful chemicals used in modern materials and products; hormones and antibiotics fed to cattle; industrialised agribusiness, agricultural pesticides and fertilizers; harmful food processing and fast food. In particular what are the causes of the cancer epidemic? We do know that the inhumane conditions in which animals are reared for our food are playing a major part in pandemics, as discussed earlier. Not enough is spent on research to find out the crucially important answers. Little money is to be made out of such essential research.

However, it looks certain that a considerable percentage of the diseases of wealthy countries have their origins in diet and lifestyle. Take cancer. The World Cancer Research Fund UK's recent report attributes over 40 per cent of breast and bowel cancer cases in rich countries are preventable through diet, physical activity and weight control alone. Simple measures like cycling to work and swapping fatty foods for fruit can make all the difference for these and many other cancers, they say. Its report makes recommendations for "clean living" policies. According to the report, about a third of the twelve most common cancers in high-income countries and about a quarter in lower income countries could be prevented through diet, exercise and weight control.

> *After not smoking, it is clear that diet, physical activity and weight are the most important things people can do to reduce their cancer risk.*
>
> **Professor Mike Richards**, National Clinical Director for Cancer

The No More Breast Cancer campaign wants the link between breast cancer and everyday exposure to toxic chemicals taken seriously: 45,000 women are diagnosed with breast cancer every year. Over 12,400 women die every year from breast cancer. In women aged 35-54 years, breast cancer is the most common cause of all deaths, accounting for 17 per cent of all deaths. Some 50 per cent of all cancers could be prevented by changes in lifestyle and diet. But that would mean avoiding a vast number of toxic substances many of which we are completely unaware of.

They argue that lifelong, low-level exposure to the cocktail of hundreds of toxins and hormone-disruptors in our everyday lives, from pesticide residues in food to chemicals in consumer products and in the workplace, is linked to ever-rising rates of the disease. To date, the UK government, industry and mainstream cancer organisations have refuted this possibility.

The campaign urges the British government to mark a new approach by ensuring the substitution of all carcinogenic and hormone-disrupting chemicals with safer alternatives, as soon as they are available. 100,000 man-made chemicals are polluting our environment. Five hundred man-made chemicals are thought to disrupt the hormones in our body and mimic the role of oestrogen, a hormone closely linked with the development of breast cancer. At least 300 man-made chemicals have been found in human blood and body tissue. Cancer-causing substances and hormone-disrupting chemicals are included in this 'toxic burden'.

Parkinson's disease. It now emerges that people who work with pesticides are 80 per cent more likely to develop Parkinson's disease. Gardeners and farmers who use pesticides as part of their job are up to three times more likely than others to develop Parkinson's, according to a new study.

Sums spent on research into the causes and prevention are puny compared with expenditure on developing new drugs and treatments, where the money is to be made and glamour is attached, says Dr Samuel Epstein, Founder of the Cancer Prevention Coalition. Again, government is often part of the problem, not the solution. They support research that benefits big corporations.

Equally shocking patterns of deformities and illness exist in poor rural people in countries where well-known Big Cos extract oil and minerals, and spray crops without adequate precautions that would be required in advanced economies. Shocking nineteenth century working conditions are being exposed amongst workers producing cheap garments and other products for well-known Western brands.

On top of this, there is the damage to the environment, local businesses and to communities; anxiety, stress, insecurity and mental illness; and huge social costs resulting from globalisation, constant takeovers, reorganisations, centralisation and relocation. All to what end other than profit for the few?

Psychopathic corporations and leaders. Dr Robert Hare, Canadian psychologist, noticed the similarities between the characteristics of criminal psychopaths and the behaviour of big corporations and some of their leaders. Amongst these characteristics are:

- Callous unconcern for the feelings of others
- Incapacity to maintain enduring relationships
- Deceitfulness, repeated lying to others for profit
- Incapacity to experience guilt
- Failure to conform to social norms with respect to lawful behaviour

It is easy to think of examples in the way global corporations, particularly those without ties to a particular community or country, behave in the pursuit of lower and lower costs and increasing short-term performance. A few leaders, like criminals, really do display these characteristics. However, mostly it is the system in which they work and their role in it that results in this behaviour and gives them little alternative if they stay in the game. They are not bad people. I am always struck by what decent human beings most top people are. I well remember sitting at dinner beside the chairman of a well-known, global company I shall not name. He would be a good father, partner, neighbour and friend. Yet his company produces harmful products and pursues unethical policies in marketing them. There is a split between the man or, more rarely, woman and his/her corporate role.

Many people at the top are completely out of touch with ordinary people and ordinary lives. They lead insulated lives, surrounded by similar people including politicians and celebrities. In a sense they are culpable "innocents" who are, or choose to be, almost completely unaware and out of touch with reality. We have seen this recently in disgraced bankers holding on to their huge bonuses, pay-offs and pensions without any apparent feelings of shame.

The narcissistic leader is another common phenomenon. They love attention. Maybe they did not get enough as children. I name no names. You know who fit this category!

Patriarchy and false values underlie the unsustainable system. Such values are based on a definition of what it is to be a success, to be a leader and what is cool. The prevailing values of top leaders tend to favour heroic, top down leadership and decisiveness; put money and power before human needs. Ends justify means and there is an inclination towards violence, in word or deed. They *"do what is right"*, regardless of the views of others. It is the conviction that one knows best; one cannot trust others and, therefore, one has to take charge. Such beliefs may be denied but are never hidden from perceptive people. Patriarchal leadership is dysfunctional because it undervalues others and encourages them to undervalue themselves. It leads to flawed strategies because they are not inclusive. Patriarchy is far from exclusive to the male gender. "Patriarchy" describes this mindset. Feminine energy is more about nurturing life, caring, relationships and consensual ways of resolving problems.

Corporations are not moral beings, like humans. Corporations are there to maximise short-term profit and for the benefit of shareholders, not to be responsible global citizens. The duty is to shareholders not stakeholders. CEOs of quoted companies cannot put social responsibility first. That would often mean "suicide". What they can do is limited, hence, the proliferation of CSR and the denial and "green washing" of the past half century. For example Africa is a tiny 1.3 per cent of the world market for drugs. 80 per cent of the drugs market is in the rich countries where 20 per cent of the world's population live. Making cheap drugs to combat sub-Saharan epidemics, as compared to drugs for Western household pets, is a low priority. Of 1,400 new drugs developed between 1975 and 2000, only 13 were for tropical diseases and 3 for tuberculosis. This is pragmatic in the short-term. When Anita Roddick floated her company on the stock market, she learnt this lesson.

Externalising costs is a key principle. Corporations succeed by externalising costs, getting the public, the taxpayer, government, society and the environment to bear them. Cheap food is a prime example. Another example is the packaging used by supermarkets. The cost to the consumer, in taxation and council tax to pay clean up bills, and to the environment is not reflected in the price. Often small retailers and traders use paper bags which you can use in your compost bin or can be recycled. Studies carried out in 2007 established that excess packaging, as well as plastic carrier bags, cost the average family about £470 a year. Councils pay £32 in landfill tax for every tonne of rubbish they throw into landfill. This will steadily rise. The Local Government Association argues supermarkets should pay towards the collection of their packaging as an incentive to cut back. Only when the public finally say "No!" and firm international controls on corporations are instituted will they give in.

Corporate Charters. In the eighteenth and early nineteenth centuries, corporations like the East India Company were granted charters that set out specifically what they were required to do and their limitations. That system was eroded in the nineteenth century and corporations, especially in the USA, became immensely powerful. Laws gave corporations increasing autonomy and limitations were swept away. Oil and automobile interests bought up and closed down train and tram systems to pave the way for cars, buses and airlines. In the USA, extreme abuses of power gradually resulted in constraints and the recession led to the New Deal followed by post war federal agencies and regulation. However, restrictions were steadily eroded in the era of Ronald Reagan, Margaret Thatcher and George Bush Junior.

People should be the sovereign authority. The power of unelected, unaccountable corporations largely supported by timid governments has led to a global crisis of enormous proportions. Mary Zepernick points out how long and how much energy it takes to fight one single issue, often more than a decade, whilst more new issues constantly arise. Regulation is not effective. Regulatory agencies are too weak and expensive. Fines are too small to be treated as more than a business cost. Big business and government need to serve the needs of people. Citizens have to gain control over both big corporations and government. Mary advocates a return to the Charter for large corporations. Such a charter defines what the corporation is there to do, what it may and may not do and its relationship with citizens.

Rabbi Michael Lerner proposes:

Every corporation doing business within the US (whether located here or abroad) with annual income of over $20 million must *receive a new corporate charter every twenty years, and these new charters will only be granted to corporations who can prove a history of social responsibility as measured by an Ethical Impact Report.*

One might question "twenty years" as too long. The Tikkun community he founded proposes a Social Responsibility Amendment (SRA) to the US Constitution. The SRA will create a new system of Social Responsibility Grand Juries (SRGJ) composed of 25 citizens whose task would be to decide whether or not the corporation should be granted a new charter. He does not expect the amendment to be passed "any time soon" but it will stimulate the necessary debate about the principle.

A first step in developing that third path is to seek a New Bottom Line – so that we judge institutions productive, efficient and rational not only to the extent that they maximize wealth and power but also to the extent that they maximize our capacities to be caring, ecologically aware, ethically and spiritually sensitive, and capable of responding to the universe with awe, wonder and radical amazement at the grandeur of creation.
Rabbi Michael Lerner

We need a global economic system and new global institutions that focus on meeting human needs; protecting the planet; tackling poverty, disease and violence; giving everyone the chance to enjoy meaningful work and a healthy and fulfilling life. There is a growing consensus that to achieve them each country, with support from richer ones, needs the freedom to develop its own unique way to create a sustainable society in which there is well-being, health and education for all its citizens.

Corporations will not voluntarily transform themselves. It requires fresh governance and enforceable laws at national and global level. To get international agreement to this will take some doing! It may seem a daunting but there are a lot of us. Part Two will suggest how it can be done.

Further reading

- Corporate Watch, *Ethical Consumer*.

Chapter 6

Seeing the Underlying System Clearly

February 2009

Understanding what gets in the way of progress

> *Systems blindness seems to permeate all facets of Western society today*
> **Bob Doppelt**

We need to see the system clearly and address the underlying issues if we are to succeed in tackling the threats to our existence and create a better, sustainable and just world. It is no use trying to change things by addressing symptoms. Problem solving and quick fixes don't work, as New Labour's history demonstrates. Why have so many campaigns to fight poverty and injustice largely failed, years of concerts, Live Aid, Live Earth? The lesson is we need to transform the system and focus on the inspiring possibility of a world people yearn for.

The Possibility for Greater Happiness

- A global economic system designed to meet human needs, to create well-being, not excessive power and wealth for a small minority
- Everyone has enough and the opportunity for a healthy and fulfilling life – no one is hungry
- Our climate is stabilised
- We start restoring, respecting and nurturing the

diversity of the ecosystem on which all life depends
- We pursue health, instead of a culture of dependency on the medicine; people and businesses take responsibility for health and well-being
- Difference and diversity are valued and celebrated
- Injustices and mistakes are acknowledged; conflicts resolved without violence
- We put an end to war, the threat of nuclear annihilation, and military economy
- Terrorism is a thing of the past
- Leaders understand they are servants

Why are we so slow to respond to the global crisis, when effective action is urgently needed? Why, when faced with a threat far greater than WWII, are world leaders struggling to agree to a coherent strategy? The paradox is that to save ourselves we have to give up focusing on self-interest and instead focus on the greater good. We humans change and learn slowly. But this time change is urgent and we need to learn fast!

Apparently 41 per cent in the UK do not accept the overwhelming scientific consensus that global warming is largely man-made and almost a third of us think the link is not proved. Only 28 per cent think it is happening and is the world's most serious problem; just over half think it is serious but other problems are more serious.

It's partly that we in the West have never had it so good. We don't want to give up the way we live. We put our own interests first. It's hard to admit that a mindset in which so much has been invested for so long is not working.

Primitive ways of reaching decisions. Part of the problem lies in the way we reach vital decisions. Leaders don't listen to whistle-blowers. They marginalise, bully, penalise or fire people who express the dissenting views. This results in "group think", the thinking of the herd of sheep that runs over the cliff. The whip system in Parliament is an example. Anything that constrains independent thinking and principled, courageous action is dysfunctional. Adversarial debate is outdated, inadequate for dealing with the crisis we face today. We need ways of deliberating that use the full diversity of views, not opposing each other but listening, seeking a complete picture and reaching a consensus about what action is in everyone's best interest and has widespread support.

We witness this dysfunctional process daily. People are weary of it.

Dysfunctional Processes

- Abusive debate
- Bargaining, bullying and threats
- Blaming others and denying responsibility
- Defence and denial
- Expelling or killing dissenters
- Gathering together the like-minded, "One of us"
- Group think
- Marginalising and penalising dissent
- Reluctance to let go of power or advantage
- Resistance to change
- Suppression of truth

There is a better way, the way of the most effective leaders, servant leaders.

A Better Way

- The focus is on the possibility of something far better than the now
- The aim is a shared vision consensus that meets the needs, wishes and hopes of everyone and offers win-win solutions
- All the creative intelligence available is used – all the knowledge, expertise, understanding and experience
- Conflicting views that we may not wish to hear are encouraged
- Decision-making involves the whole system, all stake-holders
- Diversity and difference are valued and respected
- We have open minds and continually learn
- Honest feedback about behaviour is given
- Mistakes and past injustices are admitted and apologies made
- No blame or abuse
- People agree to listen to each other with respect
- People appreciate each other and celebrate
- Personal responsibility, commitment, integrity, truth and authenticity are cardinal principles
- Conflict resolution and reconciliation are practised

We shape and then are shaped by institutions. That is how a dangerous monoculture develops and organisations and government gradually become corrupted. It explains how good able men, like corporate leaders, participate in unethical, unsustainable business practices and bankers engage in the dodgy ones responsible for the credit crunch and the growing recession. People are appointed to head up inquiries or commissions who whitewash. Ministers who toe the party line believe in their own integrity despite evidence to the contrary. Power has a tendency to corrupt. Most people have good intentions and care, especially about their loved ones. But clearly, there is something dysfunctional in the human psyche that has to be reckoned with. Safeguards have to be built into our institutions.

Today our institutions are designed to achieve the wrong purposes; consuming and producing more, and making corporations and relatively few people richer and more powerful. Instead they should be designed to meet our needs sustainably, lift the poor out of poverty and benefit everyone without damaging the Earth on which all life depends. We get caught in pointless pursuit of ever higher levels of income, consumption, competition and overwork. We are subtly subjected to propaganda, brainwashed into believing we'll feel better with more and bigger and it leads to greater happiness. Clearly it never does. The pressure on us is to display wealth, be cool, compare ourselves with others and we end up feeling bad. We have a sense that there is no alternative. The pressures to conform are enormous. Anyone who fundamentally questions or challenges the system is marginalised and portrayed as weird. The media is a major part of it.

This figure sums it up.

Free Market Capitalism and Big Business Out of Control

- Belief in "Great God Growth" and economic growth and having more stuff
- Fuels climate change and consumes more than "spaceship Earth" can provide
- Destroys the ecosystem and diversity on which all life depends
- Pursuit of cheaper everything

- Not making us happier or creating more well-being and security
- Systematically transfers wealth from poor to super-rich. Bears down on people who make things, serve and feed us
- Big Co's externalise cost, abuse power, subvert democracy, dominate the media and keep us misinformed and mesmerised
- Big government, big tech fixes – not small solutions or precautionary principle. Ideology – not what works
- Centralising power and diminishing democracy at all levels and civil rights
- Mono-thinking creates mono-culture, mono-everything, "clone towns"
- Supported by a huge military economy that does great harm and diverts us from the biggest fundamental challenges we have ever faced

Essentially we are robbed and disempowered – how can we be so gullible?

Underlying the global economic system is an unsustainable debt money system. The financial crisis makes that clear.

An Unsustainable Money System

- Debt Money : 95% of our money created by banks , "creating money out of thin air"
- Creates massive debt burden especially for poor countries
- Debt systematically transfers wealth from poor to rich
- Inherently unsustainable – need to repay debt and

interest drives unsustainable development

- Lack of regulation and due diligence e.g. sub-prime crisis, credit crunch, recession, bailouts i.e. the taxpayer pays
- Perverse taxation: bears down on poorer people, fails to reward the sustainable and penalise the unsustainable
- UK personal debt £1.35trn exceeds GDP £1.31trn
- Unstable financial markets, about 90% transactions are speculative
- Vast avoidance and evasion, UK tax havens, laundering and blue suit corruption, a denial of responsibility, an industry

The big irony is that governments are trying to get us out of the mess caused by borrowing and debt, by borrowing our way out of it and creating more debt! There is an alternative: only central banks create money.

> *An economy that does not enslave people to debt is one in which they retain their freedom and empowerment.*
> **Brian Good vin**, "Resilience", *Resurgence,* July /August 2009

In Part Two, I put forward proposals for radical system change. However, before doing so, I offer a summary of Mahatma Gandhi's far-sighted thinking which contains many of the solutions to the crises which we face today.

Further reading

- Bob Doppelt, "The power of sustainable thinking", *Ecologist,* 20 February, 2009.

Chapter 7

Gandhi's Thinking Provides Inspiration for the 21st Century

February 2009

His is a completely revolutionary way of thinking. It is striking just how relevant Gandhi's thinking is today. His arguments for the primacy of local self-determination, local food and appropriate technology are prophetic.

Arguably, he was the most successful and influential change agent of the 20th century. He got the British out of India and influenced some of the greatest leaders of our time. He called his campaign **"All rise"** meaning everyone benefits; everyone takes responsibility. He understood the need to find out what it was like for ordinary people and created a growing groundswell for change. His key principles were truth and non-violence. If only politicians, journalists and business leaders would try this. It takes courage.

Gandhi's thinking could not be more relevant at a time when we fear we are moving closer than ever towards irreversible global warming. We face the potentially devastating effects of climate change; increasing competition for scarce resources; economic and social injustice; fear and insecurity generated by out of control violence in many places; nuclear proliferation and the threat of international terrorism using dirty bombs. State violence and bullying are not answers to these problems.

Gandhi was a whole system, living systems thinker. His systemic analysis of the world's problems is as relevant today as when he lived. He offers a systems approach to tackling these problems rather than "fixes" that don't work. Gandhi is a guide to those who wish to change things for the better.

Gandhi's thinking is essentially about a sustainable way of life, an economic system based on trusteeship for universal welfare and a society in which everyone gains rather than one in which the few become rich at the expense of the many. It is a system of interelated thought.

Gandhi has much to teach us. His ideas were a response to his time and need adapting for our time. He influenced Martin Luther King, Nelson Mandela, Archbishop Desmond Tutu and Aung San Suu Kyi and others who inspire us today. Many of his ideas have already born fruit. He had little chance to implement his ideas in India because he was assassinated soon after independence was achieved. He feared that India might rid itself of the British only to perpetuate a "brown" form of exploitation still based on British and European values. Most of his successors, including Nehru, who supported Gandhi in the political struggle, did not share his economic views and believed the future of India lay in industrialising like the West. Nehru ruled India for 17 years and laid the foundations of the Westernisation, which predominates today. Visiting London in 1935, when asked what he thought of Western Civilisation, Gandhi said, *"It would be a good idea."*

Gandhi illuminates the situation we are in now and how we can respond to the environmental crisis, poverty, violence and international conflict.

Gandhi's movement, called *Sarvodaya* or "All rise" means remaining firm on the Truth and actively resisting Untruth, using only non-violent means. *Sarvodaya* is Sanskrit for *"the welfare of all"*.

Gandhi's Eleven Principles are the core of his thinking and provide the basis for what we would call a sustainable society and way of life. If all leaders received a Gandhian education, what a difference it would make to the world!

They are:

1. **Non-violence or love:** ***Ahisma***
2. **Truth:** ***Satyagraha***
3. **Fearlessness:** ***Saravatra Bhaya Varjana***
4. **Self-organisation or self-rule:** ***Swaraj*** Self-regulation means self-knowledge and taking responsibility.
5. **Non-stealing:** ***Asteya.*** Part of this is **Non-consumerism:** ***Asangraha.*** This requires ecological humility; realising that waste is a sin against nature and that nature's cycle should be followed. It is about having enough.
6. **Sacred Sex:** ***Brahmacharya***
7. **Physical work:** ***Sharirashram***
8. **Avoidance of bad taste:** ***Aswada.***
   i. *Sattva:* simplicity
   ii. *Rajas:* glamorous
   iii. *Tamas:* depressing
9. **Respect for all religions:** ***Sarava Dharma Samanatva***
10. **Self economy or Local economy:** ***Swadeshi*** decentralisation.
11. **Respect for all beings:** ***Sparsha***

***Here is an expansion of the principles*:**

Non-violence or love: Ahisma

> *To deal with abuse of power, you confront love of power with the power of love.*
>
> **Satish Kumar**

It means resisting oppression non-violently through love: non-violence in thoughts, words and deeds. Gandhi got a response from the British, rather than a reaction, because of non-violence and the power of large numbers of people. Liberation does not mean killing people. Problems are not solved using the same mindset that created them. We can see this clearly in Iraq and

Afghanistan. Change of heart ended apartheid in South Africa.

Nelson Mandela once said that in a world full of violence and strife, Gandhi's message of peace and non-violence holds the key to human survival in the 21st century.

We need non-violence as a worldview, non-violence towards nature, women, workers in organisations and animals. The imposition of factory agriculture and inhuman conditions in factories and offices is violence. Gandhi admitted we'll never reach Utopia; humans are aggressive as well as compassionate. We need to develop non-violent ways of dealing with violence and soldiers of peace to deal with conflicts.

Hitler was a product of our military education and an unjust settlement after WWI. The roots of the Middle East conflicts lie in the history of the Crusades, Western foreign policy, injustice and exploitation and the greed of the ruling classes of oil rich Arabian states. Saddam Hussein was built up and supported by the West. We need to look at the system that creates violence and produced Hitler and Saddam. There was no *essential* difference between Bush and Saddam. We run a war economy. Violence is not working in Iraq or Afghanistan. Violence only creates more violence. Today to destroy ourselves completely is a growing risk. If ever there was a time to have the courage to try non-violence, it is now. It may be difficult but it is not impossible.

Satish Kumar argues for a global *Peace Council*, rather than a *Security Council*, to which recognised spiritual leaders are appointed, "Wise Elders" who have the interests of the world, rather than corporate or national interests, at heart.

We may doubt Gandhi's method, but it worked; he got rid of the British. Today's campaigns against nuclear power, nuclear weapons, militarism and war are Gandhian.

Truth: Satyagraha. Lack of truth is a daily issue. Political and corporate leaders mislead the public to achieve their will and are in denial when it goes wrong. It does not work. Truth and integrity are vital for bringing about change non-violently.

Pursuit of truth is an open-ended journey requiring respect for all points of view, however hard to articulate. It requires exceptional courage, especially in politics and business organisations. Gandhi subtitled his autobiography *"My experiments with truth"*.

Linked to truth is respect for all religious traditions – ***Sarava Dharma Samanatva*** – and tolerance for beliefs with which we disagree. We need to see that beliefs from different cultures and traditions have a common essence.

Gandhi believed in bringing about fundamental change through:

1. constructive programmes
2. resistance: non-violent

We lose integrity if we merely protest. Our lives need to demonstrate integrity and reflect our mission. The basic principles of transformation are: create readiness; readiness grows out of popular demand; spot when there is sufficient groundswell ready to take action; without readiness, you wait and prepare the ground. When Gandhi returned to India from South Africa, he travelled for six months, visiting and learning from the poorest people in the villages. That is a model for today's leaders.

Satyagraha is a way of life: *"Life is a continuous conversation with the universe"* – dialogue, not monologue; then change will occur. The lessons for change agents are:

1. Patience
2. Learn to spot the opportunity
3. Learn to endeavour, endure, face difficulties
4. Be fearless.

Fearlessness: Sarvatra Bhaya Varjana. Non-violence requires us to speak our truth and that requires courage; fear causes violence. It stops people from acting powerfully, speaking out and being true to themselves. Gandhi was not afraid of death. We can become fearless by seeing each situation as an opportunity for learning, developing confidence that we will overcome difficulties.

Self-organisation or self-rule: *Swaraj*. We can learn from nature, a self-organising, self-correcting, self-healing and self-managing system. It requires mutuality and reciprocity. The village is the first form of government. We need, not *"trickle down"* but *"trickle up"*. We need to start on a small scale, applying self-organising first to ourselves; then in our families; our village or community. This maximises the potential for creativity, innovation and diversity. The process moves up from community to town or city to regions, national governments, arrangements like the EU and finally world government. This is similar to the participatory budgeting process in Puerto Allegre, Brazil and the community based system in Cuba. It is an application of the principle of Subsidiarity. The recent Sustainable Communities Act in UK, intended to give greater power to local communities, lays the foundations for moving towards such a system in UK. The roots need to be intimate, giving maximum power at the bottom, co-ordinated at the top. Needs should be met locally wherever possible.

Since WWII government has drawn more power to itself. Now it is clear: this is not working. There are growing calls for decentralisation and devolving power. Central control impedes successful change; takes away responsibility and initiative from people who best understand their communities' needs and how to meet them. Hence the importance of the bottom up campaigns – Pressure Works, Unlock Democracy's Network's "*Power to the People*" proposals, headed by Baroness Helena Kennedy, and the Local Works campaign for a Sustainable Communities Bill. Gandhi proposed that tax be collected locally, most retained locally, only sending smaller amounts to the next level, as in Puerto Allegre in Brazil (Participatory budgeting in Puerto Allegre). It would be better to have Social Forums in every part of the world, where local problems are better understood.

Non-stealing: *Asteya.* This goes far beyond not taking what does not belong to you. The Earth and natural things are sacred. Earth, fire, air and water are sacred elements. It is theft when family farms are destroyed by agribusiness, livelihoods are destroyed by globalisation, crafts are destroyed by industrialisation and big trawlers overfish. It is theft when food, seeds, trees and plants are patented; when commons like water are privatised, rivers diverted. Salinisation is caused by excessive irrigation or large amounts of water taken by drinks companies like Pepsi and Coca Cola.

Greed by a few individuals, excessive remuneration and abuse of corporate power are theft. Global sourcing that involves exploitation of poor workers and displacement of local workers in order to cut costs is theft. Gandhi says accumulation and overconsumption are stealing from God. ***Asteya*** is a way of consuming only what nature can replenish, having enough, consuming only to meet our vital needs, knowing that other peoples and creatures need to have their share, I only take my share: *"Living simply, so that others may live, a way of generosity,"* as Satish Kumar says.

Non-consumerism: *Asangraha.* Part of this is ecological humility, realising that waste is a sin against nature and that nature's cycle should be followed. Satish says: *"Greed has become a creed, a new religion!"* Consumerism is theft and causes crime.

Sacred Sex: *Brahmacharaya* means loving sexuality within a healthy human relationship. Sexuality is a source of energy and creativity. This explains why tyrannies of mind, for instance many religions, have often suppressed it throughout history. Sexuality appropriately practised is part of love of God.

Trivialisation and commercialisation of sex, pornography and sexual exploitation stem from disrespect for the sanctity of sex. Sacred sex is based on commitment, responsibility, celebration and joy.

Physical work: *Sharirashram*

> *Sharirashram means the practice of daily labour. Physical work is a form of worship, a spiritual practice. It is a healing process and an antidote to alienation and exclusion… Our hands have a tremendously transformative power… A deskilled society is a degraded society.*

Making things by hand, creating, doing ordinary things like cleaning, working with the soil and growing things is embedded in the human psyche. When affluence, industrialisation and technology take us away from using our hands, this separates intellectual from manual workers and does us physical and spiritual harm. Separating mind and body denies us our identity as human beings.

Avoidance of bad taste: *Aswada* Three Qualities of Life are:

Sattva – simple
Rajas – glamorous
Tamas – depressing

There is much here for leaders, so easily corrupted by power, celebrity, wealth and honours.

Sattva means simple, how life is. Rajas is glamour and ceremony. Tamas is dark, depressing. In everything we can see the three qualities. Living in the here and now, having a conversation with nature is Sattvic. Sattvic food is healthy, simple, fresh and local, easy to digest and nutritious. Organic can be Sattvic – not cruel factory farming with large, distant abattoirs and unhappy animals. Meat, produced with cruelty, is Rajasic. Meat is sustainable when consumed in moderation, to supplement our diet or when there is no alternative, provided killing is done with respect and humility. Rajasic is the banquet or when food becomes more important than the people who cook it, a display, a statement, showing off. The same applies to clothes, cars and houses. A temple or church can be Sattvic or Rajasic. Prisons, the Home Office building, a nuclear bunker, nuclear weapons are Tamasic. All three qualities are present in everything and you can appear one way but in your heart be something else.

Power can be Sattvic when it comes from spirit inside; Rajasic when from status or position; Tamasic when power and beliefs are imposed.

Respect for all religions: ***Sarava Dharma Samanatva*** means in a nutshell that *"all religions tell the same truth"*.

Self-economy or Local economy: ***Swadeshi*.** Gandhi saw that industrialisation was sweeping the world. He predicted that it would destroy creativity, diversity, culture, agriculture and replace it with industrial farming.

Swadeshi provides an answer to the destructive effects of globalisation that contribute to poverty and debt in countries like India and starvation in Africa. There are similar effects on food, farming, communities, diversity and livelihood in UK and continental Europe. The campaigns of the New Economics Foundation, Local Works, the Soil Association, Garden Organic, Slow City, Slow Food and LETS Local Exchange Trading Systems and Transition Towns are *Swadeshi*.

Under this principle, whatever is made or produced locally is produced first and foremost for people of that locality. The primary motivation of business and entrepreneurs must be not to damage society or the environment but to serve the community by meeting needs, rather than creating wants. The local community should be a microcosm of the macro world (with its own craftspeople, technicians, clothing-makers, farmers, food producers, musicians, artists, etc.). The local community or nation should have power to decide what is imported into or out of it, not some distant authority like the WTO.

The principle is not against cities, but against sprawling suburbs and megalopolises. Cities of one to two million would be flanked by greenbelts and sufficient farmland to provide food. Gandhi wanted a system for a post-industrial society which provided a balance between city and rural – 20 per cent of people living in cities and the rest in villages. He wanted to educate planners and architects to create cities that provided their own food within 30 to 40 miles' radius, like Havana today. Herbert Girardet's *CitiesPeoplePlanet – Liveable Cities for a Sustainable World* and Transition Town initiative are 21st century expressions of these principles.

Gandhi was not against trade but he believed trade with distant countries should be the icing on the cake and basic food and clothing should be produced locally.

Respect for all beings: *Sparsha.* Scientific solutions like nuclear power represent an arrogant and blinkered view of the natural world of which we are part. Genetic engineering, terminator seed technology and patenting life forms show a desire to dominate natural processes.

Satish Kumar says:

> ***Sarvodaya*** *requires us to put nature at the centre. We are part of nature and there is no separation. No one is above or below. Worms are as important as trees. Everything plays its part. The mango tree teaches us about unconditional love as it feeds animals, wasps, birds, humans and worms. Nature is not there to serve our needs. We do not have dominion over nature or the Earth. The ecological crisis stems from the view that we do. We do not even have power over our own bodies or when they will die. We can receive the gifts*

of nature but not exploit nature. We need to liberate our minds from:

Nationalism
Racism
Colour
Sexism
Species-ism.

Gandhi held the view we all rise together and we are completely interdependent. Over 20 billion years we are all made of each other, all the food we have eaten, the air we breathe, our parents, ancestors and all our teachers. The well-being of one is dependent on the well-being of all. Diversity and unity are integral to unity and two sides of the same coin. The Advaita tradition argues everything is divine and there is no two-ness – we are all one. We cannot live happily whilst violence and injustices are going on. Every human being is a microcosm of the universe – there is no separate self.

Most movements for preserving nature spring from a utilitarian viewpoint and are inspired by fear rather than love. We have to make peace with nature and give up all cruelty towards animals, poisoning of the Earth with chemicals and make peace with the Earth.

Other Gandhian Ideas

Appropriate technology. Gandhi was not against technology. Appropriate technology is an important concept – technology that serves rather than harms human beings. We need to ask, *Technology for what?* Then choose whatever best meets need and purpose. Clearly the mass production of cars cannot be done locally. Technology should aid, not replace human hands. This means technology for service, not greed, with gratitude and humility towards nature. The aim of new technology should not be increased power, ego gratification, excessive profit and consumption. Change should not be for change's sake or to create obsolescence. More, faster and faster change may mean more rapid destruction of the planet.

Appropriate scale and markets. It makes sense to have a global market for some things; but for others regional, national or local market may work best. This means neither small nor large scale but *appropriate scale*, choosing whatever scale is best for different purposes. Wherever possible, food should be produced organically and grown locally. Food, the source of life, health and spiritual well-being is not a commodity and generally should not be industrialised. We should not be separated from the process of growing and cooking food.

Appropriate scale also applies to organisation structures. They need to be as small as possible for the purpose to make them democratic and inclusive.

Money. Gandhi believed currencies should be created, not by banks, but by communities and government:

Local
National
International

Money is a means of exchange and should be subservient. Instead, it dominates and people are enslaved by debt. Speculation in money markets and the stock exchanges causes damaging instability for enterprises, their stakeholders, savings and retirement pensions. Free market capitalism obstructs long-term stewardship, which is seen as a constraint on the fullest short-term exploitation of people and capital for share growth, profit and dividends. Making a few people super-rich damages the rest of humanity. The harm cannot be undone by setting up charitable foundations. James Robertson's radical ideas on monetary reform, debt and taxation are in Gandhi's tradition. Also, LETS – Local Exchange Trading Systems or Schemes, local community-based mutual aid networks in which people exchange all kinds of goods and services with one another, without the need for money.

Our political system. Gandhi advocated *participative* not *representative* democracy. Instead of a system in which parties fight elections, he favoured voting for people who contribute well and are highly thought of, have the required skills. A system like this would prevent the huge cost of election campaigns that corrupt democracy. Hence the importance of the UK *Power to the People* report under the chairmanship of Helena Kennedy and Unlock Democracy's continuing campaigns to bring about a fairer and more participatory democracy.

The Venerable Samdhong Rinpoche, Prime Minister of the Tibetan Parliament in Exile, says that under their system for parliament there are no parties. Individuals do not propose themselves as candidates for election but are nominated on the basis of their contribution to society.

Cohesion. Gandhi's philosophy is about synthesis and integration. The Indian idea is cohesion, bringing together polarities – outer and inner – matter and spirit. Western tradition analyses and separates. This explains the contemporary lack of *joined up thinking,* which constantly gets in the way of efforts to tackle climate change and the successful implementation of sustainable strategies. Another example is not recognising the importance of feeling at work. When feeling, intuition, joy and spirit are brought into work, everything fits together. Gandhi stood for integration and cohesion.

1. ***Yagna*****:** meaning soil or the replenishment of nature.
2. ***Tapas*****:** replenishment of soul.
3. ***Dana*****:** replenishment of society.

Western society is based on exploitation and indebtedness to nature. Replenishment means: we take wood, we replace it with a tree. We use soil, we replenish it. Industrial society does not believe in replenishment and waste is dumped. In Gandhian language, this is a sin against nature. Humans need to be part of nature's system. ***Yagna*** is the responsibility of every living being. ***Tapas*** means silence, rest, meditation, walking, putting our feet in water, sitting in the forest and accepting ourselves for who we are, being ourselves. In silence we use our whole self, not just our voice and brain. Every morning and evening Gandhi would go into prayer. He gave himself one day a week for replenishment, to retreat, reflect, introspect and listen to his inner voice. ***Dana*** means giving back to society, taking care of society and its replenishment.

Conclusions and Implications

The biggest threats we face are violence and destruction of planet Earth on which life depends. Gandhi provides insights and guiding principles to help us avoid these disasters and create a sustainable, fairer, less violent world and a new world order fit for our time.

Acknowledgements

This chapter first appeared as my Schumacher Society Challenge Paper, *All Rise – How Gandhi's thinking can help us in the 21st century,* slightly modified here. It owes much to talks and discussions on the course on Gandhi and Globalisation given by Satish Kumar, Vandana Shiva and the Venerable Samdhong Rinpoche, Prime Minister of the Tibetan Parliament in Exile held at Bija Vidyapeeth, Vandana Shiva's International College for Sustainable Living at Navdanya Farm near Dehra Dun, November 24th – 7th December 2006. Vandana's farm and college embodies Gandhian principles, as does her field work in India and campaigns against the industrialisation of agriculture, commodification of food and water, patenting of seeds, plants and food and abuse of corporate power. I also draw on Gandhi's eleven principles, or Eleven Vows as he called them, described in the last chapter of Satish Kumar's autobiography *No*

Destination and his *The Three Qualities of Life* and Gandhi's *Hind Swaraj or Indian Home Rule.*

Further reading:

- Gandhi, M K, 1938, *Hind Swaraj or Indian Home Rule,* Jitendra T Desai, Ahmehdabad, India.
- Gandhi, M K, *Eleven Vows,* National Gandhi Museum & Library, New Delhi.
- Kumar, S, 2000, *No Destination: An Autobiography,* Green Books, Dartington, Devon, UK
- Kumar, S, 2006, *The Three Qualities of Life – a compass to realign reality,* the Viveka Foundation, New Delhi.

Part Two

A Vision for a Better World:

Possibilities for a better future: What needs to be done and how we can make it happen

Chapter 8

Greening the World

March 2009

What needs to be done about climate change, Peak Oil and ecological destruction – Paradigm change, green transport, green heat and power, nuclear power or not, good models.

We have the opportunity to create a world that is sustainable, just and free from poverty and violence in which everyone has the chance of a fulfilled life. All over the world people are doing what is needed – in Cuba, Ecuador, Germany and Scandinavian countries such as Denmark, Norway and Sweden. Where technology can help, it is there and just needs to be developed and used. It is a matter of choice. Will we choose to do it? We have had ample warning as to the consequences if we don't.

We have to develop green, ecological economies. This means learning from nature. Our processes are linear, destructive, wasteful, and out of balance. Nature wastes nothing. It recycles everything and renews itself. We are part of nature and we need to be part of that process. Nature's processes are circular: creation, growth, maturity, decline, death, recycling and rebirth. Everything is interrelated, in balance and in harmony. That is why people feel healed in nature. Yesterday I heard Rupert Isaacson story of how his autistic son Rowan was calmed and healed by horses in Mongolia.

We get our "kicks" from more: more money, more power, more consumption, more excitement, more gadgets, new, the latest, faster, further, bigger, cheaper, more complex, not better, healthier, fairer, happier, more fulfilling. We are bemused. Our business leaders and politicians are all "on it" without realising it. Growth, they think, is the solution to everything.

This is the meaning of sustainability:

Living without compromising the needs of the future

Principles are needed to guide decisions. Without them, a coherent strategy is not possible.

Basic Principles

- Work towards limiting our carbon and ecological footprints to a sustainable world average
- Use renewable resources wherever possible
- Minimise use of non-renewable resources, use them efficiently and they should be recycled
- No more renewable resource should be used than can regenerate in the same period
- Release of materials into the environment should not be greater than the environment's capacity to absorb them
- Toxic substances should not be used or disposed of in ways that are a threat to future generations
- The precautionary principle should be applied and incalculable risks, such as nuclear power, *should not be taken*

What are the implications? We need to move away from *"bigger, further, faster and more"* to moderation. It is not a move from one extreme to another but a better mix. We need a change from one way of thinking to another. It will be a revolution driven by the multiple crises the world is confronted with.

A Paradigm Shift

Here I summarise the paradigm shift we need to make. My source is a book I strongly recommend , written eleven years ago but still providing the thinking required today – *Greening the North – a Post-Industrial Blueprint for Ecology and Equity*, Wolfgang Sachs, Reinhard Loske, and Manfred Linz, eds, 1998, Zed Books. The book describes eight paradigm shifts:

A Paradigm Shift

- Moderation in time and space
- A green market agenda
- From linear to cyclical production processes
- Well-being rather than well-having
- Intelligent infrastructures
- Regeneration of land and agriculture
- Liveable cities
- International equity and global solidarity

Moderation in time and space – Moderate speeds, shorter distances and regional scale. Transport and travel would be more regional and local, de-emphasising long distances and intensifying shorter links and more sustainable forms like trains, buses, cycling and walking and substituting electronics for travel.

A green market agenda. Move from market euphoria and growth. Place more emphasis on local than on global division of labour. Move from everything calculated in financial terms to protection of climate, ecology, environment, including well-being. Value the social, historical and cultural. Support health, community, fulfilling work and security. Avoid large-scale uninsurable risks and liabilities. Reuse existing capital, rather than whole scale demolition and new build. Ban toxins. Enable decentralised, locally based generation of electricity and heating. Steer with taxation and subsidies reflecting all these objectives; taxing the unsustainable, not the sustainable, enterprise or jobs.

From linear to cyclical production processes. Follow nature's example, not wasting and valuing diversity. Create an economy founded on solar and nature's energy and the principle of recycling; longer product cycles, emphasis on durability, service and repair. Instead of competition based on constant innovation, larger market share, ever shortening product cycles and lower price, initiate ecological leadership based on meeting real human needs. Produce more and more products and materials locally and regionally in decentralised workshops and mini-mills, providing skilled and rewarding work again. It is unsustainable to ship products and waste around the world. Involve human creativity in selling utility and services rather than products – for example individual transportation rather than cars – opening up fresh possibilities.

Well-being rather than well-having. This opens up the possibility of a complete change in values, to meeting post materialistic needs, moving from affluence to, for instance, conserving, informed eating, freedom from toxins, local and regional orientation, using instead of owning, rich in time, and the elegance of simplicity.

Intelligent infrastructures. Today's infrastructure projects are lavish and massive, both on the surface and underground, consuming vast resources, giving rise to enormous wasteful throughput, emissions and waste. Ultimately these projects will be demolished leading to even more waste. Magnitudes have more than doubled in Germany, for instance, since the sixties for motorways (260 per cent), networks for gas (230 per cent), water (206 per cent), electricity (398 per cent) and transportation of goods by road (159 per cent). A switch is needed from a throughput economy to meeting human needs. As the magnitude increases for roads, the congestion and delays get worse. The switch needs to be ***from*** magnitude and constant growth ***to*** services meeting human needs, saving the planet and bringing about global justice. This means energy saving, eco-efficient products and services and better local and community infrastructures – just the opposite of what is happening! It means a shift to energy suppliers becoming energy efficiency service companies, integrated resource planning, decentralised and least cost planning (LCP) of heat and power that can lead to big savings. The same can be done for water supplies with fewer dams and less groundwater extraction. The concept of service orientation and orientation to what is close at hand can be applied to mobility with fewer journeys and road schemes e.g. cycling, car-sharing and buses. Instead of building ever larger housing estates, there needs to be a shift towards "functional intermingling" of housing, work, shopping, leisure, recreation, food growing, land and buildings, local power and energy linked to both housing and offices.

Regeneration of land and agriculture. In Europe 75 per cent of the population, 80 per cent in the UK, live in densely populated urban areas. However, these are heavily dependent on the countryside for food, water, air, materials and recreation. City and countryside are interrelated. We need to move from a parasitical relationship between the two towards regionalism. We have depleted and neglected the countryside and damaged the capacity of farmers to feed us by underpaying them. Industrial farming methods have harmed the soil, the ecosystem and polluted our water. The countryside, trees and plants, play a major part in absorption and regeneration, renewing soils, water and air. This requires respect for the ecosystem, a shift from monoculture to diversity, from plantation to woodland, from linear agribusiness to organic cultivation, from food as a commodity and heavily processed food to healthy food, from globalised supermarket to regional farmers' market. We need to be reconnected with food as the source of health and energy; learn how to grow and cook again. It means producing food in our gardens, allotments and community gardens.

Liveable Cities are described in Chapter 13: *Sustainable Cities, Towns and Communities.*

International equity and global solidarity. It is most important that we manage our transition in a way that does not harm the rest of the world, already suffering greater poverty as a result of the downturn, but brings about greater equity. Chapter 9 describes how we can create greater equality through a fairer global economic system, global co-operation and involving poorer nations as equal partners.

Strategies

To avoid catastrophic climate change and secure energy supplies, governments need to take urgent action to implement a coherent strategy on a massive scale. The two largest industries causing CO2 emissions are energy i.e. heat and power, and then transport. Here are outlines of what can be done:

Heat and Power

The Lib/Con Coalition is committed to the target to generate 20 per cent of electricity from renewable resources by 2020. Many people are strongly opposed to plans for new nuclear power – see Chapter 4, Section A – and coal fired stations with carbon capture and storage (CCS). The CEO of Centrica warned that carbon capture storage (CCS) equipment is unlikely to be ready to make big cuts in Britain's emissions before 2030. The following describes elements of a coherent strategy to ensure this target is achieved without either of these options.

Renewable power is a more responsible option. It matches peak consumer demand. It is argued that wind power is usually greater in mornings, evenings and winter. Spending disproportionately on coal and nuclear undermines potential investment in renewables. A better match for renewables is hydropower. We also need to link our grid with other countries such as Denmark, Germany, Spain and Portugal which are far enough away to have different wind and weather patterns that can complement ours. That will make it possible to smooth fluctuations in renewables on a reciprocal basis. The UK and northern Europe need to work with the Mediterranean, Africa and the Middle East to help them to help them develop solar power and link it to our grids, see below under Natural Advantages and Solar Powering.

Generating electricity from waste. According to the National Grid, biogas made from waste could be used for generating electricity and heating in half the UK's homes. *"Biogas has tremendous potential for delivering large-scale renewable heat for the UK but it will require government commitment to a comprehensive waste policy and the right commercial incentives,"* said Janine Freeman, head of National Grid's Sustainable Gas Group. *"It provides a solution for what to do with our waste with the decline in landfill capacity and it would help the UK with a secure supply of gas as North Sea sources run down."* The cost of developing the infrastructure for biogas was estimated at £10 billion, while the cost per unit of gas was found to be similar to that of other renewable energy sources. Manure, slurry and food can be used to create enough energy in the form of biogas to heat and power more than two million homes in Britain, according to Defra.

Government needs to support and encourage the development of an industry supplying all the technology that is needed. The various technologies and options are well known. In some we are in the lead but, unfortunately, having to rely on export markets because of lack of government commitment to renewable energies and support. They have given preference to coal and nuclear power. Substantial incentives including sustainable taxation are needed to make things happen. In some cases development is needed. Large-scale production will bring down the cost. There is no shortage of solutions which, when combined, could make dirty coal and dangerous nuclear power unnecessary.

Natural advantages. Areas like the Mediterranean, Africa, the Sahara desert and the Middle East have huge potential for large-scale solar power generation. Britain with its long coastline with wind, tides and wave and Scottish hydropower has enormous natural advantages. The whole of the North Sea, balanced by hydropower in mountainous areas such as Norway and the possibility of storing water behind dams, offer similar advantages. All offer potential for large-scale national and regional "smart grids". Similar collaborations are likely to take place all over the world. At the local level, similar ways of using natural advantages are likely to emerge. Together they could make nuclear power redundant.

Solar powering. Solar powering the Mediterranean area could create links in a power grid that will ring the Mediterranean Sea. Sharing electricity over this "Mediterranean Ring" could secure Europe's power supply with clean renewable energy, accelerate North Africa's development and knit together two worlds that seem to be racing apart. It has to be said that early experiments in North Africa in 2005 experienced difficulties.

Combined heat and power. Combined heat and power, either at large installations such as power stations or in smaller community, residential or office developments, can also make a contribution by avoiding wasted heat and energy, especially when the heat and power are derived from renewable sources.

Sustainable Power Networks and Smart National or Regional Grids. We need to re-engineer our electricity distribution grid to accommodate small and medium scale, local, combined heat and power generation and power from domestic and office roofs. Current national grids were created in a different age for different needs and sources of power. They can be modernised and expanded for moving electricity from where it is generated to where it is needed through a unified national smart grid. The grid is smart in the sense that it can monitor and balance both the load and the fluctuating power from diverse sources such as sun, wind and wave from different areas, accommodate distributed energy from local areas and, in the future, capitalise on a massive national fleet of clean, plug-in cars. Such a new grid would encompass both the long-distance, high-voltage transmission lines and the lower voltage distribution systems that connect the power to customers. Updating grids will save wastage and money, increase reliability and protect consumers from outages, and make possible a clean electricity system. It will move renewable power from where it is generated to wherever it's needed, whenever it's needed. Investing in modernisation of the grid will create thousands of jobs for workers. Such schemes are being considered in North America, Europe, the European North Sea area and could be applied to solar powering the Mediterranean area, embracing European, Middle Eastern and North African countries and, for that matter many, other regions of the world.

Smart meters help householders manage their consumption better and save the cost of visits by the meter man, or woman.

Smart appliances. At the GridWise lab, a refrigerator, washer, dryer, dishwasher, water heater and even coffeemaker are all doing their bit for the national power grid.

Massive savings could be made by turning off unnecessary lights at night in cities throughout the world, especially late at night. Large savings can also be made by reducing energy use and heat loss by various means including constructing carbon neutral new buildings and retrofitting existing buildings which are by far the biggest challenge for the nation.

The most sensible approach seems to be a combination of approaches, reflecting the geography and ecology of different regions or areas, taking into account the amount of wind, nearby seas and the existence of supplies of wood or biomass. Large power stations supplying through a national grid waste two-thirds of the heat and energy they generate. Smaller more local power stations are able to supply the heat they generate to neighbouring buildings. The following is a summary of the main technologies, for large and small scale application, in roughly descending order of size:

Heat and Power

- Concentrated solar power (CSP) technology in sunny countries.
- Pan-European offshore electricity network to even out fluctuations in North Sea wind and wave turbines.
- Wind turbines, on land and increasingly at sea, wave, tide and solar PV power.
- Smart national and regional power grids that can balance both fluctuating demand and the fluctuations of different sources of green energy.
- Saving energy by turning off unnecessary lights at night in cities.
- Decentralised renewable energy supplying communities with both heat and power.
- Power generation by small and large-scale hydropower.
- Turning factories, homes, offices, farms and other businesses into generators of heat and power – mini neighbourhood power stations.
- Community power generation schemes.
- Rooftop generation – but generally excluding micro turbines which are not financially viable for most homes.
- Homes as mini-power stations, e.g. using sun and light, selling what they do not need.

- Better feed-in tariffs to make domestic and small business generation more attractive for people.
- Adapting the national grid to facilitate feed-in.
- Biomass for both small scale heat and power generation – but not large-scale growing of crops for biofuels – that diverts land from food.
- Woodlands managed as local sources of fuel.
- Micro-generation through small turbines and photo-voltaic panels.
- Solar panels and ground source for heating.
- Combined heat and power.
- Heat pumps.

Sources: Geoffrey Lean's *10 ways to save the world, Independent on Sunday*, 15 March 2009 and Oliver Tickell's *Renewing our obligations, The Guardian*, Saturday, 27 September 2008.

Transport

A holistic transport policy, of which the following innovations can be a part, has great potential to contribute to a more sustainable, happier, safer and healthier life. The development of engines that emit much less CO2 or are powered by alternatives to fossil fuel has tremendous potential to reduce greenhouse gas emissions and enable the world to adapt to Peak Oil.

Trains, powered by electricity instead of diesel, especially electricity generated from renewable sources, will make an increasing contribution. Braking systems on electric trains that return power to the supply for other trains are already used on our railways. Regenerative breaking, as this is called, and kinetic energy, the energy a moving object possesses because of its motion, is also being used in hybrid cars.

Freight. The big question is how freight haulage and deliveries will be powered. Electric vehicles as yet are far from providing a complete answer for ether personal travel or freight purposes. It is likely that both our travel habits and road haulage will be fundamentally transformed.

Hydrogen fuel cell buses. In December 2008, two design teams shared the London Mayor's competition prize for a new eco-friendly London Routemaster. Two designs will be passed on to bus manufacturers, following a competitive tendering process, to develop a final design which could be in service by 2011. However, David MacKay casts doubt on the hydrogen fuel cell solution in the near future.

Hybrid cars. Honda and Toyota have been successfully selling these for years. Honda, General Motors, Nissan and Toyota are building new, smaller hybrid models. Whilst hybrids offer fuel savings of some 20-30 per cent, smaller vehicles made from lighter materials offer just as much. So, whilst giving impressive savings, hybrids may be only an interim solution.

Electric cars offer considerable scope for short journeys. They are widely used in Denmark and Norway. Current electric cars are limited in range and capacity and a lot of development is needed. Most are impractical for more than short distances and there are safety concerns about the G-Wizz, a two-seater. Reva Electric Car Company (REVA), market and technology-leader in EV (electric vehicle) personal transport in India, announced the launch of lithium-ion batteries that would cater to the European market. The two-seater Mini's range is 156 miles but it has only two seats because of the size of its batteries. But most car journeys in UK are less than 40 miles. In 2011, Nissan will offer a family-sized battery electric hatchback. By 2015, a range of family-sized electric and hydrogen fuel cell cars should be available. Bearing in mind the relatively short range of current cars we'll need to think carefully about how best to meet our individual needs. Relatively high prices may make it preferable to hire.

Networks to support Electric and Hybrid vehicles. Renault and Peugeot Citroen have announced a deal with French electric company, Electricite de France (EdF), to develop and market green vehicles. The plan is to build a cross-country network to support plug-in electric vehicle charging stations. The charging stations would have smart technology that would recognize individual cars and directly invoice the owner for any charges. This partnership between the car makers and EdF reinforces the strong French stance and commitment to being a leader in green transportation. The message is *"We need green transportation now."*

Shia Agassi, founder of Better Place, developed the idea of marketing electric cars like mobile phones, taking out a contract for miles. It is being tried out in Israel, Denmark, Japan, Hawaii, Seville and San Francisco. He says it isn't just about making all-electric vehicles. His big idea is for electric car networks throughout the world, using clean electric energy. An infrastructure will be needed, including charging stations, battery swap stations, and the software to make it as easy as possible for the user. London Mayor Boris Johnson wants to greatly expand charging points around London. His working group is developing a plan along the lines of the Autolib electric car rental scheme planned for Paris for 2010. Of course it depends how the electric power is generated!

Car share schemes are developing on a substantial scale in the USA with Zipcar leading the market, smaller, not for profit organisations, and Hertz and other car hire companies getting involved. Bill Ford said, *"The future of transportation will be a blend of things like Zipcar, public transportation and car ownership."* A survey of "Zipsters" found that 80 per cent want to drive an electric vehicle.

It's a safe bet we'll have a range of green options by 2020. Meanwhile plug-in hybrids rechargeable at home may suit us.

UK Campaign for Better Transport. The following summarises the comprehensive proposals of the UK Campaign for Better Transport source: the *Green Car Congress, USA.* The full report is available from the Campaign for Better Transport.

Transport Policies for Cutting UK Transport GHG Emissions by 26 per cent by 2020 provides a comprehensive package of transport policies that could reduce UK transport sector greenhouse gas emissions by 26 per cent by 2020 from 2006 levels. It argues that current government policies, including intensive improvements to vehicle efficiency, will achieve less than a 5 per cent reduction in CO_2 on 1990 levels by 2020. The Campaign's proposals, in line with overall aims to achieve 80 per cent reduction in emissions by 2050, are:

- Cut overall CO2 emissions from transport by 26 per cent by 2020 on 2006 figures.
- Cut passenger travel emissions by 32 per cent.
- Cut freight emissions by up to 19 per cent.
- Make cars 25 per cent more fuel efficient.
- Cut car traffic by 15 per cent; and
- Cut domestic aviation emissions by 30 per cent.

It recommends policies ranging from increasing walking to reducing aviation and deep sea shipping. They vary in impact but are mutually supportive and need to be implemented as a package.

Vehicle technology and low-carbon fuels. The UK has about 27 million private cars, with a refresh rate of about 15 years. Policies to encourage technological change in the vehicle fleet include:

- **First year charges on cars** related to their level of emissions, to increase annually to 2020 and applied per gram above an efficiency reference level, at least 130 in 2012, 100 in 2015 and 90 by 2020.
- **Efficiency reference level to rise annually** as technology

becomes available so the charge on less efficient vehicles rises in real terms.

- **Air conditioning** and other power consuming devices to be included in carbon emission g/km (grams per kilogram) calculations.
- **Vans** brought within car standards scheme.
- **Fuel duty** to rise in line with predicted improvements in efficiency to avoid rebound effect.
- **Vehicle Excise Duty increases to be slowed down** as the least effective means of changing purchasing behaviour.
- **Reduce work-related car travel.** Work-related travel accounts for 37 per cent of total CO_2 emissions from passenger transport: 24 per cent from commuting and 13 per cent from travel in the course of business. People are taking long journeys by themselves: 91 per cent of car commuting and 87 per cent of business car trips.
- **Tax changes** are recommended for business use of private cars to reward low carbon vehicles and reduce incentives for high business mileage; active traffic management systems to make longer road journeys more efficient; tax breaks to promote cash back and green bonus schemes that reward people for not driving to work; government serving as an example for supporting low-carbon commuting and business travel.

Similar actions are needed to reduce shopping related travel.

Reduce journey lengths and transfer short car journeys to walking and cycling. Between 1985 and 2005 average annual mileage per head within the UK increased by 35 per cent. This is the result of the interaction of transport policies with land use planning. Car journeys of less than five miles account for 20 per cent of passenger transport CO2. Shifting some of these to walking and cycling will help cut congestion and obesity and improve health too.

Land use policy is a key component. The market for land, and decisions about how it is used, depend crucially on transport. This is a two-way relationship; transport demand arises from land use and land use patterns are made possible by the availability and cost of transport networks. However, there is an intervening factor at work; behavioural choice, in other words, how people react to the many different combinations of location and methods of travel which are available to them.

- **A national funding scheme for smarter transportation,** of £200 million a year for 10 years, with specific initiatives for:
- **shopping** (including home delivery, local collection centres, local outlets, local sourcing;
- **schools** (including walking and cycling initiatives but with school safety zones and non-statutory school bus initiatives in rural areas);
- **workplaces** (including established techniques to encourage video conferencing, car share, public transport, cycling and walking); and
- **leisure facilities**

Walkable Streets. Policies such as a new "Walkable Streets" fund provide cycle priority networks and bike hire schemes in major towns and cities, along with reformed street priorities and street design to increase safety and make walking and cycling a real option for short journeys.

Planning policies should reduce the need to travel and support higher density development around high-frequency public transport. Policy statements on economic development and shopping should include a stronger focus on developments in, rather than outside, town centres.

Longer term policy recommendations include:

- **New parking policies,** including maximum parking levels in new commercial developments, reducing over time and charges for car parking over these limits, with the revenue going to reductions in business rates.
- **Better local services and shops in new developments:** housing developers should give endowments rather than one-off planning gain deals to fund these.
- **Use eco-towns and eco-developments** to show it's possible to create developments where people can choose not to own a car.
- **Expose real transport costs of other decisions:** Government decisions on the location/centralisation of health, education, leisure and other facilities (like post offices) should take full account of increased transport costs and emissions and the results of such analyses should be made public.
- **Increase public transport trips.** Improving public transport in association with the other policies already mentioned would produce a "total sustainable travel offer" to allow households to replace second and third cars and to target other journeys producing large CO_2 emissions, such as "chauffeur" trips where parents act as unpaid taxi drivers (15 per cent of passenger transport CO_2).
- **Cut freight emissions.** Freight transport accounts for 36 per cent of UK transport CO_2 emissions: 23 per cent for trucks, 12 per cent for vans and 1 per cent for rail freight. Emissions from this segment are growing faster than emissions from cars. The report recommends:
- **Road charging for trucks,** with incentives for greater efficiency and reductions in vehicle duty.
- **Increasing rail freight by increasing capacity** on the rail network and using the planning system to locate new freight warehousing next to rail lines.

- **Increasing water freight and reducing its emissions** by promoting the use of more local ports, use of biofuels and more efficient ship designs.
- **Reducing van emissions** through encouraging cleaner vehicles and fuels through tax breaks and regulation, as now applied to cars, and also driver training and vehicle maintenance.

Cut aviation emissions. The report recommends tackling emissions from the aviation sector by:

- **Reducing demand.** The government should promote video conferencing as part of business travel initiatives, and the current Air Passenger Duty should be replaced by a charge per aircraft, adjusted by weight and distance.
- **Rail enhancements including high speed lines,** for the longer term, planned as an alternative to short distance flights.
- **Domestic aviation should pay fuel duty and VAT** with money raised used to cut other taxes and charges and invest in rail.

Conclusions

Amongst the conclusions I draw about the future of our energy are as follows:

Our Energy Future – Global

- A combination of radical reduction in energy use and waste and lifestyle change
- More efficient technology and new sources of energy
- An exciting, challenging and expensive transition
- Better ways to travel, better conditions in our towns,

cities and countryside, better health, greater tranquillity, in short a better life

- New enterprises and new jobs
- Different nations and bioregions within them will develop their unique solutions and take advantage of natural advantages
- The most promising renewable source for large-scale use is concentrating solar power using moving mirrors, molten salt, steam, and heat engines from desert sources, where there is plentiful sunshine, large areas and low population densities

The way forward for the UK. David McKay reaches some uncomfortable conclusions about the way forward for the UK. He calculates that the UK will need to reduce its consumption of "stuff", a high proportion of which is currently imported at a cost of at least 40kWh per day per person. For renewables such as biomass, wave power and wind power to make a significant contribution, required are country-sized solutions. To meet 25 per cent of current energy consumption, 75 per cent of the UK would have to be covered with biomass plantations, not an unacceptable solution. To provide 4 per cent of our current consumption through wave power would require 500km of our Atlantic coastline. Wind power would need similarly large areas and for that reason would be best located out at sea.

Provided economic constraints and public objections are resolved, the average EU energy consumption of 125kWh/d per person can be provided. But the UK needs to reduce it by electrifying transport and electrifying heating using heat pumps. Electrifying transport will require a substantial increase in electricity generation.

For the UK, the best plan for green sources of carbon free

energy will make use of a combination of many different sources, national, regional and local community schemes, that take advantage of our natural advantages of sea, coast, wind, water (hydro), wood together with pumped heat, a substantial source, photovoltaic panels and heat and power generated from waste. David McKay confirms that a plan that does not make large use of coal and nuclear will require a significant part of our needs to be met in collaboration with other countries in the North Sea area and solar power from the Mediterranean region.

New buildings, like the German Passivhaus, can be carbon neutral, requiring no energy for heating. However, as has been pointed out earlier, the big problem in countries like the UK is the very large legacy of "leaky" buildings requiring retrofitting that many people will find difficult to afford. For the domestic user, David McKay believes that turning down the thermostat is the single most effective strategy. Roof top solar heaters can supply half of a family's hot water. In general, domestic roof mounted micro-wind turbines are too expensive to be viable, and never pay for themselves. Combined heat and power in buildings, generating local electricity and heat, are only slightly more efficient than the standard way, if fossil fuel is used. It is much better to generate from heat pumps using electricity.

Sustainable Energy: Without the Hot Air has been a valuable source (MacKay, 2009).

A New Green Deal

If we want all this to happen, a Green New Deal is needed, as proposed by the Green New Deal Coalition initiated by the New Economics Foundation (nef). This offers not only a way of greening countries like the UK but also a way of reviving the global economy as a whole, providing new green jobs and combating escalating unemployment (next chapter).

Action Resources

The vested interests opposing these reforms may seem overwhelming. But ordinary people far outnumber them. We need to get proposals like these into the minds of our new coalition, other governments and negotiators in future UN and other Summits. Be part of a mass global movement to lobby and participate in demonstrations: Use Stop Climate Change Chaos Coalition, New Economics Foundation (nef), Christian Aid, Greenpeace, Operation Noah, Oxfam and the World Development Movement.

Chapter 9:

Transforming the System to Create a Sustainable and Just Global Economy

March 2009

A Steady-State economy; A Green New Deal; Contraction and Convergence; Fee and Dividend; Global governance: global institutions and fair global trade

> *The part played by orthodox economists, whose common sense has been insufficient to check their faulty logic, has been disastrous to the latest act.*
> **J. M. Keynes** (1936)

At the beginning of the 21st century, human beings face two fundamental challenges. We need to:

- **Reduce our consumption to a sustainable level.** The Earth is finite. There is a limit to what it can provide. At the moment we are consuming more than the planet can provide and our numbers are increasing. We are consuming nature's capital instead of living off what it can create from it.
- **Distribute the resources of the world fairly.** The North has been taking far more than its fair share for centuries. It's both a pragmatic and a moral issue. Can we live easily with ourselves if we do not do the right thing or use our ignorance as an excuse?

Our guiding principles should be:

Don't

- ***use natural resources faster than they can be replenished by nature***
- ***deposit wastes faster than they can be absorbed***
- ***release or bury anything toxic***

The crisis requires international government action on the scale of Franklin Delano Roosevelt's New Deal to turn around the 1930s Great Depression or the UK coalition government's strategy to enrol the whole UK population and its manufacturing resources in a national war effort at the beginning of WWII. Significantly there was rationing. In 1940, UK factories rapidly converted to producing aircraft, tanks, munitions and other products needed by a nation at war. Women were mobilised to work in these factories. Eighty thousand women joined the Land Army. There was the *"Dig for victory"* campaign, encouraging to people grow their own food in their *"Victory Gardens"*, garden squares and parks in London were turned over to food production. Six thousand nine hundred pig clubs were formed and potato peelings were regularly collected to feed pigs. When USA joined in, it produced Liberty Ships at an astonishing rate. All these determined actions demonstrate what we can rapidly do in a crisis. They are models for today. When human beings realise their backs are against the wall, all their creativity and genius come into play.

> *The West should have a war on global warming rather than a war on terror.*
> **Stephen Hawking** on ITV News, 17 January 2007

Here I summarise four paradigm shifts:

1. ***A Steady-State Economy***
2. ***A Green New Deal***

3. *Contraction and Convergence, Fee and Dividend*
4. *Global governance: global institutions and fair global trade*

Part 1: Steady-State Economics

Steady-State Economics is almost unthinkable. It is by far the most challenging, radical and controversial proposal in this chapter. That is how conventional thinking makes it appear. It could equally be described as common sense.

There are two unpalatable truths. One, we have to drastically reduce our consumption of the Earth's natural resources. We need to bring down average individual CO2 consumption to 2 tonnes per person per year and average eco-footprint to 1.7 global hectares, a per capita "fair share" of the planet's resources. In the UK, where the average person currently has an ecological footprint of around 5.4 global hectares, or three times the global per capita target, we need to reduce our ecological footprint by two-thirds. The other unpalatable truth is that human population cannot be allowed to continue growing at the rate of 80m a year which it is estimated will lead us to 9bn by 2050. We need to bring it down to a sustainable size.

Spaceship Earth, our beautiful, miraculous home has limits as has been said many times. We are using up our children's and their children's legacy from nature. We ignore this at our peril. It is hitting back hard and we must take notice. We need to acknowledge that we are animals, not higher than other animals, and we are part of a self-regulating, interconnected ecological system.

We need to re-define what a "higher" standard of living means; not more stuff but a higher quality of life for everyone in the world. It means giving up some things that are not important to our well-being. Do we really need the current rate of technological innovation? Would it be better to have innovation created greater all round well-being? Much innovation is to more money rather than serving us. My new printer lasted less than 18 months, was obsolete when it broke down and could not be fixed. Since I bought it, numerous new versions were born. Dealing with the manufacturer cost me days of stress. Luckily, the retailer replaced it free of charge.

Less is more and more is less

Less can mean less stress.

Politicians and economists are wedded to continuous economic growth as measured by (GDP). Ever "faster and more" gives us more stress, higher cost and more debt. We see that most clearly in motorway enlargements and bypasses and the increasingly complex, disruptive and intrusive new applications of technology, many of which overrun time and cost estimates and keep breaking down or failing to meet the original need. Governments want to save the economy, save jobs by restoring economic growth and unfettered free trade. But that is using methods that destroy jobs and got us into the fix in the first place. G20 leaders repeatedly say there must be "no protectionism", nothing must stop growth. Growth is the only solution, never mind the planet's limited capacity or the possibility that the planet may be unliveable for human beings later in this century. If all else fails we'll move to other planets!

Herman Daly, an ecological economist, proposed the idea of Steady-State Economics in 1977 in his book, *Steady-State Economics*. It caused a sensation when it put forward his radical, yet commonsense view:

Enough is best

His thinking is captured in the *New Scientist* Special Issue, dated 18th October, 2008, entitled "The folly of growth – how to stop the economy killing the planet". What politician would dare to advocate steady-state economics at this time of deepening global recession? To those of us conditioned by the doctrine of continuous economic growth, the notion of steady-state economics is alarming. It immediately brings up the question: ***How can we provide jobs and redress growing unemployment without continuous economic growth?***

The answer partly lies in recognising that GDP is not the most appropriate measure of development. In 1965 Kenneth Boulding in *Earth as a Spaceship* pointed out that GDP is largely Gross National Cost. What is needed is Qualitative Development for which there are other more appropriate measures than GDP, some of which have already been mentioned. Two important new books, Tim Jackson's *Prosperity without Growth* and Lester Brown's *Plan B 4.0 – Mobilizing to Save Civilisation,* explore how we can achieve a different kind of prosperity in the twenty-first century. There are enormous opportunities for enterprise and new, rewarding jobs including training in the required skills. The UK government could make bail-outs to industries conditional upon a rapid shift to what is needed.

There are massive opportunities in transforming our transport system, green vehicles, green manufacturing, retro-fitting housing and offices, developing green heating and power generation, services to householders and businesses and most of all in building a better, fairer and more sustainable UK and global society. Many specific examples of the copious business opportunities were given in the previous chapter. It is the Government's job to help business and citizens to manage this transition as rapidly as possible. Sweden and Denmark are getting on with it and prospering.

So in more depth, what would a steady-state economy look like and what needs to be done?

Here I draw on several sources of important ideas, including articles from the *New Scientist* special issue, already mentioned, and other writings by Herman Daly and the late John Attarian. Here are proposals based on these sources:

- **Set Limits.** Scientists set sustainable consumption and emissions limits; allow growth only so long as it does not breach these limits.

- **Taxation.** Change taxation: gradually abolish income tax which is a tax on enterprise and work, and instead tax precious resources like oil and fish at source; that will raise the cost and encourage more careful use. This will encourage increases in efficiency and developments in technology that will enable us to get more out of precious resources. Introduce a carbon tax on oil fuelled travel that will trigger huge investment in transport infrastructure, green vehicles and renewable energy.
- **Help to poorer people.** Provide a citizens income – more about this and how to fund it in the next chapter. End tax havens through which half of all world trade passes. Set upper and lower limits to income inequality, currently a factor of 10 to 20 in universities, civil service and military and over 500 in US corporate sector – bring this down to 30. Above all, we need to tax fossil fuels at source to reduce their use and redistribute the dividend to citizens and investment in green energy, see Fee and Dividend below.
- **Banks.** Insist that banks, in exchange for bail-outs, must devote a percentage of their loans to environmental projects at below-market rates and make up the difference by charging polluters higher rates. The enormous superstructure of finance cannot be supported in steady-state economy and the focus becomes investment in sustainability, quality of life improvement, replacement and repair. Banks need to gradually raise the percentage of money required to be kept in reserve, as in former times. Require banks to get their income as intermediaries and from service charges.
- **Sustainability.** Provide financial incentives for retrofitting homes and other buildings and research on alternative

energies; institute Cap and Trade, see next section below.

- **Economy of maintenance and repair.** Making short-lived disposable goods is no longer economical as raw materials become more expensive and we pay for environmental costs. Develop new models of ownership such as leasing. Switch to a policy of products are built to last. There is more maintenance and repair instead of production and rapid obsolescence through excessive innovation.
- **New work patterns.** Without rapid growth there may be more part-time employment. More local work is likely which feeds money into local economies and may be less subject to the insecurity resulting from global ownership and sourcing for lowest labour cost. More people will work as co-owners instead of workers.
- **Reform free trade.** Support the abandonment of excessive free trade, with foreign or transnational corporations ignoring social and environmental costs and abusing their power. Countries should have freedom to decide how their economies operate and how much they engage in international trade as opposed to becoming more self-sufficient; development of regional trade areas.
- **Measures of national welfare.** Develop measures of happiness and sustainable development to replace GDP. GDP, really Gross National Cost, as the single measure of progress, includes many externalised costs that are avoidable such as disposing of waste, cleaning up pollution, the cost of accidents and disease, the cost of crime, the many other indicators of social distress and malfunction.
- **GDP grossly undervalues key resources.** Herman Daly pointed out in 1968 that minerals production represented only 1.7 per cent of GNP and total fossil fuels 2.0 per cent. This is a further illustration of how the most important

resources are underpriced and how both price and GDP grossly distort the value placed on such resources. Often they are heavily subsidised, as in the case of oil, which encourages their unsustainable and wasteful use.

- **The poorest countries are often those with the richest mineral and other natural resources.** But the population gain little benefit. These "commons" are in effect "stolen" by rich countries and corrupt rulers. These peoples should fully benefit from and have far more control over their resources, which should also be regarded as "global commons".
- **Ultimately the world population has to stabilise and reduce.** When women are given choice and good education they tend to have fewer children. As poverty and violence are addressed, migration will reduce.

Some of these solutions are elaborated later in this and succeeding chapters.

Part 2: Stabilising and Reversing Global Warming

To reverse the rise in carbon emissions and stabilise global warming requires action at a global level. Progress cannot be achieved by a national government alone. This means setting an overall limit to emissions now to halt the inexorable rise; setting a clear timetable for rapid reduction; determining how these cuts are to be equitably allocated globally and then allocating rights for future emissions, again in as equitable a way as possible.

"Contraction" and "convergence" (C&C) is a way of bringing about the reductions in consumption and emissions. First, to avoid too abrupt and painful a shift, emission rights would be allocated based on the current pattern of world output so that rich countries would have higher entitlements than poorer ones. Then, through a process of convergence, emission rights would move progressively towards an equal distribution on a per capita basis. How to allocate these rights within a country would be left to each nation to determine.

"Cap & share" (C&S) is another method. Under this system, emission entitlements are not decided by national governments. Instead each person would receive an annual entitlement which they could use as they saw fit. Trading would be part of the scheme. Individuals who wanted to consume more would have to buy from individuals willing to sell. Energy companies would have to buy emission entitlements to function. This would lead to a massive redistribution of wealth from richer to poorer individuals and countries. Such redistribution would make a big contribution to bringing about global economic and social justice and eradicating poverty.

Fee and Dividend. James Hansen, reflects on the UN Copenhagen Summit in his article "Copenhagen has given us the chance to face climate change with honesty – A carbon-use dividend for everybody must replace the old, ineffectual 'cap-and-trade' scheme", *The Observer*, 27 December 2009, describes the outcomes as minimalist. He sees this as an opportunity for more honest and effective action. Like many others, he sees "Cap-and -trade" beloved of big corporations and governments as ineffectual, a *"modern indulgences scheme"*, a way of avoiding responsibility for radical action to reduce fossil fuel use. Agreements to cap have not had sufficient effect, nor are they likely to do so. Goals for future emissions reductions are unlikely to be effective, whether legally binding or not. People will continue using fossil fuels whilst they are the cheapest form of energy. Oil prices externalise and do not include the social cost: the damage fossil fuels do to human health, to the planet, our children and future generations. Governments have to face down the energy companies and tax fossil fuels at source, making them more expensive than green energy. The tax would be applied at mine, wellhead or port of entry, creating a dividend that can be used to fund green energy, making it cheaper, and research and development. Fifty per cent of the dividend could, he suggests, be distributed to the public directly through their bank accounts depending on their carbon footprint, thus encouraging efficiency in use. "Cap-and-trade," he argues, is in effect a tax but it creates no dividend.

Not only could this measure be effectively enforced; it would help conserve a precious resource and provide the funds for the great the transition societies will have to make.

Part 3: A Green New Deal

The Green New Deal Group proposals got into minds all over the world and are said to have inspired UNEP's Global Green New Deal and influenced President Obama's Green Economy Initiative outlined below.

The UN Environment Program (UNEP)'s "Global Green New Deal" proposes that world leaders invest the equivalent of one per cent of the global gross domestic product to revive world economy and put a brake on global warming. According to UNEP, investments of one per cent of global gross domestic product, about $750bn, could finance a "Global Green New Deal". Five environmental sectors should be the goals of immense investments. These: energy efficient buildings, renewable energies, better transport, improved agriculture and measures to safeguard nature. This call for action was sounded by UNEP, the UN Environment Program, when leaders of the world's biggest economies, G20, met in London on April 2, 2009.

The opportunity must not be lost
Achim Steiner, head of the UN Environment Program (UNEP)

A Green Economy Initiative is also proposed by US President Barack Obama as part of his American Recovery and Investment Plan.

Key Features:

- Double the production of alternative energy in the next three years.
- Modernise more than 75% of federal buildings and improve the energy efficiency of two million American homes, saving consumers and taxpayers billions on energy bills.
- Help to create five million new jobs by strategically investing $150 billion over the next 10 years to catalyse private efforts to build a clean energy future.
- Within 10 years save more oil than currently imported from the Middle East and Venezuela combined.
- Ensure 10% of our electricity comes from renewable sources by 2012, and 25% by 2025.
- Put one million Plug-In Hybrid cars (cars that can get up to 150 miles per gallon) on the road by 2015, cars that we will work to make sure are built here in America.
- Implement an economy-wide cap-and-trade programme to reduce greenhouse gas emissions 80% by 2050.

Gordon Brown, to his credit, sought to influence European Leaders with similar proposals.

A Green New Deal. The Green New Deal Group proposals call for comprehensive, joined-up action by politicians to tackle "triple crunch" of credit, oil price and climate crises. The following is an edited version of these proposals. The full version is available from the New Economics Foundation (nef)..

Seventy-five years after President Roosevelt launched a New Deal to rescue the US from financial crisis, a new group of experts in finance, energy and the environment have come together to propose a "Green New Deal" for the UK. As the Green New Deal Group launched their proposals, new analysis suggested that from the end of July 2008 there were only 100 months, or less, to stabilise concentrations of greenhouse gases in the atmosphere before we hit a potential point of no return. This is the moment when the likelihood of irreversible changes in the climate becomes unacceptably high.

The Green New Deal is a response to the "triple crunch": a combination of a credit-fuelled financial crisis, accelerating climate change and soaring energy prices underpinned by encroaching Peak Oil, and to the lack of comprehensive, joined-up action from politicians. It is increasingly clear that these three overlapping events threaten to develop into a perfect storm, not been seen since the Great Depression, with potentially devastating consequences.

Green New Deal Proposals

- Massive investment in renewable energy and wider environmental transformation in the UK, leading to
- The creation of thousands of new green collar jobs
- Reining in reckless aspects of the finance sector – but making low-cost capital available to fund the UK's green economic shift
- Building a new alliance between environmentalists, industry, agriculture, and unions to put the interests of the real economy ahead of those of footloose finance

The "Green New Deal" is designed to power a "renewables" revolution, create thousands of green-collar jobs and rein in the distorting power of the finance sector while making more low-cost capital available for pressing priorities. The most serious global crisis since the Great Depression calls for reform the like of which has not, yet, been considered by politicians. This entails re-regulating finance and taxation plus a huge transformational programme aimed at substantially reducing the use of fossil fuels and, in the process, tackling the unemployment and decline in demand caused by the credit crunch. It involves policies and new funding mechanisms that will reduce emissions and allow us to cope better with the coming energy shortages caused by Peak Oil.

The Green New Deal requires action at local, national, regional and global levels. Focusing first on the specific needs of the UK, the Green New Deal outlines an interlocking programme of action that will require an ambitious legislative programme backed by a bold new alliance of industry, agriculture, labour and environmentalists.

Proposal's set out in the group's report include:

- **Executing a bold new vision for a low-carbon energy system** that will include making "every building a power station".
- **Creating and training a "carbon army" of workers** to provide the human resources for a vast environmental reconstruction programme.
- **Establishing an Oil Legacy Fund,** paid for by a windfall tax on the profits of oil and gas companies as part of a wide-ranging package of financial innovations and incentives to assemble the tens of billions of pounds that need to be spent. These would also include Local Authority green bonds, green gilts and green family savings bonds. The monies raised would help deal with the effects of climate change and smooth the transition to a low-carbon economy.
- **Ensuring more realistic fossil fuel prices that include the cost to the environment, and that are high enough to tackle climate change.** This will provide funding for economic incentives to drive efficiency and bring alternative fuels to market and for safety nets to those

vulnerable to higher prices via rapidly rising carbon taxes.

- **Minimising corporate tax evasion** by clamping down on tax havens and corporate financial reporting. A range of measures including deducting tax at source for all income paid to financial institutions in tax havens would provide much-needed sources of public finance at a time when economic contraction is reducing conventional tax receipts.
- **Re-regulating the domestic financial system.** Inspired by reforms implemented in the 1930s, this would imply cutting interest rates across the board – including the reduction of the Bank of England's interest rate – and changes in debt management policy to enable reductions in interest rates across all government borrowing. This is designed to help those borrowing to build a new energy and transport infrastructure. In parallel, to prevent inflation, much tighter regulation of the wider financial environment is needed.
- **Breaking up the discredited financial institutions** that have needed so much public money to prop them up in the latest credit crunch. Large banking and finance groups should be forcibly demerged. Retail banking should be split from both corporate finance (merchant banking) and from securities dealing. The demerged units should then be split into smaller banks. Mega banks make mega mistakes that affect us all. Instead of institutions that are "too big to fail", we need institutions that are small enough to fail without creating problems for depositors and the wider public.

The Green New Deal Group urges UK Government to take action at the international level to help build the orderly, well-regulated and supportive policy and financial environment that is required to restore economic stability and nurture environmental sustainability, including:

- **Allowing all nations far greater autonomy over domestic monetary policy** (interest rates and money supply) and fiscal policy (government spending and taxation).
- **Setting a formal international target for atmospheric greenhouse gas concentrations** that keeps future temperature rise as far below 2°C as possible
- **Giving poorer countries the opportunity to escape poverty without fuelling global warming** by helping to finance massive investment in climate-change adaptation and renewable energy

In this way we can begin to stabilise the current crisis, and lay the foundations for the emergence of a set of resilient low carbon economies, rich in jobs and based on independent sources of energy supply. The Green New Deal will rekindle a vital sense of purpose, restoring public trust and refocusing the use of capital on public priorities and sustainability. In this way it can also greatly improve quality of life. There is an immediate imperative to restore faith that society can survive the dreadful threats it now faces as a result of the triple crunch. The Group believes we can deliver a crucial national plan for a low-energy future. The absence of any such plan at present leaves the country very vulnerable.

The Green New Deal Group: **Larry Elliott**, Economics Editor of the Guardian, **Colin Hines**, Co-Director of Finance for the Future, **Tony Juniper**, former Director of Friends of the Earth, **Jeremy Leggett**, founder and Chairman of Solarcentury and SolarAid, **Caroline Lucas**, Green Party MP, **Richard Murphy**, Co-Director of Finance for the Future and Director, Tax Research LLP, **Ann Pettifor**, Campaign Director of Operation Noah, **Charles Secrett,** Advisor on Sustainable Development, **Andrew Simms**, Policy Director, **nef** .

Part 4: Reform of Global Institutions and Global Governance

Many current proposals are updated versions of John Maynard Keynes's proposals, key aspects of which were blocked by US negotiators at the Bretton Woods post war conference in July 1944, who had the upper hand because Britain was bankrupt and hugely indebted to the USA.

The chief features of the Bretton Woods system were an obligation for each country to adopt a monetary policy that maintained the exchange rate of its currency within a fixed value – plus or minus one per cent – in terms of gold and the ability of the IMF to bridge temporary imbalances of payments. In the face of increasing financial strain, the system collapsed in 1971, after the United States unilaterally terminated convertibility of dollars to gold. This action caused considerable financial stress in the world economy and created the unique situation whereby the United States dollar became the "reserve currency" for the 44 states which had signed the agreement.

Present global institutions such as the World Trade Organisation, World Bank and International Monetary Fund are unrepresentative and dominated by the interests of big business and rich countries. Attempts to reform these institutions, make them properly representative of all nations, change their underlying rigid free market, free trade ideologies and make their policies fairer are strongly resisted. Similarly, five permanent members, the US, UK, France, Russia, China, plus ten non-permanent members, constitute the UN Security Council. Also EU policies are unfair to poor countries.

In *The Age of Consent,* George Monbiot put forward comprehensive proposals for the necessary reforms and how to bring them about. These include a World Parliament, a Fair Trade Organisation to replace the WTO to enable poor nations to catch up with rich ones, regulation of the largest corporations, a new international security system to replace the Security Council, an updated version of the proposed International Clearing Union to stabilise capital flight, currency fluctuations, indebtedness and trade balances.

New Economics Foundation's Centre for the Future Economy: Proposals for a Future Global Economy

Comprehensive proposals were put forward in *From Old Economics to New Economics: Radical Reform for a Sustainable Future,* November 2007 by Stephen Spratt and Stewart Wallis (nef), also available on my website. The following is an edited version:

We need an economy that serves people and planet. The need for a radical transformation of the global economy to tackle poverty has been recognised for over a decade. Now widespread awareness of climate change, Peak Oil, growing shortages and threats to the ecosystem gives the need for radical action far greater urgency. We need a shift from an economy that consumes us to one that serves people and planet. It needs to be, as Adam Smith would have agreed, a *"moral economy"* based on moral principles. These principles would include social justice, social and economic rights for all, valuing the feminine and the "caring economy", sustainable development for planetary systems and future generations and the fostering of diversity and systemic resilience at all levels. The goal would be to increase individual and collective well-being.

The economic system has become the problem. It is not just that it is "not fit for purpose"; it causes serious and potentially fatal harm to all life on the planet. The assumptions underlying the current system are false:

- We can keep growing the global economy indefinitely
- More money or wealth equals more happiness
- Markets are equitable: clearly not the case when there are power differentials. As power differentials increase markets become even more inequitable.

A sustainable world needs to be based upon "*development which meets the needs of the present without compromising the ability of future generations to meet their own needs*" and economic justice and non-violence. It also requires recognition of the informal economy and unpaid work to which women make the major contribution.

A sustainable and just global economy. Such an economy would be designed to achieve these ends:

- At a global level we halt and reverse our carbon emissions.
- We safeguard our ecosystems; give poor countries the room to develop in their own unique way, enable those in rich countries to scale back and live more sustainable and less materialistic lives. This is an opportunity. Despite the fact that our wealth has doubled since the 1970s, we are no happier.
- Trade reflects the environmental costs of production and transportation.
- Businesses bear the full environmental costs of their activities.
- Sustainable and progressive corporate behaviour is linked to the "bottom line" and becomes the mainstream idea driving innovation and progress.
- The financial system is re-designed to support sustainable and progressive business activity; it serves the real economy of the future with finance flowing into those activities society most needs and values.
- Institutions foster co-operation that would lead to the best outcomes.
- Space is opened up for people to participate to a much greater extent in local and national life.
- Decisions are taken at the most appropriate level; this is as locally as possible in most instances.
- Local communities gain democratic control over their public services and also the economic development of

their areas.

Institutional reform is essential to the creation of a sustainable, just and non-violent world economy in which people's best instincts are fostered and allowed to blossom rather than being constrained and shaped by commercial imperatives. Greater personal, local and national autonomy and self-sufficiency are most likely to create the resilience needed in a world our economy. Similarly, by decentralising democracy, people need to be encouraged to take personal responsibility for their lives and engage in their local communities. Behaviour that increases well-being is encouraged; other behaviour discouraged. Institutions powerfully influence attitudes and behaviour. We need to create institutions that encourage people's better instincts such as co-operation and mutual respect, rather than competition and survival of the fittest mentalities.

International trade and finance. At present, trade in goods and services and financial flows are tilted heavily in favour of rich countries' interests as opposed to the developing world.

Trade injustice is due to:

- Major barriers to developing country exports to developed countries
- Subsidisation of developed country agricultural products lowering world prices and damaging local country markets
- Developed countries forcing developing countries to open their markets, making them more open than their own.
- Imposing agreements on investment and services that favour rich corporations and countries.
- The dominance of major international companies in many markets and the lack of competition laws to constrain their behaviour.
- Huge inequalities of power, knowledge, education,

training and access to capital between and within nations.

Inequalities in finance are due to:

- Massive scale of financial in- and out-flows relative to real economies that have highly destabilising effects
- Inherent volatility of international flows largely driven by speculation
- International financial crises which devastate emerging developing economies
- Tendency for crises to spill over from one to other developing economies
- Focus on what developing economies should do rather than the need fordeveloped economies to regulate
- Strong discouragement of capital controls in favour of liberalisation
- Trade Related Investment Measures (TRIMS) prevent developing countries insisting that foreign investors use some local procurement.

"Good" trade as opposed to "bad" needs to be defined. The International Institute for Environment and Development (IIED) says:

> *Sustainable trade takes place when the international exchange of goods and services yields positive social, economic and environmental benefits reflecting four core criteria of sustainable development:*
>
> - *It generates economic value.*
> - *Reduces poverty and inequality.*
> - *Regenerates the environmental resource base.*
> - *Is carried out within an open and accountable system of governance.*

For this to happen these are prerequisites:

- Basic levels of social and economic rights for all peoples
- Factoring in environmental costs in all transactions
- Removing economic injustices
- Regulating transnational corporations (TRNCs)
- Regulating international financial institutions
- Effective capital controls to a) prevent damaging speculative flows that are anathema to sustainable development; b) encourage positive flows that support sustainable development global governance to create and maintain this system
- Radical rethink of the ownership models of "natural resources" such as water, land, minerals, fossil fuels and air

The starting point for a just and sustainable trading and financial system must lie in ***basic social and economic rights and corresponding duties***. This must mean that all human beings have not only enough to eat, but fair wages, health care and good education. Southern countries must have the right to protect their markets and production crucial to ***food sovereignty***. This requires major redistribution and investment at national and global levels. This in turn requires consideration of global taxation and redistribution that is just and progressive. International trade in food products would only be developed where a) food security was already strong; and b) the product bore the true costs, both of production and the real "carbon costs" of transport. In a carbon constrained world, in which oil prices will steeply rise, long distance transportation of most goods is likely to become non-viable. There will be a huge resurgence of local markets except for goods unique to particular regions or where large-scale economies are overwhelming e.g. the production of large aircraft. A C&S system would give many developing countries with relatively abundant renewable energy sources such as solar power, together with lower wages, a relative advantage in producing some goods for transportation to the North.

Unequal power gives advantage to different trading nations. It needs to be recognised that in the current situation, relative advantage is largely determined by the unequal power of different participants in the global marketplace. Therefore markets need to be regulated. This would mean:

- removing Northern subsidies
- opening up Northern markets
- intervening in global commodity markets to achieve just outcomes for all
- changing the ***Agreement on Trade Related Aspects of Intellectual Property Rights** (TRIPS)* regime to allow generic production of life-saving drugs and banning patenting of life forms and seeds
- abolishing the ***Agreement on Trade Related Investment Measures** (TRIMs)* thus allowing governments to favour local suppliers
- regulating financial institutions in source countries
- as envisaged by John Maynard Keynes, requiring countries to implement capital controls to discourage short-term speculative flows and encourage longer-term investment supportive of sustainable development.

Regulation of Transnational Corporations TNCs

These key changes need to be considered:

1. **International competition controls.** At all levels, local, national and global, no player should control the market. On a national and international basis this might mean no more than 5 per cent of the market.

2. **Fair terms of employment.** TRCs should be obliged by international law to pay fair wages, internationally agreed benefits, allow the right to organise and also pay fair levels of taxation where they operate.
3. **International environmental regulations.** Similar obligations should apply to international environmental regulations.
4. **Inward investment.** All inward investment in a country or locality should have strict requirements on value added long-term benefits to workers and local community including local procurement, employment and training.

Global governance

The World Trade Organisation (WTO) needs radical reform so that it serves peoples' needs and all countries rather than corporations. It would:

- Apply the above rules and remove TRIPS and TRIMS from its remit.
- Provide large-scale support to Southern governments to allow them to participate on equal terms.
- Democratise WTO processes and stamp out behind-the-scenes threats and arm twisting.
- Major new, democratic global governance bodies would be created such as:
- A body to regulate competition and ensure corporate compliance to agreed global environmental and social standards.
- An environmental agency to manage the global environment.
- A new body to manage global taxation and spending.
- A reformed World Bank to handle international development projects not provided by reformed markets.

Action Resources

Once again, vested interests opposing these reforms may seem overwhelming. But ordinary people far outnumber them. We need to get these proposals into the minds of our new coalition, other governments and negotiators for futureUN Summitsand other international conferences. Be part of a mass global movement to lobby and participate in Demonstrations: Use Stop Climate Change Chaos Coalition, New Economics Foundation (NEF), Christian Aid, Greenpeace, Operation Noah, Oxfam and the World Development Movement.

Further reading:

- Heinberg, R, 2007, *Peak Everything: Waking Up to the Century of Decline in Earth's Resources.*

Chapter 10:

New Money

March 2009

Money, debt, taxation, the commons, land value tax and citizens income

I am indebted to James Robertson whose writings on the subject of money are a clear and invaluable resource, especially his *National and International Financial Architecture: Two Proposals, Memorandum* and his *G20 Agenda for April must include Monetary Reform – A Crash Campaign,* available on his website. I also much appreciate Tony Vickers' and Roy Langston's help in creating the section on Land Value Tax (LVT).

> *The process by which banks create money is so simple that the mind is repelled.*
> **J.K. Galbraith**

We need a different way of creating money

Money created by debt is at the root of the current crisis. Yet it is the least understood, least discussed, least questioned aspect of the economic system. The establishment have frozen minds on this subject. Vested interests benefit whilst the rest of us continue to think it incomprehensible, the domain of experts. We leave it to them. It is ***not*** incomprehensible. The monetary system cannot continue to be the domain of experts!

This chapter describes proposals that would release sustainable enterprise, encourage personal responsibility, instead of dependency, and create fairness. I intend to share with you the best proposals I know for reform, make them completely accessible and dispose of the idea that it is a subject for experts.

A world that was deeply in debt got more indebted, unnecessarily as I shall argue, in its efforts to solve a crisis created by debt.

> *Surprisingly few politicians, public officials, economists, sociologists, political scientists and other professionals have been interested in money as a system that might be made to work better as a whole. Perhaps it is even more surprising that few campaigners for good causes – social justice, ending poverty, dealing with climate change, a more peaceful and fairer international order, human rights and so on – seem to realise that the money system is a prime cause of the ills they oppose. The development of the money system over the years has been piecemeal – and largely in response to powerful interests – and this means that it is now not only incoherent and incomprehensible to most of the world's people, but also systematically perverse.*
>
> *It fails to make wealthier and more powerful people and organisations and nations pay for what they take from the common wealth, and it taxes the value of the rewards that less powerful people get from contributing to it.*
>
> *The reason is simple. The main interest of the goldsmiths and bankers and government servants who in the past evolved the monetary, banking and financial system, and the main interest of those who manage it today, has been to make money for their customers, shareholders and other associates, and for themselves and their own organisations. There has never been anyone whose role has been to ensure that the monetary and financial system would work efficiently and fairly for all its users – that is not the purpose of the system.*
>
> *The arrival of the Information Age should make it possible to work out a better way for the money system to evolve, so that it can be managed with the aim of making it perform efficiently and fairly*

the functions we require of it. In the context of sustainable development, the challenge for policy makers is to make sure that the money system evolves as an accounting (or scoring) system that will operate to serve common interests, and the interests of all its users.

James Robertson, *the Future of Money: If we want a better game of economic life we'll have to change the scoring system.*

Underlying the present global economic system are debt, debt money, out of control financial markets, perverse taxation and massive tax avoidance that puts up the burden of personal taxation. It systematically transfers wealth to the rich. Debt money, money created by debt, has been at the centre of the collapse of the financial system, leading a deepening recession. Our leaders were, once again, stuck in an old mindset when they need to be in a new paradigm. Governments actually created **MORE DEBT** to get us out of the debt crisis! They left an even greater legacy of debt and increased taxation and cuts in public expenditure at a time when expenditure on a green new deal is needed.

Part 1: The Debt Money System

- What the money system is
- What it does
- Positive ways forward

What the money system is:

The key notion to understand is that less than 5 per cent of money is issued by government or central banks in the form of banknotes, notes and coins. The remaining 95 per cent is debt money created "out of thin air" by banks writing it into their customers' accounts as profit-making loans, thus making large profits for themselves. It is estimated that UK commercial banks make over £20bn a year in interest from creating this bank-account money, whereas public revenue from the issue of banknotes and coins is less than £3bn a year.

It is astonishing that banks are given, free of charge, by Government and Parliament, the privilege of engaging in this vast money-making business and they then charge us and Government huge amounts of interest. They also engage in vast tax avoidance and evasion. When things go badly wrong, they are bailed out by more borrowing and by the taxpayer!

Debt is at the root of the system. Debt is an, if not ***the***, underlying issue in the system. It raises the cost of almost everything. The need to pay back the loans and pay interest fuels unsustainable economic activity and the constant call for rapid economic growth. Borrowing fuels excessive, unsustainable consumption, needlessly puts up the cost of public infrastructure investment, creates a large burden of debt and hardship, for both the relatively well off middle classes and poor people and poor countries. For example, Jamaica spends some 60 per cent of its GDP servicing debt.

What it does:

A number of astute people are realising that the money system is damaging and that there are alternatives. James Robertson and Hazel Henderson are amongst key figures. The New Economics Foundation (NEF), the US American Monetary Institute, the Christian Council for Monetary Justice and the Tax Justice Network are amongst organisations arguing for a fundamental change in the monetary system.

American Presidents Thomas Jefferson and Abraham Lincoln opposed the creation of money by commercial banks.

> *I believe that banking institutions are more dangerous to our liberties than standing armies.*
>
> **Thomas Jefferson**, US President 1801-9

Here is a summary of the adverse outcomes of the current monetary system:

A Perverse Money System

- Systematically transfers wealth from poor people and countries to rich ones
- The money-must-grow imperative compels people to make money in socially and environmentally damaging ways
- Diverts economic effort and enterprise towards making money out of money, the rising values of existing assets, and away from productive activities that provide valuable goods and services
- Exerts a systematic bias in favour of the people, organisations and nations who should be managing it on behalf of us all
- Erodes the credibility of political democracy after 200 years of progress
- Is a major source of opposition to globalisation in its present form, and thereby a threat to world peace and security.

Adapted from: James Robertson's article, quoted above

As a means of raising money for public purposes such as investment in infrastructure, such as roads, tramways, the Underground and railways for example, as well as and new hospitals, schools, colleges and universities, money created by debt is inevitably more expensive. New Labour's approach to funding was to channel costly private investment finance into public infrastructure and services thus avoiding the figures appearing in the government budget but costing the taxpayer far more.

Whoever puts new money into circulation profits from its value minus the cost of producing it, and also decides who will have first use of the money for what purposes. If almost all the money in circulation starts as debt which has to pay interest and eventually has to be repaid in full, additions to the money supply will automatically be accompanied by increased indebtedness in society, and money transactions will cost more than if all money circulated debt-free.

James Robertson

A Different Way of Creating Money

It is ironic that even more debt is being created to provide stimulus packages and hence combat the global recession. This additional debt, created to provide stimulus packages and combat the global recession, would be completely unnecessary if national reserve banks, not commercial banks, created the required funds. In the case of the UK for example, it has been estimated that additional public revenue of about £45bn a year could be collected if the Bank of England took over responsibility for creating new money.

This of course is heresy. Total restructuring of the banking system is needed to make this possible. Clearly there are enormous vested interests at stake. However, it is interesting to note that the UK Bank of England has already started doing this, using the euphemism "quantitative easing" to start pumping £75bn into the economy. As James Robertson points out, in a democratic society one would expect the national bank and the government ***not*** commercial banks to be in charge of the money supply. Money should be seen as a common resource, not the preserve of commercial banks.

This is how such a change would work:

1. Commercial banks are prohibited from creating new money.

2. National central reserve banks, as agencies of state, in our case the Bank of England, take over responsibility for creating all new money free of interest. This would also include supplying the major component of public money that consists of bank-account money mainly held and transmitted electronically.
3. The national reserve bank gives the money as debt-free public revenue to the government, to spend into circulation to achieve national objectives agreed by Parliament. This process of restricting money creation to what is required to achieve agreed national objectives would prevent political abuse through heavy spending in the run-up to elections.

Commercial Banks would then have two separated responsibilities: retail and investment banking. There would be 1) **High Street banks** providing and competing for the bank account services needed by citizens, shopkeepers and businesses; and 2) **Investment Banks** providing corporate funding and investment service which, as has been shown, can be incompatible with reliable, solid "boring banking" providing a safe place for people's money transactions and current accounts.

The benefits of these changes would be:

1. Reducing the cost of public investment projects such as hospitals, schools, and affordable housing.
2. Providing the urgent and massive government support needed for greening the economy, providing infrastructure for electric vehicles, railways, tramways and cycle lanes and the enormous cost of retrofitting the majority of UK housing stock to meet the goals of the 2008 Climate Change Act.
3. Further new jobs and support for a transition from a brown to a green economy.

4. Addressing the current economic crisis ***without incurring further debt***.

A further development, recalling the situation in Victorian times, would be to encourage local economic development through institutions such as local banks, community development banks, credit unions, investment funds and monetary initiatives like the Totnes Pound initiated by Transition Town Totnes to encourage purchasing from local retailers and businesses, Local Exchange Trading Systems (LETS) which are beginning to support local economic activity and trading. The Grameen Bank supplying micro credit to rural women in Bangladesh is a well-known example, and there are similar schemes in Africa.

For further information, see *Money: Past, Present & Future.*

Reform of the debt money system is at the root of the global environmental crisis. It needs to be on the agenda of the next UN Summit. I urge you to campaign to get it on the agenda. Use this chapter as a resource.

Part 2: Taxation

"Perverse" Taxation

Under the current system for raising public revenue, taxes are "perverse" in the sense that they do not sufficiently encourage "good" contributions to society such as sustainability, enterprise, work, healthy food, including organic food. Taxation that encourages green demand would help prevent recession induced cutbacks in green initiatives (such as BP's solar energy enterprise).

"Perverse" taxation encourages unsustainable practices such as creating pollution, using up non-renewable resources, cheap products including poor food that create social costs. Once again we see the failure of pricing to reflect the full costs to society of so-called "cheapness". Furthermore, as mentioned earlier in Part

1, wealthier people pay least proportionately and can afford expensive advice and help with a complicated and inaccessible system. Taxes bear down on middle income but especially poorer people.

To sum up:

- **By heavily taxing employment and rewards for work and enterprise** and lightly taxing the use of common resources, income tax systematically encourages inefficiency in all kinds of resource use – underuse and under development of human resources, and overuse of natural resources (including energy and the environment's capacity to absorb pollution);
- **Taxing the value added by the majority of people's positive contributions to society** (VAT), and failing to tax the **value subtracted** by the rich and powerful minority who profit most from the use of common resources, systematically skews the overall burden of tax to the detriment of the majority.
- **Organic food is beneficial not only in the dietary sense** but also because of all the ecological advantages, thus saving of cost (perversely counted as GDP!) in cleaning pollution. In the recession, we now see people spending less on organic food and supermarkets cutting out organic products which are nature, health and people friendly. This causes producers even more difficulty surviving.

Existing taxes are also becoming less viable.

For example:

- **National economies in a competitive global economy** have to reduce taxes on incomes, profits and capital in order to attract and keep investment capital and highly qualified people – both being increasingly mobile.

- **Ageing societies** will be unable to support growing numbers of economically inactive people by taxing the work and enterprise of fewer people of working age.
- **Internet trading** makes it more difficult for governments to collect customs duties, value added tax and other taxes and levies on sales, and easier for companies and rich individuals to shift earnings and profits to low-tax regimes and tax havens.
- **Tax avoidance** by big corporations and rich individuals is increasingly damaging. The Tax Justice Movement estimates that tax havens now cost governments £255bn annually and hold assets of $11.5 trillion, causing serious distortion of economic priorities and encouraging criminal money laundering.

Tax Havens

In the case of tax avoidance, international action to close tax havens and insist on full disclosure in company reporting is now a possibility following the G20 agreement in April 2009. It is worth noting that Britain is one of the largest providers of tax havens in its Crown Dependencies or Colonies. Well-known large UK businesses and business men are amongst the largest users of these facilities. Over a quarter of the world's tax havens are British property. More than half of Britain's colonial territories and dependencies are tax havens, including Jersey, Guernsey, Isle of Man, Bahamas, Bermuda and the Virgin and Cayman Islands. The Cayman Islands are now the fifth largest financial centre in the world, after New York. Tax lawyers regard the Caymans as a no-tax or zero tax haven.

From the perspective of ending poverty, tax havens are used by large companies to divert funds that would otherwise be paid in taxes to poor countries – Christian Aid estimates $160 billion a year, 60 per cent higher than all the international aid the poor world receives. The US research group Global Financial Integrity estimates $900bn. For a full account of the extent of tax havens and the cost to nations and tax payers throughout the world, go to the Tax Justice Network's website.

Would people be so happy holidaying in these places if they knew what underlies the prosperity of these destinations?

Shifting a large part of the tax burden on to the value of land (which cannot move elsewhere) through Land Value Tax may be one of the most effective responses to these problems.

Taxing the Commons

Commons are resources whose value is due to nature and to the activities and demands of society as a whole, not the efforts or skill of individual people or organisations. Land is the most obvious example. The value of a particular land-site, excluding the value of what has been built on it, is almost wholly due to the activities and plans of society around it. Commons include:

- Un-extracted fossil-fuel energy
- The electromagnetic spectrum
- The environment's capacity to absorb waste and pollution, water for extraction and use for transport, airport landing slots, carbon
- Rises in property values brought about by large public investment in infrastructure or other improvements. This happened in the case of public investment in the new Jubilee Line in London

James Robertson gives the example of a house in Chelsea in London that cost £1000 in 1910 and was worth £4.5 million ninety years later, which is an increase nearly 37 times greater than the increase in the price of a basket of basic items like bread and potatoes over the same period. For more examples see Land Value Taxation Campaign and Land Labour Campaign below.

An example of a "tax" based on common resources that was

actually implemented was the £22.5bn raised for UK taxpayers by the auction of licences to use the radio spectrum for third generation mobile phones. Other European governments enacted similar taxes. Such taxes could fund investment in renewable energy, energy saving, transport, schools, hospitals, affordable housing and a basic citizens' income and pension that could replace current complicated, expensive to administer and ineffectual measures to alleviate poverty without the need for the Government to incur the large costs of borrowing. Similarly, taxing global commons could fund global initiatives for sustainable development, alleviation of poverty and peace-keeping.

Land Value Taxation (LVT)

This section was contributed by Roy Langston, Canadian writer, policy consultant and advisor to UN Habitat's Land Value Tax/Capture Initiative (UN Habitat Organisation), with help from Tony Vickers.

Introduction

If we are to create a more sustainable and fairer world, Land Value Tax (LVT) is of major importance. It needs to be widely understood and firmly on the political agenda. I believe it constitutes a major opportunity, not generally known about or understood. Its importance has to be seen in the broader context of the Earth's commons well described in the following extract from the Earth Rights Institute's Policies. We need to lobby for it to be widely discussed:

> ***We have a "land problem"*** *Almost all of us live someplace where land values and hence housing costs are rising faster than wages. Hundreds of millions are homeless, low income working people struggle to pay the rent each month, and middle class people labour for decades to pay off mortgage debt. There is an enormous*

worldwide wealth gap between the super-rich and the rest of us. Too few people and corporations now "own" our planet.

Treating land as a for-profit and speculative commodity instead of a common heritage resource is a major flaw in the neoliberal economic paradigm. We want a FAIR market economy with lots of individual and family owned businesses and decentralized, productive, well-managed co-operatives who care about both the people and the planet.

Earth Rights Institute and our worldwide network of "new economics" partners have a handle on a key policy for building a fair economy – take taxes off working people and productive businesses and capture for the benefit of everyone the "unearned income" which attaches to land and natural resources. Research by land economists shows that this kind of "rent" is as much as one third of GDP in some countries – a more than adequate tax base to pay needed public services and even then some which could be distributed as direct citizen dividends.

The UN Habitat Agenda Section B.55 states: "Access to land and legal security of tenure are strategic prerequisites for the development of sustainable human settlements affecting both urban and rural areas. It is also one way of breaking the vicious cycle of poverty. Every Government must show the commitment to promoting the provisions of an adequate supply of land in the context of sustainable land-use policies..."

What Is LVT, and Why Is It Better?

Why are we burdened with high taxes? Most government spending tries to undo the injustice and economic damage caused by unfair and destructive taxes and the uncompensated violation of people's rights, especially the right to utilise the opportunities nature and the community provide.

Income tax, sales tax, VAT, etcetera, place a burden on the productive activity that enriches society, reducing wages and increasing unemployment and poverty. Governments try to undo this damage by spending money, but they get the money by levying more of the same bad taxes that caused the damage in the first place!

There is a better way to fund public goods, a way that makes society fairer, greener and richer, not poorer. Most people are familiar with property taxes. A land value tax (LVT) is simply a property tax on the unimproved value of land (currently about 2/3 of average property value), not on improvements. Though simple in concept, LVT offers great social and economic benefits.

A number of factors influence land value, but it ultimately comes down to ***"land rent"*** i.e. the economic advantage gained by using desirable land (for an explanation, go to my website). This advantage comes from the services and infrastructure government provides, the opportunities and amenities the community provides, and the physical qualities nature provides. Whatever the owner provides may affect improvement value, but by definition does not affect land value: the land is already there, ready to use, with no help from the owner or any previous owner. Because the supply of land is fixed and a tax on its rent does not affect user demand, LVT does not increase land rent. It is borne entirely by the landowner, and its burden cannot be shifted on to tenants, consumers, or anyone else.

LVT high enough to replace the unfair taxes that harm the economy would recover all publicly created land rent for public purposes. Land value would decline to a very low level, while wealth production would soar. After all, earned income measures what the recipient contributes to the wealth of the community, while land value measures what the community contributes to the wealth of the landowner. It is self-evidently better to tax the latter than the former.

LVT Redresses the Biggest Subsidy of All

Under the current system, productive citizens pay income tax, VAT etc. to fund the services and infrastructure government provides, and must then pay land rent (or capitalized rent as a purchase price) to landowners for access to the same services and infrastructure their taxes just paid for. The productive thus pay for government twice so that landowners can pocket one of those payments in return for nothing. With LVT, the productive pay for government only once; directly, with a voluntary, market based, value-for-value payment to access the benefits it provides, thereby cutting out the something-for-nothing payment to the landowner.

A landowner either charges tenants for what government, the community and nature provide, or gets those benefits by using the land himself. Land value is the exact measure of how much more benefit the landowner expects to get than he expects to pay in taxes i.e., how large a net subsidy he will receive from the community. As land rent amounts to about 1/5 of GDP in typical industrialized countries (more in densely populated ones), private land ownership has the effect of transferring an enormous quantity of wealth every year from workers, entrepreneurs and investors in capital goods – buildings, machinery etc. to landowners, in return for nothing. The subsidy to landowning is thus the major cause of the working-class poverty, unemployment, low wages, social problems and great inequalities of wealth typical of capitalist countries. LVT recovers the land subsidy for the purposes and benefit of the public that provides it, rather than letting landowners take it in return for nothing.

LVT consequently has an important but widely misunderstood effect: requiring the landowner to repay the benefits he gets from government and the community just by owning the land reduces its value, because it reduces the net subsidy the landowner receives at the expense of taxpayers and the people. If all the publicly created land rent is recovered for public purposes and benefit, the land will have no value at all as an asset: it will have rental value only, because the owner will not be getting any net subsidy.

LVT Can Provide a Citizens' Income, for Free

LVT clears the way to implement an effective citizens' income (see below in Part 3) without having to raise any additional tax revenue to fund it: a flat, universal, personal LVT exemption for every resident citizen, adult and child, in owner occupation, similar in concept to the personal income tax exemption, and applicable only to land the recipient is using. Land rent accounts for half or more of the poor's average living expenses, so replacing current taxes with a revenue-neutral LVT with a modest universal personal exemption would effectively lift almost all the poor out of poverty at a stroke, while costing the public treasury, i.e. taxpayers, no more than their current taxes.

In addition, because high housing costs are always driven by land value, the need to either pay for land upfront, or pay mortgage interest in addition to land rent, reducing land value towards zero by LVT tends to remove mortgage interest from the housing cost equation. As LVT also stimulates the best use of each location, it increases the supply and quality of built space, dramatically improving the supply, quality and affordability of housing, especially for the poor. So paradoxically, taxing land value at a high rate with a flat, universal personal exemption eliminates the unearned profits of land speculators, but makes owning a decent home far more affordable for the great majority of people.

LVT: Better for Communities, Business and People

A high LVT rate dampens boom and bust cycles based on land speculation. LVT makes development more compact by stimulating the most productive use of high-value downtown sites, revitalizing blighted areas, and reducing sprawl. If land is not designated for development, taxable value of sites will be low: LVT is "Development Plan led". Providing the whole Plan-making and Plan-managing processes of government are open and transparent, for example by using land value maps that are kept up-to-date and publicly available, opportunities for corruption of public officials should greatly reduce and quality of involvement of the public in planning decisions should improve. Denser development of central business districts makes public transit and other services more affordable by increasing utilisation rates. Even parks pay for themselves by increasing the land rent of surrounding areas, which is then recovered by LVT.

Would LVT encourage overdevelopment of land?

The only people who pay LVT are those who own land. Tenants (domestic or commercial) will cease paying Council Tax or Business Rates to government – but will pay land rent to the landowners who pay LVT to government, whether the land is used or not. A universal personal LVT exemption, similar to income tax allowance, would relieve those owner-occupiers who use little desirable land, i.e. mainly the poor, of any tax burden. There are only two ways to "dodge" LVT: one is by moving to less valuable land, which benefits less from government spending on services and infrastructure; the other is to sell the land to the user, who can claim his or her personal allowance. The few people who use land that has no value at all, like remote wilderness, are not benefiting much by government spending anyway: for all the benefits they get, there might as well not be any government.

LVT's effect on business is independent of the size of the business, though abolition of unfair and destructive taxes would be more favourable to small businesses, as they are generally less able to game the current tax system because they can't afford to pay top tax lawyers and accountants to find ways to avoid paying taxes. Land can't be moved, and it can't be hidden, so LVT is effectively impossible to evade. Its effect on any given business depends much more on whether the business is actually productive, or is just pocketing publicly created value. LVT makes the latter unprofitable, freeing capital and labour for genuine productive activity.

Many businesses operate inefficiently on land owned by the business, because the present tax system turns them into "speculators" (i.e. "pocketing publicly created value") more than "producers". Unless the accounts of the business (especially the asset valuations in the balance sheet) record "market value" as opposed to "value in use", they are liable to be asset-stripped. LVT encourages all economic activities to be sited in the most efficient locations for the business. Of course, planners can designate land for uses below the "highest and best" or economically optimum use, for social or environmental reasons, which will then be reflected in taxable value.

How LVT Could Benefit Small Businesses

Large companies with substantial liquid currency assets are likely to have a monthly account for its tax payments (VAT, income tax corporation tax). That means there is a lot of money in its accounts that is due to be paid to Government. There is usually at least a month before it needs to be paid. So companies play the short-term money markets with public money, often employing a whole team of staff to do nothing else. This team is a "cost centre" which is given targets to make money on the transactions it undertakes. Small business (10 employees or less), with far less liquid cash to play with, certainly cannot afford to have someone in house doing what large firms do. They generally have to pay an external accountant to handle their tax affairs, whose fees can account for more than the firm's total tax bill. Research at Bath University in 1996 showed that whilst a large firm (1000 employees or more) on average made a profit out of "Treasury", small firms on average spent £250 per employee, on top of their tax bill, handling their tax affairs. This is an inbuilt advantage for large firms, nothing to do with the efficiency of their core operations and entirely to do with the deadweight burden of current taxes. With LVT there is no equivalent inbuilt advantage to large businesses. If anything, it would favour the "nimble" operation, such a start-up business which needs land, because land prices (rents) will fall, as will the admin overheads of operating under the current tax system. The barrier to entry for many businesses is the sheer complexity and time-consuming nature of grappling with tax law, off which an army of tax advisers feeds.

Advantages of LVT

Here are just some of the benefits of taxing publicly created land value instead of privately created goods and services:

- **Reduced land acquisition costs,** because owners lose money if they hold land out of its most appropriate use. Rental values are unaffected at first, though they will likely rise later as LVT increases prosperity.
- **Higher quality of built space, especially housing.** Owners have every incentive to maintain and improve their property, as the improvements needed for productive use (including accommodation) are not taxed.
- **Less urban sprawl.** Conurbations – collections of people going about their business – produce higher land values than marginal land, which may have no value. Activities that need high-value land will concentrate where good planning wants them. This makes public mass transit systems more efficient and transport generally more sustainable. Hong Kong is a classic example: it has the highest proportion of public revenue from land values anywhere.
- **Conservation land protected:** whether for biodiversity, recreation or heritage, land whose use is legally

constrained will pay less tax. However, land accessible to public parks has a value premium (e.g. Hyde Park), the tax on which pays for the park: "beneficiary pays", is fundamental to LVT.

- **Minimal tax avoidance or evasion.** Land cannot be hidden or moved. Failure to pay results in a public debt attaching to the land title and diminishes its value by the amount of that debt – which cannot be "written off", since land cannot be destroyed (only buildings can!).
- **Higher employment levels and lower costs generally.** The "deadweight effect" of existing taxes bears most heavily on the poor, whose consumption of essentials (shelter, clothing, food) is greatly affected by the current system, which massively subsidises "rent seeking" activity by landlords. For good reason, Henry George's classic work on LVT was called *Progress and Poverty.* (See Earth Rights Institute website.)
- **The demise of what James Robertson calls "the dependency culture":** benefit payments of all kinds would decline as the poor enjoyed more opportunities and lower living costs. Most supporters of LVT would first abate income taxes on the poor, then phase out subsidies to landlords such as "housing benefit", which produces no houses and only benefits landlords!
- **Small businesses flourish, as compared to big business.** Some 40 per cent of the value of FTSE100 listed companies recently consisted of real estate (i.e. mostly land value) assets, often unconnected with the core business, while most small firms are tenants.

Why is LVT not used more often?

A recent study *Land Value Taxation: Theory, Evidence and Practice,* edited by Richard Dye and Richard England, listed several reasons:

- **Wealth, especially land wealth, accrues to the most powerful in any society.** The rich resist LVT, pleading that many of their number are "cash poor" and "cannot pay". In fact, there is a strong correlation between high lifetime income and high land wealth – very few cannot pay LVT, and these can easily be accommodated in any transition. LVT is always affordable by definition: just let the most productive user use the land, and collect the rent!
- **Annual site rental values are not currently measured or, for the taxpaying public, understood.** LVT has sometimes been abandoned because tax values were not kept up-to-date or on a rental basis. Modern technology (computer mapping and spatial analysis of market data) makes it much easier to regularly update and publish "value maps".
- **Sudden, dramatic changes in property taxes can impact alarmingly and often unpredictably on economic development.** Unless the spatial planning system and the construction industry are both robust and flexible, unintended consequences of LVT may follow. The solution is to implement LVT gradually, transparently, and on a plan-led basis.
- **There are bound to be losers as well as winners in any tax reform.**
- **Politicians are always nervous about losing votes.** The full benefits of introducing LVT may not be seen within a single period between elections, especially if it is implemented late in the election cycle. Hence a wide consensus as to those benefits is first needed, especially where the losers are powerful and well organised.
- **Elected officials as well as the voting public simply do not understand LVT** and it has been kept off the agenda.

LVT offers major possibilities about which the public should be widely informed. There needs to be a cross-party examination of it involving all stakeholders in our society to fully explore LVT.

Part 3: A Citizens' Income

It is time to do something different to end poverty in UK. Life for the fifth of the UK's population living in poverty is set to worsen because of the recession. The government defines poverty as having an income of 60 per cent or less of the median. On this basis 13.2 million people in the UK live in poverty, 22 per cent of the population. New Labour's admirable, but typically complicated and ever changing efforts to eliminate poverty in the UK, including child and pensioner poverty, did not succeed. They were largely based on tax credits, benefits and efforts to help people into work. These efforts may have contributed to the problem of poor school achievement, low social mobility and bad behaviour by making it even harder for parents working long hours to give their children sufficient support at home. The social and economic costs of our failure to develop our children are enormous. James Robertson reports that support for a Citizens' Income, as a right, continues to grow, especially in Europe but elsewhere too.

A Citizens' or minimum Income would be paid to all citizens as a right, out of public revenue. It would include state pensions and child allowances. It would replace many other existing social benefits, and eliminate almost all tax allowances, tax reliefs and tax credits. The considerable potential for administrative cost savings needs to be evaluated.

Humiliating dependency. One of the greatest benefits of Citizens' Income is that it would release many people from humiliating dependency on state handouts. Even more important, it would give citizens more freedom and encourage them to take full responsibility for their lives. A Citizens' Income would recognise that, in a society of responsible citizens, some of the public revenue arising from the value of common resources should be shared directly among them. Politicians and government officials now channel huge sums in contracts and subsidies to private sector business and finance, as well as to public service organisations, to provide citizens with public services. Much of that public money could be distributed directly to citizens to spend in a market economy that would become more responsive to their needs than it is today. The state would be able to let the market economy operate more freely, with less intervention.

At the personal level a Citizens' Income would allow people, if they wished, to reduce the time they spent working as employees and, with a basic income, make it easier to become self-employed. Or they could opt for more free time. With more time and energy to supply themselves and their families with some of the goods and services they now have to buy, they could further reduce their need for money, if they so wished. Much of the valuable work done in families and communities, such as parenting, caring for growing numbers of elderly and people with disabilities, is unpaid and does not show up in GDP.

A Citizens' Income would help in the fight against child poverty and also help students reduce their large and growing burden of debt.

I invited John Field, a member of the Royal Society of Arts Living Systems Group, and long-standing advocate of Citizens' Income, to contribute his thoughts as follows:

I have two main reasons for advocating CI:

- *It reduces the need to chase economic growth for the purpose of income distribution.*
- *It introduces the culture of sharing, recognising that everyone has a right to a minimum share in wealth created through the use of skills and technologies that are our common heritage.*

From these flow many advantages such as you have mentioned, particularly that of eliminating humiliating depen-

dency. In reducing the political need for growth, sustainable growth only becomes more achievable.

My proposals for CI are on the basis of giving everyone a right to a proportion of GDP, maybe starting with 20 per cent and moving higher as CI becomes accepted. In fact 20 per cent is roughly equivalent to what we already achieve in UK with our complicated system of benefits and by in effect allowing the first tranche of remuneration as CI for those in employment.

There is growing support for Citizens' Income. It will require massive public pressure on Governments and MPs to make it happen. Namibia is piloting a Basic Income Grant.

Part 4: Global Measures

International institutions that deal with world monetary management, public revenue and public spending also need to be more effective. They too should be based on sharing the value of common resources more fairly.

Global Currency. With the rise of the BRICS economies, Brazil, Russia, India and China, there is growing criticism of the present "dollar hegemony" of the United States. The formation of the G20 will make change inevitable. Under the current regime, the dollar is a global monetary instrument that the US, and only the US, can produce. For the privilege of using the dollar as the main global currency, the rest of the world is estimated to pay the US at least $400bn a year. World trade is now a game in which the US produces dollars and the rest of the world produces things that dollars can buy. Developing countries, like China and India, provide the US not only cheap goods but also, from their savings, massive credit. To build up their reserves, poor countries have to borrow dollars from the US at interest rates as high as 18 per cent and then lend the money back to the US in the form of Treasury Bonds at 3 per cent.

A genuine international currency, issued by a world monetary authority, is needed as an alternative to the US dollar and other reserve currencies. It would be a source of revenue to the world community, as national monetary reform would provide a source of revenue for nation states.

Global Commons and Global Taxation. The Commission on Global Governance also recognised the need for global taxation to service the needs of the global neighbourhood. It proposed making nations pay for use of global commons, including:

- Ocean fishing, sea-bed mining, sea lanes, flight lanes, outer space, and the electromagnetic spectrum
- Activities that pollute and damage the global environment, or cause hazards beyond national boundaries, such as emissions of CO2 and CFCs, oil spills, and dumping wastes at sea.

Revenue from global taxes could provide stable sources of finance for global spending by organisations like the United Nations to meet global purposes such as peace-keeping, hunger relief and climate change. Some of it could be distributed per capita to national governments, reflecting the right of every person in the world to a global Citizens' Income as a share in the value of global resources.

Benefits of a Global Citizens' Income

This approach would:

- Encourage environmentally sustainable development worldwide
- Generate a much needed source of revenue for the UN
- Provide substantial financial transfers to poorer countries by right and without strings, as compen-

sation for rich countries' disproportionate use of world resources

- Help liberate poorer countries from dependence on grants and loans from rich-country-dominated institutions like the World Bank and International Monetary Fund
- Help to solve the problem of Third World debt
- Recognise the shared status of all people as citizens of the world
- By helping to reduce the spreading sense of injustice in a globalised world would contribute *to global security.*

Taxing Speculative Transactions. Financial markets create instability for businesses, and create a focus on the short-term, share values and short-term profitability thus diverting attention from the long term and stewardship.

In 2007 daily global international transactions were averaging $3,200bn a day, only a small per cent of which, around 3 per cent in 2006, were related to world trade. The rest, well over 90 per cent, were speculative transactions which do not contribute to wealth creation, except for the speculators, and destabilise currencies. Swings in currencies due to currency (and commodity) speculation are highly detrimental to businesses and national economies. A tax on such transactions, such as less than 1 per cent, was first proposed by James Tobin in 1972 and former US Treasury Secretary Larry Summers. Since then many countries have put forward proposals for such a tax and called for international action. For example, in November 2007, the All Party Parliamentary Group for Debt, Aid and Trade published a report on financing for development in which it recommended that the UK government undertake rigorous research into the implementation of a 0.005 per cent stamp duty on all sterling foreign exchange transactions, to provide additional revenue and help bridge the funding gap required to pay for the UN Millennium Development Goals.

Amongst the various proposals are a Robin Hood Tax or Currency Transactions Tax, put forward jointly by War on Want and NEF. It would be for a 0.1 per cent tax they estimate would raise between $100bn to $300bn per annum towards achieving UN Millennium Development Goals and help to eliminate poverty (New Economics Foundation (nef) Tobin Tax). In April 2009 over 100 Civil Society Organisations worldwide called on G20 leaders to introduce a Currency Transaction Levy to meet the aid revenue shortfall and safeguard lives from the worst ravages of the economic storm (Stamp Out Poverty). One unanswered question is how such a global tax would be enforced (Global Tax – The International Debate Education Association (IDEA)). Ideally a levy would be managed by the UN but some countries in Latin America have already implemented levies. Recently some support amongst senior EU politicians has been emerging, especially in Germany.

Reducing the over $1 trillion annually countries spend on military hardware. For the London G20 Summit in April 2009, Hazel Henderson proposed reducing the over $1 trillion annually spent on military hardware:

> *The summiteers can agree on the proposed United Nations Security Insurance Agency (UNSIA). Militarism is ever-less useful in resolving today's conflicts in Iraq, Afghanistan and other guerrilla insurgencies. This UNSIA proposal, backed by four Nobel laureates, would allow countries which wished to follow Costa Rica's lead in 1947 and abolish their armed forces. Instead, countries could buy the insurance of a peacekeeping force from the UN Security Council (expanded and veto-less)... The premiums would fund a standing, properly trained UN peace-keeping force and complimentary contingents of NGO peace-making conflict-*

resolution groups.

The UNSIA proposal is taught in many university programs and was debated in the UN Security Council in 1996 (see UNSIA). *This and other proposals, including the Foreign Exchange Transaction Reporting System (FXTRS) for Central Banks* Foreign Exchange Transaction Reporting System (FXTRS), *are also described in The United Nations Policy and Financing Alternatives,* (1995) (UN Policy and Financing Alternatives and Henderson, H).

Perverse National Public Spending

Perverse subsidies are another global issue. It is estimated that $1.5 to $2 trillion a year is spent worldwide on ***perverse subsidies***, which encourage economically, socially and environmentally damaging activities. These include the subsidies from rich-country governments to their farming and agricultural sectors, most of which go to large instead of small farmers and small organic farmers who most need help. Combined with tariffs against imported food, these subsidies devastate these sectors in poorer countries and expose the hypocrisy of rich-country support for free trade. But there are many other examples of perverse subsidies such as subsidies to the oil industry which disguise the full costs of extraction and supply.

German subsidies for coal mining are so large that it would be economically efficient for the government to close down all the mines and send the workers home on full pay for the rest of their lives. The environment would benefit too. Subsidies for agriculture foster overloading of croplands, leading to erosion of topsoil, pollution from synthetic fertilizers and pesticides, and release of greenhouse gases. Subsidies for fossil fuels aggravate pollution such as acid rain, urban smog and contribute to global warming. Subsidies for road transportation promote some of the worst and most widespread forms of pollution. Subsidies for water encourage misuse and overuse of supplies that are increasingly scarce in many lands. Subsidies for ocean fisheries foster overharvesting of fish stocks. Forestry subsidies encourage over-logging and other forms of deforestation. Apart from the environmental and economic costs, these subsidies act as direct drains on economies. Perverse subsidies in just these six sectors total at least $2 trillion per year.

This enormous sum contrasts markedly with the inadequate subsidies to green energy. Systematic national and international measures are needed to reduce these perverse subsidies, year by year, and transfer the money to green energy subsidies for both consumers and producers.

Conclusion

The proposals in this chapter offer the prospect of:

1. Democratic national states performing their monetary and financial functions more purposefully and effectively.
2. Money being created debt free.
3. The market economy operating more freely.
4. People liberating themselves from their present degree of dependence on goods and services and jobs provided by big corporations and the state.
5. Rewarding people and organisations financially if they act in ways that conserve, not squander natural resources.
6. Abandoning perverse subsidies.
7. A new stage in the evolution of international political economy based on fairly sharing the value of common resources.

The G20 Group of Twenty Finance Ministers and Central Bank Governors from 20 economies who met in London on 2 April 2009 are steeped in conventional economic wisdom, out of touch with ordinary people. They focus on ***patching up*** a failed system, at enormous cost to the average person, ***rather than*** changing the system and tackling the impending environmental disaster. The power of the banking system is so great that it has diminished the power of politicians and government to act in the interests of citizens.

They are, to quote James Robertson:

> *insulated from reality by advisers from the conventional school of financial experts, who have never questioned if it's right to depend on the commercial banks to create our public money supply.*

They forgot the far greater crisis facing us: climate change, Peak Oil, depletion of the Earth's resources, economic injustice and poverty. It did not address the most fundamental issues driving humanity over a cliff: unsustainable economic and money systems based on debt. There was a lack of radical thought. This failure will have disastrous consequences for 6.7 billion people.

> *If you turn off the television, and turn on your brain, and realise what a huge scam this whole thing really is, and the brazen theft of not only your money but the money of your children and grand-children who will be paying these fraudulent debts for generations – then maybe you will find the strength and wisdom to do what is really necessary – stand up and* ***say No More!!! Take control of your democracy****, take back your money from those who are stealing it in front of your very faces, and send all of them to jail for the rest of their lives.*
>
> **Dave Patterson**, Green Island Backgrounders

Action: Help get these ideas widely discussed. Think of the complexities that would be saved that the coalition and other governments are struggling with. Brief yourself and meet your MP and MEP. Get monetary reform on to your Government and International agendas.

Support *A Sane Alternative* and James Robertson's Newsletter, American Monetary Institute, Coalition for Economic Justice, Christian Council for Monetary Justice, Jubilee Debt Campaign, Land Value Taxation Campaign, Money Reform Party, New Economics Foundation, Scottish Monetary Reform, Tax Justice Network, Tobin Tax Institute, World Development Movement (WDM).

Chapter 11

Unlocking Democracy

April 2009

Giving power to communities and people, subsidiarity, providing real choice; government that serves citizens, government that serves citizens, participation and involvement.

Unlocking democracy at all levels is vital if we are to bring about the great transformation that is needed. We need powerful democracy to overcome all those vested interests that obstruct change and endanger the lives of millions.

In the UK, we are fortunate to live in one of the better democracies but it is not good enough. Brave women and men fought hard for it over the centuries. All over the world, people have sacrificed their lives in the struggle to give power to citizens, regardless of their wealth, gender, colour, race, religion or age, and to protect it. It has been a long journey and we still have a long way to go. We also benefit from many independent "think-tanks", research organisations, campaign groups and non-governmental organisations. Although they cannot match the funds spent by big business on lobbying and advertising, their campaigns are extremely effective.

As Churchill said,

> *Democracy is the worst form of government except all the others that have been tried.*

The campaign for democratic reform in the UK is part of a process that is happening all over the world. There are constant campaigns urging people to lobby their MPs, Ministers and the Prime Minister and sign petitions. Many campaigns have resulted in successful legislation, such as the Sustainable Communities Act; through Early Day motions initiated by independent minded MPs. Friends of the Earth achieved major changes to the UK Climate Change Act 2008.

What is wrong with UK Democracy?

Dissatisfaction with and disengagement from politics has been at an all time high. It is not that people are unconcerned about political issues. They have lost faith in the political system. The new coalition will have to address a widespread belief that citizens have little influence over government, especially between elections. The Power Inquiry, chaired by Baroness Helena Kennedy, showed a widespread belief that transnational corporations had more influence on our daily lives than the government. This is unlikely to have changed.

Disengagement is at an All Time High

- Turnout of UK electors is amongst the lowest in Western countries. Turnout in USA is even lower.
- Turnout is particularly low in local government elections.
- Voting decline is highest amongst younger people.
- Turnout has steadily declined since the sixties.

What are the causes?

Causes of UK Disillusionment with Politics

- An overwhelming feeling of disempowerment.
- One of the most centralised governments in Europe.
- A widespread belief that whichever party one votes for makes little difference, i.e. there is no real choice; power rests with rich elites, transnational corporations and big financial interests.
- At both national and local level, people have little confidence in consultations which they see as "fixed", the results ignored.
- Expensive inquiries are whitewash exercises.
- Politicians are not trusted and their behaviour is widely disliked; it's seen as adversarial, abusive to one another, untruthful and lacking integrity.
- Broken pledges.
- The composition of the House of Commons does not reflect voters' intentions.
- The second chamber is still unelected and subject to patronage.
- MPs and Ministers are seen as too close to and too much influenced by corporations.
- Sums spent by corporations on lobbying government and MPs cause a lack of confidence.
- Funding of parties is highly questionable and a constant source of controversy.
- Frequent reports of sleaze and corruption in both houses of Parliament; members voting themselves overgenerous pay settlements, expenses and pensions; abusing expenses and obstructing investigations

A more representative voting system is needed. The composition of Parliament does not reflect the wishes of the people. In

2005, six voters in ten supported a party other than New Labour, yet New Labour won six out of every ten seats in the House of Commons. In 1997, only 37 per cent of people between 18 and 24 voted. Between 1964 and 2001, identification with political parties dropped from 44 per cent to 14 per cent. In the 2001 election, 52 per cent of voters did not vote and in that year and 2005 more eligible people did not voted than voted. Votes cast were New Labour 35.2 per cent, Conservative 32.3 per cent, Lib Dem 22 per cent, other 10.5 per cent. Seats in the House of Commons were New Labour 55.7 per cent, Conservative 30.7 per cent, Lib Dem 9.6 per cent, other 4.6 per cent. That is what a first past the post (F PTP) system does. Significantly, no elected institution created since 1997 has used first past the post (FPTP). Despite its promise in 1997 to hold a referendum on how we elect MPs, New Labour dragged its feet for thirteen years and did not fulfil its promise.

A fair voting system would enable a far wider spectrum of information and opinion to be contributed to policy. Arguably, there would be better dialogue, leading to better decisions. Parties would be forced to collaborate and reach consensus. Parties would no longer be able to inflict extreme policies on us; in effect, dictatorship by the party that unfairly wins most seats. Proportional representation would enable smaller parties, like the Greens, to gain more seats and a greater diversity of parties would be able to contribute. More people would feel their votes counted and their views were represented. They would have an incentive to vote for the party of their choice, rather than vote tactically or not at all.

We need deliberative processes and dialogue of the highest quality in reaching key decisions about whether to go to war, how to deal with climate change and other difficult and complex issues. This requires intellectual integrity, willingness to listen with an open mind in search of solutions that will benefit the vast majority of people in the world. Decisions need to be informed by the widest range of expertise and opinion, not outweighed by powerful vested interests or party political considerations. This is far from what we see in the House of Commons. An adversarial party political system, including "whipping" is completely out of step with the rigorous decision processes needed today. Instead we see a witty display, point scoring, blame, denial and lack of responsibility. As Jean Lambert, Green Party MEP for London, said at a meeting I attended:

> *It does not help when your job description says you have to oppose, be decisive, you cannot say things are complex or difficult – a sign of weakness, you have to have a position and the press try to push you into a position.*

The anachronistic rituals, procedures and layout of the Commons chamber are dysfunctional and do not inspire confidence. The monarchy, representing a long gone age of deference and empire, although conscientious and loved, is part of the problem. The honours system appreciates many deserving people, but is an anachronism, corrupted by party patronage and virtually automatic honours. Benjamin Zephaniah showed integrity in refusing the Order of the British Empire. He did not want to be associated with that Empire.

Undermining our hard fought for liberties. The right to peaceful protest, freedom to campaign and demonstrate, essential for democracy, has been eroded. Last year, treatment by the police of some 5,000 G20 demonstrators, the majority peaceful, raised questions about police intimidation and violence; police hit people who were sitting down, driving people into police cordons, known as "kettling", holding them for several hours and taking photographs of protestors. In July, at this year's G20 protest newsvendor Ian Tomlinson was hit from behind and died. Obviously harmless demonstrations within a kilometre of Parliament are banned without prior permission and face arrest. The extent of surveillance and government data collection causes increasing concern. The Conservative-Lib Dem government will scrap the ID cards scheme and the National Identity Register.

Equally disturbing is the growth in what are known as "private-public" areas, in private ownership and management. They may be a threat to democracy. Anna Minton, author of *"The Privatisation of Public Space"* 2006 report for the Royal Institute of Chartered Surveyors, warns the UK is "sleepwalking into a privatisation of the public realm." She says:

> *A new genuinely inclusive approach to public space and community is needed.*

Privatisation of public space is becoming an integral feature of city regeneration. In Liverpool, streets have been privatised as part of the Duke of Westminster's Grosvenor Estates Paradise Street redevelopment. Rights of way are replaced by public realm arrangements policed by US-style sheriffs. Some see these developments as threats to local cultural activities. Liberty called Paradise Street "disturbing", voicing concerns about private police forces deciding who can come and go.

Human Rights and Civil Liberties. Winston Churchill held human rights and civil liberties as sacred. Immediately after the Second World War, he restored them and initiated the European Convention of Human Rights that led to the United Nations Declaration of the Convention of Human Rights proclaimed in 1948. After the war, Labour wanted to continue ID cards, but there was considerable public opposition. The issue was brought to a head by the efforts of a small rebellious group, the civil disobedience of a small group of women and Clarence Harry Wilcock's brave stance. Wilcock's defiance led to his conviction and the High Court comment that a measure now not justified was turning *"law abiding subjects into law breakers."* The newly elected Tory government abolished ID cards in 1951.

History may is repeating itself. It is a dilemma for any government facing terrorist atrocities, but New Labour did not seem to grasp that the best defence against terrorism is to uphold, not to abuse, human rights and civil liberties. The six central pillars of civil liberty are: Right to Protest, Right to Freedom of Speech, Right to Privacy, Right not to Be Detained without Charge, Innocent until Proven Guilty and Prohibition from Torture. Under New Labour, following the events of 9/11 and 7/7, these six central pillars of liberty were systematically destroyed and whilst a climate of fear was created by media and government.

The DVD *Taking Liberties* uncovers *"stories the government don't want you to hear – so ridiculous you will laugh, so ultimately terrifying you will want to take action. Teenage sisters detained for 36 hours for a peaceful protest; RAF war veteran arrested for wearing an anti-Bush and Blair T-shirt"* and the story of an 82 year old party member, Walter Wolfgang, roughly carried out of a Labour party conference by stewards after shouting *"Nonsense!"* during Jack Straw's speech defending Iraq policy. It gives an account of police handling of a busload of peaceful protesters seeking to demonstrate against the use of UK RAF Fairford base for the US led attacks on Iraq. The police shut them in their bus, forced the driver to turn it round and sent them back to London like prisoners.

> *When governments fear the people, there is liberty. When the people fear the government, there is tyranny.*
> Attributed to **Thomas Jefferson**

The UK government's alleged involvement in extraordinary rendition and torture is coming to a head thanks to the efforts of Liberty and its response to the Joint Committee on Human

Rights Committee (JCHRC) inquiry into proposed legislation on war crimes, genocide and torture. A Torture (Damages) Bill would enable prosecution and damages in the case of UK involvement in torture taking place in other countries.

Quangos. In July 2009, there were 1162 quangos in the UK, costing the taxpayer of £64 billion, equivalent to £2550 per household. Many perform invaluable functions. However, they are unelected and unaccountable. Yet some perform governmental functions and receive funding or other support from government. They are accused of bureaucratic waste. A report by the independent Local Government Information Unit said that local quangos in England and Wales are subject to inadequate, haphazard and usually voluntary mechanisms of accountability and openness. The coalition looks set to put this right.

What kind of democracy do we want?

We need to transform our notion of politics. People need to be sovereign, not government.

The Power Report, chaired by Labour peer Baroness Helena Kennedy QC, said the parties were "killing" politics. They must learn:

> *Politics and government are increasingly in the hands of privileged elites as if democracy has run out of steam. Too often citizens are being evicted from decision-making – rarely asked to get involved and rarely listened to. As a result, they see no point in voting, joining a party or engaging with formal politics.*

It called for: a responsive electoral system for the House of Commons, House of Lords and local councils to replace the first past the post system "to ensure that all votes count by having some influence on the final outcome of an election;" 70 per cent of the House of Lords should be elected by a "responsive electoral system"; Parliament should be able to initiate legislation, launch inquiries and act on petitions; voting and candidacy age reduced to 16; a commission to encourage women, ethnic minorities, people on lower incomes, young people and independents to stand; £10,000 limit on individual donations to parties; decentralising power from central to local government; curbs on the powers of party "whips"; more powers for select committees to hold ministers to account and tighter rules on plurality of media ownership.

Participation, not consultation. Democracy needs to be, not only representative, but also participatory. It needs to involve and engage people. That means devolving power and adopting the principle of ***Subsidiarity***: an organizing principle that matters ought to be handled by the smallest, lowest or least centralised competent authority.

New opportunities for involvement through the Internet. The Internet provides new opportunities for involvement. President Obama seized this opportunity to engage younger people and people who had never been engaged in politics before. He used it to raise funds in a new more democratic way – from ordinary people – instead of relying on large corporations and wealthy people as his predecessors did. His campaign raised more than any previous one. Three and a half million people signed up to his website and he keeps them informed as part of his pledge for open government.

More power at a local level. To unlock democracy, radical legislation is needed that gives more power at a local level to local councils and communities. That is not the only way of giving people involvement but it is extremely important. Arguably it would lead to far better decisions than those imposed by remote advisors in Whitehall, county halls and borough councils. Local people are the experts on what their community needs and wants.

"Not in my back yard," NIMBYism, is a sound principle for

protecting the planet, says Satish Kumar. If you would not want something in your back yard, that is a sure indication that it is not fit for anyone's back yard.

Better informed citizens. For democracy to work citizens must be well informed. They need readily accessible, balanced information from sources that do not treat them as stupid or subject them to constant corporate advertising. Government often does its best to make a case, deny, withhold or distort information. Iraq is the outstanding example; others are the case for GM and nuclear power. Lack of integrity and due diligence ultimately become evident, result in disastrous consequences and undermine our democracy.

Bold, investigative journalism is vital. Newspapers struggle in the face of competition from the Internet and the enormous costs of fighting legal actions brought by large corporations and rich individuals. Tesco presented the Guardian with a bill for £800,000 of which £350,000 was for Tesco to explain themselves on the subject of tax avoidance. Eventually the cost would have been nearly £1m, so the case was settled confidentially. Equally important for local communities, local newspapers suffer from reduced advertising revenues. Their loss leaves communities without reliable source of local news.

Giving power to the people also requires giving citizens the right to recall representatives and, if enough people support it, a right to local or national referenda on vital issues. Constituents need the right to recall MPs and councillors outside of election time and force a by-election.

Progress has been made

Charter 88 came into existence as a response to Thatcherism and a widespread feeling that government was out of control – as now! Three hundred forty-eight activists signed a letter to the New Statesman magazine as *"a general expression of dissent"* following the 1987 General Election triumph of the Conservative

Party. Advertisements in the Guardian and Independent newspapers produced 5000 signatures and many donations by 1989. This is Charter 88's original declaration:

We call, therefore, for a new constitutional settlement which will:

- *Enshrine, by means of a Bill of Rights, such civil liberties as the right to peaceful assembly, to freedom of association, to freedom from discrimination, to freedom from detention without trial, to trial by jury, to privacy and to freedom of expression.*
- *Subject Executive powers and prerogatives, by whosoever exercised, to the rule of law.*
- *Establish freedom of information and open government.*
- *Create a fair electoral system of proportional representation.*
- *Reform the Upper House to establish a democratic, non-hereditary Second Chamber.*
- *Place the Executive under the power of a democratically renewed Parliament and all agencies of the state under the rule of law.*
- *Ensure the independence of a reformed judiciary.*
- *Provide legal remedies for all abuses of power by the state and by officials of central and local government.*
- *Guarantee an equitable distribution of power between the nations of the United Kingdom and between local, regional and central government.*
- *Draw up a written constitution anchored in the ideal of universal citizenship that incorporates these reforms.*

Ultimately some 85,000 people signed up. In 2007, Charter 88 and the New Politics Network merged to form Unlock Democracy. Strictly non-aligned it has supporters in all three main parties and the Greens. Currently there are around 4,500 members. Many more are needed to help transform our democracy. This year Unlock Democracy and POWER2010 have now joined together to campaign. Over 56,000 people have signed the Take Back Parliament Coalition petition demanding a fair voting system.

Over the past twenty years substantial progress has been made – see below.

The Charter 88 Unlock Democracy campaign

- Human Rights Act (enacted 1998) incorporating freedom from discrimination, except religious
- Freedom of Information Act (enacted in Britain 2000 and Scotland 2002, 36 years after USA in 1966.)
- Open government
- Devolution and decentralisation of power (extended in limited form to Scotland and Wales; rejected in the North by referendum)
- Reform of the House of Commons
- A democratic second chamber (limited reform – most hereditary peers were removed but life peers continue to be appointed by patronage)
- Proportional representation (enacted in the Scottish Parliament and Welsh Assembly)
- An independent judiciary
- A written constitution: a new contract between citizens and those who govern in our name

Progress has been extraordinarily slow. Reform of an unelected House of Lords was promised in the Parliament Act of 1911! There has been continuing resistance to letting go of power, secrecy and privilege. All kinds of excuses were made to resist a fair voting. Political patronage of cronies and financial supporters continues in the House of Lords and honours system. The Freedom of Information Act was watered down and there was a battle to implement it. However, the Freedom of

Information Act was an amazing achievement, a huge advantage to citizens, journalists, academics and researchers and a constant source of embarrassment to government! The revelations about MPs abuse of expenses including second home allowances is the latest example.

The most recent achievement is the Sustainable Communities Act. The current major campaigns are Electoral Reform, reform of the House of Lords, and a written constitution in the form of a Bill of Rights.

The Sustainable Communities Act 2007 is an outstanding example of what people power, skilled non-partisan campaigners working with politicians of all main parties, can achieve. Aiming for a revolution, it can give power to local communities and help reverse *"Ghost Town Britain"* (Ghost Town Britain). Initiated by the New Economics Foundation, it required a five year campaign by Local Works, a coalition of over 90 national organisations. Led by Ron Bailey, Campaigns Director of Unlock Democracy, supported by 20,000 individuals and, 1000 councils, it was backed by 365 MPs, who signed an Early Day Motion. Many people e-mailed their MPs and gave money. Ron Bailey and Steve Shaw, Local Works Campaign Co-ordinator, are working to encourage councils to opt into the Act and use it to enhance local democracy. One hundred twenty councils have done so. Sustainable Communities Act (Amendment) passed into law in April 2010 greatly strengthens the Act by creating an on-going "rolling" programme for communities and councils to submit proposals to government. It now includes Parish and Town Councils in the Act's process. If you wish to see more power given to local communities, you need to keep up the pressure to get government and local authorities to implement it. For more details, go to Local Works.

The following summarises the briefing on Act by Local Works (full text available at Unlock Democracy).

The underlying principle is:

Citizens and local councils are the experts on their own problems and the solutions to them.

The aim is to empower local communities and make government do more to help promote sustainable communities in the following four categories:

1. **Local economies** e.g. promoting local shops, local businesses, local public services and local jobs
2. **The Environment** e.g. promoting local renewable energy, protecting green spaces
3. **Social inclusion** e.g. protecting local public services and alleviating fuel poverty and food poverty
4. **Democratic involvement** e.g. promoting local people participating in local decision-making

Relevant proposals are made by a community or a local authority under the four categories above. It is the role of *central government* to help. This is how it works:

Double Devolution. The Act sets up what is called a "double devolution" process so that local people can drive central government action to promote sustainable communities:

1. The Act gives the government a legal duty to "assist local authorities in promoting the sustainability of local communities." Councils will be invited to make proposals to central government as to how it can help them promote the sustainability of local communities. So it is local authorities, **not the government**, that are in the driving seat as to what the government must do.
2. The Act specifies that local authorities cannot make suggestions to central government without involving "local people". Councils must set up (or recognise if they

already exist) "panels of representatives of local people" which **must** include people from usually under-represented groups: ethnic minorities, young people, older people, tenants, etc.

It is not another meaningless consultation exercise. The Act sets up a double devolution process where local authorities must "reach agreement" with proposals made by their communities via the citizens' panels. Government must "co-operate" and "reach agreement" with the Local Government Association who will represent all the proposals that are made by local authorities. This new and unprecedented decision-making process gives the Act real teeth!

Local Spending Reports. Government *must* publish local spending reports that will provide a breakdown by local area of *all* public spending (i.e. central and local). This "opening of the books" has never been done before and is likely to generate much debate as central agencies and quangos have to show how their money is spent locally. Local authorities can use these spending reports to then argue for the transfer of specific monies and their related functions from central to local control. Once under local control these new resources and powers could be used to promote local shops, jobs and services like Post Offices, local food, etc.

Councils that opt in must then set up citizens' panels and must "reach agreement" (again, this is NOT just another consultation exercise) with local people, regarding the proposals on promoting local sustainability that local authorities will ultimately submit to central government. The whole process re-occurs on an annual basis. So, Councils that do not opt in to the first round will have a chance to do so.

Examples of what the Act could be used to help communities achieve are:

- Keeping essential community services like Post Offices open.
- Promoting small businesses by increasing the rate relief they receive.
- Forcing large out-of-town superstores to pay local domestic rates on their huge car parks.
- Promoting local renewable energy e.g. by removing the restrictive barriers relating to the local grid.
- Promoting local food and other products e.g. by giving rate relief to businesses that earn 50 per cent of their turnover from selling local food and goods.

You may need to put pressure on your local authority to adopt the Act and use it. Local Works can help you.

The Way Ahead

- Unlock Democracy continues to campaign for:
- Fair, Open and Honest Elections
- Rights, Freedoms and a Written Constitution
- Stronger Parliament and Accountable Government
- Bringing Power Closer to the People, the Sustainable Communities Act is an important step towards this goal
- A Culture of Informed Political Interest and Responsibility
- A written Constitution e.g. Bill of Rights
- War Powers
- A Citizens' Convention

These are Unlock Democracy's proposals:

Electoral Reform for the House of Commons and House of Lords. Unlock Democracy wants all UK elections to offer real choice and fairness. They want a proportional system that broadly reflects the votes cast for each party in an election. Several electoral systems satisfy these requirements, including the Single Transferable Vote (STV) and various open list systems. One of the issues is how to provide a constituency link with a local MP. For readers who want an explanation of the different PR systems, their advantages and disadvantages, an excellent summary is provided by the Electoral Reform Society. Unlock Democracy have summarised the policies of the main political parties. The Coalition plans a referendum on AV on the 5 May 2011. AV would not produce as representative results as Single Transferable Vote (STV) or open lists.

A Written Constitution: a Bill of Rights

The following is an edited summary of: *"Unlock Democracy evidence to the Joint Committee on Human Rights inquiry into a British Bill of Rights" obtainable from Unlock Democracy.*

Charter 88 played a leading role in making the case for the Human Rights Act, for the first time incorporating the European Convention of Human Rights into UK law. Unlock Democracy has campaigned for a written constitution, setting out the limits of what governments may and may not do in our name. They argue that a written constitution must contain a Bill of Rights, thereby granting every citizen a legal remedy, should they need it, if their rights are infringed by the State.

Unlock Democracy seek a written constitution that serves and protects the people. That constitution would define the roles of, and relationships between, the Executive, Legislature and Judiciary. It would determine how, and to what extent, power is shared between representatives at local, national and United Kingdom levels, and with international organisations. It would enshrine basic liberties and human rights for all.

Bill of Rights

1. **To Check the Power of the Executive.** The need for citizens to have the power to limit the actions of government is as great now as it has ever been. Until now,

experience of politics is a House of Commons dominated by one political party and that ensures government gets its legislation through the Commons. The House of Lords, fatally weakened by the lack of any democratic legitimacy, is browbeaten into accepting this legislation and the Crown automatically gives assent. Far too often, therefore, the checks and balances on the powers of the Executive are too weak to be effective. That leaves citizens out of the picture vulnerable to repressive legislation, e.g. limits placed on the right to silence by previous Conservative Governments, restrictions on trial by jury and detention without charge of alleged terror suspects.

2. **To Create a New Britain.** Constitutional changes since 1997 make the need for a Citizens' Constitution even more urgent. New Labour continued the process of centralisation. Many features once characteristic of the British constitution have either been removed or irreparably damaged:

- **we no longer have a unitary state**
- **the sovereignty of Parliament has been undermined** by the Human Rights Act
- **Cabinet government is no more than a convenient fiction**
- **politicisation of key sections of the civil service** has continued

With the exception of the rule of law, all that is left of the old constitution are its least desirable elements: winner-takes-all elections and Prime Ministerial power. The latter has become greater than ever.

Constitutional reform has taken place in a piecemeal fashion. Radical change has been made with no overall sense of the kind of country reforms were designed to build. Each reform has been enacted without a real idea of how it would impact on the others. For example, we have had:

- **Devolution** to Scotland, Wales and London whilst the England question has remained dangerously unanswered. The result has been a destabilising sense of unfairness in England
- **a Human Rights Act** which the Government insists does not impact on the sovereignty of Parliament and has yet to capture the public imagination, few seeing its relevance to them
- **Reform of local government** that actually reduce its openness and accountability
- **Top-down reform** which has helped to foster growing voter disenchantment and cynicism with politics in a period of unprecedented constitutional change.

If voters are to become citizens they must have a fundamental document without which they remain powerless to exercise control over those who govern in their name between general elections. As a member of a European Union, the need for Britain to be clear about its self-definition is all the greater. The process of creating a Bill of Rights would help to foster this. The time has come for a new constitutional settlement. Unlock Democracy wants to see a citizen-led Bill of Rights. This is what the process should do:

- be created with **maximum public involvement**
- **guarantee political equality** and help society aspire towards social equality
- **protect democratic representation in and authority over government** and public affairs
- provide a framework for the **stable rule of law**
- **ensure that individuals can claim and protect their rights**
- **empower citizens as individuals and members of**

communities of all types, defending every citizen's right to be free from discrimination

- **define being a "good citizen" as exercising the power to say "no",** to hold authority of all kinds to account, and to resist as well as endorse and assist elected authority
- **describe what citizens share and protect the differences we enjoy;** indeed, it should map and enable differences and help to ensure they are protected as a common, living inheritance.

Citizens' Convention. Citizens have not been sufficiently involved in the changes that have taken place and have insufficient understanding of them or appreciation of their value. A Citizens' Convention is the means for providing this much needed involvement. It is important to have a debate about social and economic rights and whether they should be included in any new Bill of Rights. Hence a Citizens' Convention is an important part of the process of creating a Bill of Rights.

War Powers

This is a short, edited extract from Unlock Democracy's *War Powers and Treaties Consultation* available from *Unlock Democracy*:

Stronger powers are needed for Parliament to veto or approve the deployment of troops and to increase Parliament's role in the ratification of treaties. In a democracy, decision-making should be open to scrutiny, accountable to elected representatives and ultimately to the people. The decision to send troops into armed conflict is one of the most serious any state can make. A decision-making process that is unaccountable and cannot be effectively scrutinised is unacceptable.

The strength of feeling about the way Britain was taken into the Iraq war was shown recently when Peter Brierley, father of a dead soldier, Lance Corporal Brierley, 28, killed in

Iraq, refused to shake Tony Blair's hand at the reception following the memorial service at St Paul's. He said:

> *I understand soldiers go to war and die but they have to go to war for a good reason and be properly equipped to fight. I believe Tony Blair is a war criminal. I can't bear to be in the same room as him. I can't believe he's been allowed to come to this reception. I believe he's got the blood of my son and all of the other men and women who died out there on his hands.*

Parliamentary approval for the deployment of troops became a major issue in the context of the decision to take part in military action in Iraq. For the first time, a vote in Parliament related to the proposed military action. Some believe that better parliamentary scrutiny would have led to a different decision. Parliamentary scrutiny is part of the constitutional principle of accountability both to Parliament and the people and ensuring that all issues are debated and scrutinised. Clearly information about the deployment of armed forces should not be made public. Ways of enabling Parliament to approve the deployment of armed forces, without endangering endanger the lives of service personnel or national security, are described below.

Parliamentary scrutiny would include the decision as to whether to deploy troops but also crucially the plans for the conflict. One of the key issues arising from the troop deployment to Iraq was the lack of planning for eventualities after the initial military operation. The significant military experience in Parliament, particularly in the House of Lords, could have been much more effectively utilised. Examples from abroad suggest that it is possible to ensure the security of the armed forces whilst also allowing for scrutiny of executive decision-making.

Unlock Democracy proposes a new select committee based on the model of the German Defence Committee. The Defence Committee in Germany is a departmental select committee, established in Basic Law, which, in addition to the scrutiny of Bills and defence related matters, has power to act as an investigative committee and consider any defence matter of its choosing. The Defence Committee works in co-operation with the Foreign Affairs Committee, with access to relevant security information.

Unlock Democracy propose a similar **"Joint Defence Committee"**, to act as an "honest broker" between the executive and Parliament. It would have a similar policy remit to the existing House of Commons Defence Select Committee the key differences being:

1. It would consist of ***members from both Houses*** to ensure that expertise from the House of Lords is utilised
2. The chair would sit on the Intelligence And Security Committee, giving it ***access to all relevant security information***
3. The committee would have the ***power to act as a committee of inquiry*** and therefore to require the presence of persons and papers
4. It would have the specific role of ***monitoring the armed forces and any plans for deployment***
5. It would act as a ***guardian for the rights of service personnel***
6. It would have ***permanent legal advice***
7. The committee would be ***able to meet in camera*** if either the chair of the committee, the Prime Minister or the armed forces deemed it to be necessary for the security of service personnel or in the interests of national security
8. Papers would be confidential but, unlike the Intelligence and Security Committee, the committee would be ***accountable to Parliament and not to the executive.***

The Citizens' Convention Bill, July 2007, a private members bill, unfortunately not enacted, sought to commit the Government to establishing a Citizens' Convention which would actively involve people in deliberating on how to improve the way the UK is governed. The Government would be required to co-operate with the Convention in deciding on the implementation of those recommendations. The Bill would have committed the Government to consult widely on how the Convention should be composed, take all reasonable steps to ensure people from the most unrepresented and marginalised sections of society would be heard. Meetings and other mechanisms would involve citizens in all parts of the United Kingdom. Unlock Democracy continues to support initiatives to develop new processes for engaging the public in constitutional change and are still campaigning for a constitutional convention.

But all these institutional changes won't make much difference until politicians, journalists and people simply learn to behave differently. Nelson Mandela is right:

Simple Principles According to Which We Have Conducted Our Own Life

Indeed whether it be in the smallest community or the highest councils of nations or the world, there is a need for those simple principles according to which we have conducted our own life. These include accepting the integrity and bona fides of everyone no matter how they may differ from ourselves; loyalty no matter how much the circumstances regarding those to whom one is loyal may have changed; frankness and honesty no matter how embarrassing that may prove; and a presumption that however we may differ there are more important things we share. In other words what is required is that the mutual respect that underlies the mere possibility of negotiation should always inform the way we relate to one another as representatives of different nations

> *and different sectors of the world community.*
>
> **Nelson Mandela**, *Independent Lecture*, Dublin, 12 April 2000.

The adversarial tradition in politics is outdated for the crisis we face today. Collaboration, dialogue, statesmanship and integrity are needed as never before.

We may be at a turning point. The first peacetime coalition for more than eighty years may usher in a refreshing trend to pluralism. It seems to be working. The Big Society and the Your Freedom website invite citizens to get involved. The coalition moved quickly to propose reforms including a referendum on the Alternative Vote (AV) system. AV is far better than First Past the Post (FPP) and a step in the right direction. Ultimately we need to press for the Single Transferable Vote (STV) which offers voters the best representation. The package includes the following:

Coalition Plans

- Referendum on the AV system for general elections
- Five year fixed-term Parliaments, the prime minister not able to call poll date
- 55 per cent of MPs required to vote for the dissolution of Parliament and to trigger an election
- Committee to look at fully PR-elected House of Lords
- Cut in number of MPs and equal size constituencies
- Right of the public to "recall" corrupt MPs
- Statutory register of lobbyists
- Scottish Parliament to get more powers under
- Referendum of devolution of further powers to Welsh

assembly

- Review of Scottish MPs voting on England-only legislation
- Ban on "non-doms" sitting in Parliament
- Reform of political donations and party funding

Source: BBC News 13 May 2010

Action Above all support Unlock Democracy, Local Works, Liberty and Amnesty International. Sign the Take Back Parliament petition. **Support** Fair Trials International (FTI), New Politics Project, One World Trust, Open Democracy, Operation Black Vote, Power 2010, Pressure Works, Redress human- rights, Simultaneous Policy – a global political platform. ***Use*** WriteToThem. Go to Electoral Reform Society for an explanation of the different voting systems and the Institute of Government for a review Big Society. There are similar organisations throughout the world.

Chapter 12

Feeding the World

May 2009

A real green revolution, food sovereignty and security, eco-agriculture vs. agribusiness, GM vs.organic, bioregionalism and localisation vs. globalisation, sustainable distribution.

The Backdrop to feeding the world is this:

The Backdrop to Global Food

- We are consuming about 30 per cent more than planet Earth can provide, allowing 10 per cent of bio-capacity for nature reserves
- World population, now 6.7bn is expected to reach 9bn by 2050, leading to a big increase in demand, unless we change our eating habits
- Food waste and overeating in the North is massive
- In the North we are losing our food growing and culinary skills; we lack contact with nature
- Climate change is causing drought, desertification and a more turbulent climate
- Peak Oil: declining supply and rising cost will affect industrialised agriculture and global food distribution; the costs of farm machinery, fertilisers, herbicides and pesticides and everything in which oil is embedded will rise
- We are degrading the Earth: destroying the soil and ecosystem; industrialised agriculture is causing salini-

sation

- Pesticides and herbicides harm our health; pandemics may originate in inhumane, industrialised animal husbandry
- Large corporations dominate the production of key foods
- Peasant farmers are losing their land and drifting to cities

World Hunger and the situation we are in

The World Health Organisation estimates one-third of the world is well-fed; one-third is under-fed; and one-third is starving. Nearly a billion people are hungry. One billion are overweight. Both are victims of poor diet, though in the case of the overweight as much because of an unhealthy lifestyle, caused by overuse of the motor car, new technology and changing ways of working. Poor diet and unhealthy lifestyle often exist in the same family or household. In the USA and UK poor diet is associated with race and class. These problems are spreading to developing countries and even continental Europe where there are more sensible food cultures. Worldwide, two billion people lack essential micronutrients, such as vitamin A, iron and zinc. Most of the poorly fed are young women and babies. The Indian subcontinent has nearly half the world's hungry people. Africa and the rest of Asia together have about 40 per cent. In parts of India 50 per cent of children are still malnourished. Every year 15 million children die of hunger. For the price of one missile, a school full of hungry children could eat lunch every day for 5 years.

Hunger and malnutrition are the number one risk to health worldwide, which is greater than AIDS, malaria and tuberculosis combined. As well as hunger resulting from an empty stomach, there is also the hidden hunger of micronutrient deficiencies which make people susceptible to infectious diseases, impair physical and mental development, reduce their labour productivity and increase the risk of premature death. Hunger puts a crushing economic burden on the developing world which stands to lose from a population whose physical and mental development is stunted by hunger and malnutrition.

Increasing population and decreasing rainfall and soil fertility make Africa uniquely vulnerable to famine. Climate change is expected to make a bad situation worse through more frequent droughts and floods. Hunger and malnutrition are getting worse, as a result of climate change, Peak Oil, overexploitation of the environment and degradation of the Earth. Recession has led to less aid for important projects such as building roads to help farmers get their produce to market. The rising price of oil is causing higher food prices, partly because of increases in the cost of fertilisers and pesticides and growing crops for biofuels. Other causes are natural disasters, drought, wars and civil wars which drive people off their land. Western Governments contribute to wars and civil wars through unethical foreign policies and armament sales. Strictly even-handed interventions are essential to foster conflict resolution without resort to violence. Too little is invested in such initiatives.

World food prices are rising: wheat prices increased 130 per cent and soya prices by 87 per cent 2007-2008. Fertilizer prices are rising. Meanwhile, the profits of the top three fertiliser companies rose 139 per cent during 2007 and profits from the top three seed and pesticide corporations rose 91 per cent.

Whilst hunger and malnutrition in the world are growing, food waste in the North is enormous. Supermarkets cause suppliers to return as much as half their good vegetables and fruit to the soil just because it does not look right. Allegedly supermarkets throw away large quantities of good food unnecessarily. Householders throw away a third of what they buy, often because they have been encouraged to buy more than they need by sales promotions.

The United Nations Millennium Development Goals for the 21st century aim to halve the proportion of hungry people in the world by 2015. But the obstacles in minds and institutions are considerable.

Misguided trade policies put local farmers out of business by enabling wealthy countries to dump food products on poor countries at low prices which undercut local farmers. This is often the unintended consequence of aid. In Haiti, for example, local farmers cannot compete with food aid such as rice from USA. That damages local food production and drives farmers off the land and into the cities where there is no employment and conditions are desperate. Poverty in Haiti leads to people cutting down trees to make a living from charcoal. As a result of deforestation, good soil washes into the Caribbean. It is a vicious circle that will take years of wise policies and the right kind of aid to reverse.

Unhealthy eating in rich countries results from poverty and excess. Fast food, diet simplification, decline in the eating of pulses and the use of refined carbohydrate and unhealthy fats lead to ill-health. In part this comes from the industrialisation of food, turning food into a commodity, mass retailing, competition and an emphasis on low prices instead of value and nutrition. The same issue applies everywhere: lack of respect for food and those who grow it. Mass produced food has often been stripped of important ingredients. To be healthy, human beings need a complex variety of fresh, nutritious food. Children who eat more diverse foods develop better height for age scores which are a good measure of healthy development.

As a general rule, the more that food is processed, the less good it does you. Organic muesli made from unprocessed grains and other whole ingredients is far better for you than cereals processes by filling them with air or separating their constituents. Today's breakfast cereals were born when it was realised that more money could be made by separating out different constituents of the grain thus creating a variety of products. Grain could be blown up as in the case of popcorn, rice crispies, cornflakes or puffed wheat. In processed cereals the raw grain is refined and roughage is taken out. Further harm is done by adding a lot of salt and sugar. Various additives make the product taste or look better, increase its shelf life or restore vitamins. The same was done to bread, ultimately producing white sliced bread tasting more like paper. Potato crisps are another example; processing a nutritious vegetable, adding lots of salt and putting it into a packet.

It's called ***adding value***! Business schools teach this way of making more money. In the case of food, it is ***taking out value*** and creating social costs. Another business opportunity is opened up; the growing vitamins and other supplements industry, necessary to compensate for the poor nutritional quality of our food. Smart business! Another cost is added to the household budget. We'd be far better off in every sense with the original unprocessed food.

Cheap food is more expensive! Ultimately it is poorer people and small farmers who suffer most from cheap food policies. The biggest cost is ill-health and that means higher taxes to pay for health care. This perverse practice steadily destroys local supplies everywhere. When a global food crisis looms, it's crazy to drive farmers out of business for a few pence on the price of milk or a few extra pounds of profit ***and*** we buy our milk from across the water, contributing even more CO2 emissions. We are increasingly driven into hands of food multinationals. Is that wise? The same applies to importing potatoes from Egypt and apples from France or Italy. The UK has the best natural conditions for growing apples. ***In a sane world,*** products that damage our future and produce social costs would be heavily taxed. A Social Cost Added Tax (SCAT) would be applied to the producers and distributors to help pay the social costs of "cheap food" and thus healthy food would have a lower price.

History of the Green Revolution

The Green Revolution began in 1945 and the term was first used in 1968. Essentially it was to produce an abundance of cheap food to feed the world after the privations of WWII. It ushered in what became large-scale industrial agriculture, now referred to as agribusiness. It involved the use of oil-based fertilizers and pesticides and nitrates as well as ever larger, more complex, oil-powered machines. The pioneers who introduced the Ferguson and Massey tractors that replaced horses were idealistic and believed they were helping to feed the world. At first the tractors were small and did less damage to the soil. But tractors and combine harvesters grew bigger and bigger until we now have huge satellite directed machines that operate in giant prairie fields. In countries like the USA, industrialised agriculture involves transportation over great distances – even of the bees required to fertilise Californian fruit trees. Globalisation now means that food is shipped over vast distances, sometimes with sound justification, sometimes just the opposite.

It couldn't have happened without abundant cheap oil. It took the drudgery out of agriculture. The Green Revolution succeeded in its aims in rich countries. In general, it caught up with and surpassed the needs of the global population for the first time. But it largely bypassed Africa. Whereas worldwide the average person today has 25 per cent more food than in 1960, in Africa they have 10 per cent less. However, as is so often the case with large-scale technological, science based revolutions, there were enormous unintended consequences. Amongst such unintended consequences were wine lakes, grain-mountains and loss of seed diversity. But we now know more; we're in the 21st century, a different situation, a different world.

A warning for those who believe world hunger can be solved by GM food! The Green Revolution also led to the steady destruction of a complex, intelligent, interconnected ecological system. European soil is badly degraded. More and more, industrial agriculture has destroyed the habitat of wildlife, including the bees and other insects essential for pollination. Since the 1950s over 90 per cent of traditionally managed, flower-rich hay meadows have disappeared, largely due to a shift from hay-making to silage production of food for cattle. The loss of meadows, hedgerows and ditches has had disastrous effects on bumble bees, honey bees and other insects needed to fertilise our crops.

The Green Revolution destroyed the natural balance that kept disease and pests under control. Soil was stripped of nutrition vital for plants. Our water supplies became polluted and required expensive filtration. Rivers became full of chemicals harmful to fish and the seas are increasingly affected by the runoff from field to river and other detritus. We are being deprived of essential mineral nutrients previously derived from the soil. There is more and more evidence of poisons in our bodies and our passing them on to our babies. Lack of research means we do not know the full extent to which this harms us; undermines our immune systems or causes growing epidemics such as cancer; effects on our fertility and children's behaviour. Unlike research to produce profitable new pharmaceuticals and develop medical technologies, such research is not in the commercial interests of Big Pharma. Often research exposing harms has been suppressed. But we do know that pesticides have terrible effects on poor people working in the fields in countries where precautions are less rigorously imposed; often resulting in cancers and shocking deformities in their children.

We have to rethink everything about how we feed ourselves. The globalisation of food cannot continue in its present form. We cannot allow millions to starve and continue as we do without regard for the consequences and the cost in terms of human suffering. Charity makes us feel better but is "first aid" that does not get to the root of the problem; a global economic system of exploitation that keeps people impoverished, dependent and disempowered. It is our responsibility to be informed, to understand the system and change the way our food is grown, prepared and distributed. If we ignore this challenge we face growing starvation, disease, civil unrest, mass-migration and resource wars.

Key Issues

What is the case for organic food?

Whether organic food is more nutritious and healthier (more research is needed), the case for organic food is broader. The Soil Association's poll of organic consumers provides their main reasons for choosing organic food:

Why Organic Food?

- **It is better for the planet and all life on it.**
- Quality and taste
- To avoid pesticide residues
- Better animal welfare
- Fair prices/wages for farmers
- Wildlife conservation
- To avoid food additives
- To avoid GM ingredients
- To know where food comes from
- Concerns about climate change

Is there a role for GM?

This is a hotly debated issue with many people believing that

GM provides the answer for a hungry world. Governments, there to protect us, are subjected to the lobbying by the GM industry, with vast sums of money to spend compared with more objective organisations. In *The Observer* 6 June 2010, it was revealed that a GM lobby helped UK's Foods Standards Agency (FSA), established to protect citizens, draw up a crucial report and influenced the UK Government in making overstated projections of world food needs.

Why GM Freeze?

GM Freeze summarises the apparent consensus amongst independent researchers. Similar views are also reflected in the UN World Food Programme described later in this chapter.

Genetic modification has the potential to cause massive social, economic and environmental effects worldwide. Some imported foods with genetically modified (GM) ingredients were introduced into the UK in the late 1990s without any public consultation or labelling. Widespread public concern followed and as a result of consumer pressure, UK supermarkets and food processors largely removed GM ingredients from their own-brand products. Despite the fact that most consumers do not want to eat GM food and many outstanding questions about its long-term effects remain, the British Government has given the go-ahead for the commercial growing of GM maize in the UK and consistently votes in favour of approval of new GM products at the European Union. Patents are being granted which give monopoly control of the world's genetic resources for food and farming to a few private corporations. Only the refusal of shoppers to buy GM food in the late 1990s prevented an avalanche of products reaching supermarket shelves.

However, the threat of poorly tested GM food and feed imports remains and constant vigilance is needed to ensure there is no creeping GM contamination in our food chain.

Biotechnology companies claim that genetic modification will "improve" our food, increase crop yields and reduce use of chemicals on farmland. But the need for this technology has not been proven. So far there is no convincing evidence of any "benefits" other than profit for the biotech industry. Genetic modification has dominated research and development to the extent that viable alternatives such as organic or other forms of sustainable farming have been neglected.

Genetic modification in food and farming raises many fundamental environmental, social, health and ethical concerns:

- GM has resulted in chemical resistant "super weeds".
- Pesticide residues in animal feeds are not monitored so we do not know what is being eaten.
- There is increasing evidence of the failure of segregation to prevent spreading contamination of conventional or organic crops and wild plants over long distances, and potential damage to wildlife.
- The effects on human health of eating these foods remain uncertain.
- There are questions about lowering nutritional content, damage to animal guts, problems with immune systems, impairing the fertility of mice.
- Some scientists are calling for much more rigorous safety testing.
- GM companies say we need GM animal feed to keep animal feed prices down but the costs are still going up.
- Because more GM is being rejected, more goes into animal feed but without labels; we don't know which dairy or meat products come from these animals. In 2006 NOP poll found that 87 per cent of those polled wanted labelling to help them avoid GM animal feed.
- It is clear that further research into all these issues is vital.
- Furthermore the public has not been properly involved in

decision-making processes, despite strong public support for the precautionary approach to GM in the UK and the EU.

Much more time is needed to assess the need for and implications of genetic modification in food and farming, and the increasing use of plant patents by corporations to secure their future markets.

GM Freeze believes that the following measures must be implemented before any further commercial use of GM:

- A system where people can exercise their right to choose products free of genetic modification
- Public involvement in the decisions on the need for and the regulation of genetic modification
- Prevention of genetic pollution of the environment
- Strict legal liability for adverse effects on people or the environment from the release and marketing of genetically modified organisms
- Independent assessment of the implications of patenting genetic resources
- Independent assessment of the social and economic impact of genetic engineering on farmers
- GM ingredients must refer to any ingredients that have been genetically modified or that contain derivatives from GM crops or organisms

"Golden rice" is an example. Introduced in India, it failed to deliver the promised nutritional benefits. As Vandana Shiva argued, the problem this rice was supposed to address was not deficiencies in the existing varieties but difficulties arising from poverty and loss of biodiversity in food crops. These are aggravated by the corporate control of agriculture based on genetically modified foods. By focusing on a narrow problem (vitamin A deficiency), she argued, the golden rice proponents were obscuring the larger issue of a lack of broad availability of diverse and nutritionally adequate food sources. It is alleged that exports of Chinese rice and processed foods were contaminated, despite government controls and a ban on GM exports. Japan, New Zealand and Australia now ban GM rice.

Holistic agro-ecological approaches. At the Feeding the World Conference, London, 12th November 2008,(organised by the Organic Research Centre in association with the *Ecologist*, Friends of the Earth, GM Freeze, UK Food Group, Slow Food UK and The Sheepdrove Trust), Dr Michael Antoniou, of King's College, London, explained that the GM transformation process is highly mutagenic, causing thousands of mutations with unknown consequences including impaired crop growth, reduced yields, reduced nutritional value of food, toxic effects and reactions in humans and animals. Fortunately there already exist many highly nutritious and tasty types and varieties of food crops that are naturally adapted to grow under harsh conditions and on marginal lands. "Marker assisted selection" (MAS) is generally accepted as a far more powerful, holistic, biological approach for further development in expanding non-GM biotechnology. It is a tool for safely developing new varieties from existing ones and their wild relatives. Recently scientists decoded the genome of an ancient wheat from which they believe new disease resistant varieties with higher yields can be developed.

Eric Kisiangani of Practical Action in Nairobi, Kenya argues that small-scale agriculture is by its very nature adaptive to climate change as has been demonstrated over millennia by farmers saving and exchanging seed and growing a wide variety of crops to manage risks. In Africa's complex farming environment, instead of advocating quick technology-fixes, more space for research into more effective crop protection, alternatives to GM and critical reflection ought to be supported. Efforts to promote GM technology, which brings large profits to corporations, take away attention from the more fundamental problems affecting African small-scale farmers. Dr Julia Wright, formerly of Garden Organic, reported that in Cuba an agro-ecological approach has transformed the micro-environment into a water-rich one, creating an environment that no longer suffered from drought.

Climate Change and Peak Oil will make the current food system unsustainable. Oil is embedded in agriculture, food production and distribution. Prices of fertilisers, insecticides and pesticides are likely to rise.

Are farmers paid enough? For example, the UK's 125,000 farm workers are amongst the lowest paid despite their high productivity and importance to our food security; they receive the smallest percentage of profits in the food industry; milk marketing co-operatives are closing, unable to pay their members. Their sons and daughters do not want that way of life. There are amazing exceptions like Rebecca Hoskin who decided to return to her family farm and make it a *Farm for the Future* – see YouTube. The fortunes of farmers everywhere are insecure because commodity prices are unstable and pressures are always upon them to reduce prices even below their costs. So they resort to increasingly unsustainable forms of animal husbandry.

Food sovereignty and security are essential requirements to which every nation has a right. Sovereignty means each nation has a right to protect its own food production and choose how it feeds its population. When we are threatened with the consequences of climate change, Peak Oil and the limits of spaceship Earth to provide for an increasing population, food security is a major global issue. Food security is at risk because of the industrialisation and globalisation of food and agriculture and its domination by a few enormous TRILLIONs – in agriculture, food production, distribution and retailing.

Andrew Simms, Policy Director of the New Economics Foundation (nef) says that 75 per cent of the world's food is grown from only 12 plant types and 5 animal species (Soil Association). Production methods are now such that 95 per cent of all the food we eat in the world today is oil-dependent. Diesel is used by farm vehicles and we must take into account the carbon footprint of chemical fertilisers used by most non-organic beef farms and energy required to transport a cow to the abattoir and process it.

Food security is very much an issue in the UK although many people may not realise this. In the UK, we import 90 per cent of our fruit, half our vegetables. Seventy per cent of animal feed in EU is imported. This leaves us extremely dependent on imports and vulnerable to the effects of climate change, declining supplies of oil and gas and hence rises, growing shortages of food and major fluctuations in commodity prices. Fluctuations in commodity prices will seriously affect our farmers unless we take appropriate measures. We are vulnerable to strikes amongst transport workers and other interruptions to world transport or trade. A few years ago, when truck drivers protested against fuel price rises, we had only three days' food stocks or nine meals per person in the supermarkets. Growing world demand for food as a result of population growth will affect us too. We are also vulnerable to the effects of international conflicts and possible wars.

Apparently the UK Government has no contingency plans.

Can huge transnational organisations be allowed to dominate food production? One of the most telling accounts of corporate domination of world food, supported by government subsidies, our money, is given in the Institute of Science in Society sustainability report the *Food, Inc.* Horror Movie.

Big food, drink, agribusiness and agrichemical businesses, often combined into conglomerates, bear heavy responsibility for poor diet and ill health all over the world. They have resisted change for a very long time and continue to do so, spending vast sums on PR, advertising and lobbying. The power wielded by large corporations, used unscrupulously, disempowers communities and erodes their autonomy. It creates clone towns and clone countries. It diminishes local initiative and localisation which we are now learning that we need. They undermine democracy. Supported by unfair world trade policies and governments, they expand into poor countries without considering the adverse consequences. These approaches have diminished food security, local resilience and seed and crop diversity. They contribute to the shift of population from rural areas to large cities where the poverty of landless people is extreme. They damage local food production, push people off their land and increase poverty. The imposition of large-scale Western agriculture undermines self-reliance, self-respect and traditional agriculture based on generations of experience. Old knowledge and expertise is lost.

A global food system dominated by a few corporations is dangerous. The system is designed to maximise the power and profit of a few enormous food, seed, and agrichemical and retail corporations. Too much power corrupts. Can we entrust our food supply to such companies? Can we rely on them to tell the truth? Do we really want to leave ourselves exposed like this? What if they collapsed like the banks? Every one of us is extremely vulnerable. In his book, *The End of Food*, Paul Roberts says:

> *Since the Thatcher Revolution in England in the 1970s and the Reagan era, what is called "free market" economics has been raised to the level of religious dogma in the industrial world, starting with Britain and the US. With the spread of GM seeds, this "marketization" process has taken on a dangerous new dimension.* (Roberts, R, 2008)

The Organic Consumers Association says that fewer than half a dozen giant multinational companies control the world market in GM seeds: Monsanto, Cargill and DuPont of the USA, Syngenta of Switzerland and one or two other smaller players. Monsanto is by far the dominant player, selling some 91 per cent of all GM seeds and most herbicides, with a total monopoly of GM seeds for certain crops like soybeans. Monsanto has been at the very heart of the biofuels lobby. Cargill is one of three companies controlling nearly 90 per cent of world grain trade. According to Food and Water Watch, Cargill contributed to the 2008 food crisis through its dominance in the cereal market and trading in food and energy futures markets.

The size and market share of big food corporations must be limited. The domination of supermarkets equally needs to be limited and a fair playing field created for small farmers and shopkeepers. In North and poor countries alike, this is needed in the interests of security, diversity, the ecological system and communities.

What is the future of international trade? What are the implications for food and poor countries? It's clear that the current level of international trade is unsustainable. The FEET index throws light on what to do. Transport Emissions are measured in grams CO2/tonne-kilometre and then Foreign Exchange Earnings per Transport tonne known as the FEET index.

Freight Emissions (grams CO_2 / tonne-kilometre)	
Air	
• Short-haul	1580
• Long-haul	570
Road	
• Van	97
• Medium truck	85
• Large truck	63
Ship	
• Roll on/Roll-off	40
• Bulk	10
Rail *	15

Sources: Sustain report *Eating Oil – Food supply in a changing climate*. And *Freight on Rail Partnership.

Poor countries need foreign currency. But some trade may harm their economies and their people, especially their small farmers, ***and*** have an adverse effect on the world's sustainability. Often the financial benefits never reach the farmers simply because commodity prices are very low, compared to the profits from export/import trading, distribution and retail. Potential benefits to farmers and the general population are frequently siphoned off through corruption. According to Supachai Panitchpakdi, Secretary-General of UNCTAD, trading in commodities, like food, rarely brings benefits to poor countries.

A high FEET rating shows when a product is very beneficial in the contribution to currency relative to CO_2 emissions. The figures compare food with Software, Wind-up Baygen radios and tourism:

Foreign Exchange Earnings per Transport Tonne	
• Software by electronic mode	Extremely high
• Wind-up Baygen radios by road/sea	Very high
• Good quality wine by road/sea	High
• Apples by road/sea	Medium
• Grapes by road/ sea	Very low
• Tourism by return air	Very low

The general message is clear: the lighter, less bulky the product and the more sustainable the mode of transport, the better it is for the planet; the small farmer and local people will usually benefit more from local production and sale. In general, that is a win-win everywhere. It makes more sense to have international trade in high value, low weight items like software and other expensive products rather than charcoal and other cheap, high weight and bulk or high CO2 items.

Despite the insistence of politicians to the contrary, international trade needs to be the exception rather than the rule. That is a difficult adjustment to make but we must make it if the human species is to survive. We also need to introduce the notion of *"Work and Enterprise Sovereignty"* so that nations are not powerless to protect work and jobs in the face of global sourcing for lowest cost and least protection for workers. Otherwise, it's a race to the bottom. Governments are beginning to realise that some takeovers by foreign companies, like the recent takeover of Cadbury by Kraft, are not in the national interest.

Bioregionalism. Almost certainly bioregionalism will be a major part of a transformed global economy by developing prosperous and sustainable local and regional economies, so as to reduce the need to transport goods over vast distances, secure adequate resources everywhere and address the huge differences in well-being. Bioregionalism could play a large part in building self-sufficiency and releasing creative energy.

Wikipedia defines bioregionalism as:

A political, cultural, and environmental system based on naturally-defined areas. Bioregions are defined through physical and environmental features, including watershed boundaries and soil and terrain characteristics. Bioregionalism stresses that the determination of a bioregion is also a cultural phenomenon, and emphasizes local populations, knowledge, and solutions.

In UK, bioregionalism could rejuvenate less prosperous regions and address the overconcentration on London and the South East. It could help overcome joblessness and the waste of skills and lives in the North. Less new building would be needed in the overcrowded South East, where nature's resources and infrastructure already severely overstretched.

Whole system change is needed. Miguel d'Escoto Brockmann, President of the UN General Assembly, at the High-level Event on the Millennium Development Goals, 25 September 2008, referring to the goal to eliminate poverty, said that for the first time in history we have the capacity to do this. However, unfair trade practices, developed countries' lavish agricultural subsidies, not only of food exports to poor countries but also of fertilisers, delay development and shut poor countries out of markets while high taxes on poor countries' products amount to a "perverse tax". The Assembly must garner the strong sense of solidarity and awaken the political will to turn this crisis into an opportunity to transform a world system that denies the poor a right as basic as the right to food. He noted the World Bank's conclusion is that 75 per cent of the increase in food prices stems from the rapidly growing demand for biofuels.

Here are edited extracts from his address:

- **Only a fraction of international aid is earmarked for improving agricultural productivity.** Faced with today's world food crisis we must speak out on behalf of our brothers and sisters and say, "This is not right." Now is the time to help the poorest countries to boost their food and agricultural production. Together these factors have shaped a food production system that puts private economic interests ahead of people's basic dietary needs.
- **The essential purpose of food, which is to nourish people, has been subordinated to the economic aims of a handful of multinational corporations** that monopolize all aspects of food production, from seeds to major distribution chains, and they have been the prime beneficiaries of the world crisis. A look at the figures for 2007, when the world food crisis began, shows that corporations such as Monsanto and Cargill, which control the cereals market, saw their profits increase by 45 and 60 per cent, respectively; the leading chemical fertilizer companies such as Mosaic Corporation, a subsidiary of Cargill, doubled their profits in a single year.
- **At the same time, in response to the financial crisis, major hedge funds have shifted millions of dollars into agricultural products.** These funds control 60 per cent of the supply of wheat and other basic grains. Most of these crops are purchased as "futures". In other words, speculators have beenincreasingly active in food-related financial markets.
- **Today, 3 billion 140 million people live on less than $2.50 a day.** Of these, about 44 per cent survive on less than $1.25 a day, according to a new World Bank report issued on 2 September 2008. Every day, more than 30,000 people die of malnutrition, avoidable diseases and hunger. Some 85 per cent of themare children under the age of five.
- **The top 10 per cent of the world's people possess 84 per cent of the world's wealth,** while the rest are left with the

remaining 16 per cent. Yet we have the technical and productive capacity to adequately feed the whole planet. It is a matter of reorienting our priorities.

Ways Forward

Global proposals

The World Food Programme

This 2008 report was prepared by the International Assessment on Agricultural Knowledge, Science and Technology for Development. It is a truly independent assessment. The process used to create this report was "path-breaking" in the sense that it was ***truly inclusive*** and embraced governments, major research institutions, industry and NGOs or civil society groups and stakeholders from all over the world. Its work on GM, for example, involved hundreds of scientists and experts whose rigorous work was peer-reviewed. It has been widely accepted, approved by 57 governments in somewhat watered down form. It took three years to complete and involved analysis of 114 projects in 24 African countries. However, Canada, Australia, the UK and USA did not sign the formal report and the USA claiming it unbalanced. GM companies, though initially involved, withdrew their support because of its conclusions.

The report called for rich countries to contribute $500m (£255m) to address a growing global food crisis in which staple food prices had risen up to 80 per cent in some countries and there were riots in many cities. According to the World Bank, 33 countries are in danger of political destabilisation and internal conflict because of rising food prices. The authors said the world produces enough food for everyone, yet more than 800 million people go hungry.

The general message is that small-scale farmers and agro-ecological methods provide the way forward to avert the current food crisis and meet the needs of local communities. More equitable trade policies, increased investment in science and technologies and sharing knowledge that support agro-ecological approaches in both small farm and larger scale sectors are needed. For the first time, it says, there is an independent, global assessment that acknowledges that farming has diverse environmental and social functions and nations and peoples have the right to democratically determine their best food and agricultural policies.

In his article *Organic farming 'could feed Africa'*, on the Third World Network site, Daniel Howden says:

> *Conventional wisdom among African governments is that modern, mechanised agriculture was needed to close the gap but efforts in this direction have had little impact on food poverty and have done nothing to create a sustainable approach… The research conducted by the UN Environment Programme suggests that organic, small-scale farming can deliver the increased yields which were thought to be the preserve of industrial farming, without the environmental and social damage which that form of agriculture brings with it. The study found that organic practices outperformed traditional methods and chemical-intensive conventional farming.*

Robert Watson, director of IAASTD and chief scientist at the UK Department for Environment, Food and Rural Affairs said:

> *"Business as usual will hurt the poor. It will not work. We have to applaud global increases in food production but not everyone has benefited. We have not succeeded globally."* Governments and industry focus too narrowly on increasing food production, with little regard for natural resources or food security. *"Continuing with current trends would mean the Earth's haves and have-nots splitting further apart. It would leave us facing a world nobody would want to inhabit. We have to make food more affordable and nutritious without degrading the land."*

General Conclusions

- **Protection of soils and habitat** Science and technology should be targeted towards raising yields but also protecting soils, water and forests.
- **Investment in agricultural science** is urgently needed to find sustainable ways to produce food.
- **Incentives for science to address the issues that matter** to the poor are weak.
- **Little role for GM** as currently practised. The short answer to whether transgenic crops can feed the world is 'no'. They could contribute but we must understand their costs and benefits.
- **The global rush to biofuels** was unsustainable; diversion of crops to fuel can raise food prices and reduce our ability to alleviate hunger; negative social effects where small-scale farmers are marginalised or displaced from their land.

Individual members and NGOs comments

- **Failure of industrial farming** A sobering account of the failure of industrial farming; small-scale farmers and ecological methods provide the way forward to avert the current food crisis and meet the needs of communities.
- **Small-scale farmers** and the environment lose under trade liberalisation. Developing countries must exercise their right to stop the flood of cheap subsidised products from the North.
- **Fossil fuels** We need an agriculture that is less dependent on fossil fuels, favours the use of locally available resources and explores the use of natural processes such as crop rotation and use of organic fertilizers.

- **Bio-energy** Biofuel crops compete for land and water with food crops, are inefficient and can cause deforestation and damage soils and water. Biofuels from renewable sources that do not compete with food or damage the ecological system and reusing spent fats are no problem.
- **Biotechnology** The use of GM crops, where the technology is not contained, is contentious, the UN says. Data on some crops indicate highly variable yield gains in some places and declines in others.
- **Climate change** While modest temperature rises may increase food yields in some areas, general warming risks damaging all regions of the globe
- **Trade and markets** Subsidies distort the use of resources and benefit industrialised nations at the expense of developing countries.

Sources: *Organic farming 'could feed Africa'*, Howden, D, Third World Network; "Change in Farming Can Feed World – Report", by John Vidal, environment editor, *The Guardian*, Wednesday, 16 April 2008

The United Nations Environment Programme study – A Green revolution could feed the world

The United Nations Environment Programme study entitled *The Environmental Food Crisis: Environment's Role in Averting Future Food Crisis,* issued in February 2009, added to the picture. It found that yields more than doubled when organic or near organic practices, which improved soil quality, were used; yields jumped by 128 per cent in East Africa. This report also favours organic methods for feeding the world proposed by the World Food Programme and it cites the evidence of successful small-scale farms in Africa. It predicts that organic agriculture will continue to grow, despite the economic crisis, and that sales of certified organic produce could reach close to $70bn 2012, up from $23bn in 2002.

> *There is evidence within the report that the world could feed the entire projected population growth alone by becoming more efficient while also ensuring the survival of wild animals, birds and fish on this planet.*
> **Achim Steiner**, UNEP executive director

He continues: *"We need a Green revolution in a Green Economy but one with a capital G."* Increasing the use of fertiliser and pesticide-led production methods of the 20th century is not the answer. *"It will increasingly undermine the critical natural inputs and nature-based services for agriculture such as healthy and productive soils, the water and nutrient recycling of forests, and pollinators such as bees and bats."*

Bottom-up Initiatives

Common themes. All over the world, initiatives are emerging that put the emphasis on local food.

The Hunger Project: Empowering women and men to end their own hunger.

The Hunger Project (THP) began in 1977, triggered by the first Rome World Food Conference. It has initiated projects in many countries, constantly re-inventing itself and learning from experience. THP only works in countries into which it has been invited. Its focus is on chronic, persistent hunger. Typical top-down and charitable approaches are believed to fail in achieving lasting improvements. The Hunger Project develops a grass-roots, decentralised, holistic, people-centred approach after a thorough review of the situation on the ground and finding out what keeps chronic persistent hunger in place.

The underlying principle is self-sufficiency. It is undoing the effect of colonialism. Rather than providing financial aid, help is offered through training leaders and help in building community centres. It encourages communities to get financial and other support from the country authorities themselves. The Hunger Project uses an approach called Strategic Planning in Action (SPIA) and a process called VCA – Vision, Commitment and Action. Selected villagers are trained in VCA and later become leaders and trainers in their communities, thus reaching many more people.

About 20,000 villages in Asia, Africa and Latin America have applied SPIA to empower people to achieve lasting improvements in health, education, nutrition and family income. Women grow the majority of food for household consumption in Africa and are almost completely bypassed by official efforts to improve food for households. In 1999, the Hunger Project launched a new initiative demonstrating effective training and credit, empowering tens of thousands of African women food farmers and awakened policy makers to the fact that Africa's future depends on their future. THP promoted high standards of leadership in Africa through the creation of the Africa Prize for Leadership and created local activities managed by the villagers through the creation of Epicentres.

South Asia has the highest rates of childhood malnutrition and its women suffer severe subjugation. In 2000 the Hunger Project launched an initiative to provide leadership training to 70,000 elected women, built networks of on-going support and mobilised the media for public support. In 2003 the Hunger Project launched a campaign based on the AIDS and Gender Inequality Workshop to empower people to protect themselves and alter behaviours that spread the disease. This has trained 600,000 people. In 2004, Jean Holmes founding president of the Hunger Project was appointed to serve on the UN Millennium Project Hunger Taskforce. She used this opportunity to focus attention and launch a campaign to transform the way the world "does" development, recognising that bottom-up, gender-focused strategies are the only viable way to achieve the Millennium Goals on a sustainable basis. The Hunger Project works with their own Millennium Project's Country Directors in strategic action to achieve its aims.

Dr Makanjuola Olaseinde Arigbede – In Search of Food Sovereignty

This description of his work draws on an article by Jocelyn Jones and Louis Loizou in their World Family Ning.

Food Sovereignty is central to the work of Dr Makanjuola Olaseinde Arigbede. I met him at a weekend event in the Brecon Beacons, *Walk Your Talk,* organised by the Association of Sustainability Practitioners. He came to my meeting about the need to change the global economic system. We saw eye-to-eye and became firm friends. I saw a leader of profound integrity, great courage with a radical understanding of what is wrong with the system as it affects ordinary and poor people all over the world.

Dr Olaseinde Arigbede, a medical doctor and neuroscientist, former postgraduate fellow of University College Los Angeles, chose to become a smallholder farmer in his native Nigeria thus discovering the hardships of the poor, the challenges of farming, the resilience and innovative capacity of those who have tended the land for millennia. In this way, he earned the credentials and insight to lead smallholder farmers in their struggles. Olaseinde and Oladunni, his wife and partner, cultivate a beautiful farm of maize, pineapples, yam and cassava, and much more.

They are joint National Coordinators of the United Small and Medium Scale Farmers' Associations of Nigeria, a peasant federation and umbrella organisation for civil society organisations, a "voice for the voiceless" with branches in most of Nigeria's 36 states, a strong Women's Platform and a vigorous Youth Platform. In December 2008 Students of USMEFAN, supported by their elders, organised and presented the Global Youth Festival for Food Sovereignty at Obafemi Awolowo University, Ile-Ife. They celebrated with debates and discussions, music and drumming and theatre. Students and farmers came on long treks from north, west and east Nigeria.

World Family. During a visit with Jocelyn Jones in Brighton, UK, the idea of forming World Family emerged. World Family's focus is on developing collaborations with African farmers to avert the dangers of land grabs, agro-fuels and the patenting of life by genetically modifying peoples' seeds. The underlying work is to support smallholder farmers everywhere to produce food in a way that is ecologically sound, sustainable and fits in with their culture – Food Sovereignty. This is only possible if many young people take up farming.

World Family links together farmers' associations and connects them with interested people, advocacy organisations and resources that free and do not bind them. Current membership is mostly from Africa, the UK and USA. It is essentially about people-to-people solidarity. Celebration through music, dance, theatre, film and discussion is key.

World Family has grown to include two other groundbreaking schemes in Africa:

Better World Cameroon. This community-based organisation focuses on training young people in biodiversity conservation and natural resource management, raising public awareness of biodiversity and its great contribution towards food security and poverty alleviation in Cameroon. Many projects are planned particularly in the field of Permaculture.

The Gambia Community Empowerment Project (GCEP) inspired by local families addresses widespread poverty and unemployment in The Gambia. Its community centre provides workspace to tradespeople and artisans, in exchange for training to empower self-sufficiency in the youth.

At Nyéléni à Sélingué village in Mali, over five hundred

women, men and youth activists from 80 countries met to share their knowledge, experiences, and hopes for a world free of hunger, injustice, and corporate greed. The Bámbara legend of Nyeleni, the peasant woman who resisted oppression and taught her people how to feed themselves, provided the deep cultural symbolism that led the way to dialogue, learning, and political alliances between sectors and across industrial divides. **Declaration of Nyeleni: World Forum on Food Sovereignty.** When they had done their work they made a declaration available in full at the Land Research and Action Network website. Here is a summary:

- **Food sovereignty is** the right of peoples to healthy and culturally appropriate food produced through ecologically sound and sustainable methods, and their right to define their own food and agriculture systems.
- **It puts those who produce, distribute and consume food at the heart of food systems and policies** rather than the demands of markets and corporations. It defends the interests and inclusion of the next generation.
- **It offers a strategy to resist and dismantle the current corporate trade and food regime,** and directions for food, farming, pastoral and fisheries ***systems*** determined by local producers.
- **Food sovereignty prioritises local and national economies and markets and empowers peasant and family farmer-driven agriculture**, artisanal-fishing, pastoralist-led grazing, and food production, distribution and consumption based on environmental, social and economic ***sustainability***.
- **Food sovereignty promotes transparent trade that guarantees just income to all peoples** and the rights of consumers to control their food ***and*** nutrition. It ensures that the rights to use and manage our lands, territories,

waters, seeds, livestock and biodiversity are in the hands of those of us who produce food.

- **Food sovereignty implies new social relations free of oppression and inequality** between men and women, peoples, racial groups, social classes and ***generations***.

Food sovereignty is of the very essence of Human Freedom. For Olaseinde's key statements go to *My World Family Ning: Video – Discussions with Olaseinde.*

The following account is adapted from Practical Action's website.

Practical Action was founded in 1966, under a different name, by the radical economist Dr EF Schumacher in the belief that his philosophy of "Small is Beautiful" could bring real and sustainable improvements to people's lives. Their aim is to contribute to bringing about a world free of poverty, through poverty reduction, environmental conservation and technology choice. Practical Action believes the simplest ideas can have the most profound, life-changing effect on poor people across the world. For over 40 years, they have been working closely with some of the world's poorest people using simple technology to fight poverty and transform lives for the better.

The approach is holistic. They don't start with technology, but with people. Tools to provide long-term, appropriate and practical answers must be firmly in the hands of local people: people who shape technology and control it for themselves. Practical Action believes that the right idea, however small, can change lives. It can create jobs, improve health and livelihoods, and help people have better lives. The focus is on four key areas:

- **Reducing vulnerability** of poor people affected by natural disasters, conflict and environmental degradation.
- **Making markets work for the poor.** Helping poor people to make a better living by enabling producers to improve

their production, processing and marketing.

- **Improving access to services.** Helping poor communities gain access to basic services: water, sanitation, housing and electricity.
- **New technologies.** Helping poor communities respond to the challenges of new technologies, helping them to access effective technologies that can change their lives.

Practical Action is implementing over 100 projects worldwide. Their consultancy and educational work further extends their reach. In total, in 2006/2007, they outreached to some 664,000 people.

Through their work, they demonstrate alternatives, share knowledge and influence change.

- **Tackling the underlying causes of poverty by campaigning** to influence policies, institutions and processes. Through campaigning and advocacy, Practical Action aims to achieve greater and more lasting impact from their work.
- **Technical Information Service,** Practical Answers, aims to provide a means of accessing the wealth of technical information held by Practical Action, through technical briefs or the resource centre.
- **Education** offering a range of support services for teachers and young people in the UK looking to address sustainable development within their teaching and learning.
- **Lessons from Practical Action's grassroots experience** are also spread through consultancy services and publishing activities.

Micro Credit

Micro Credit inspired by Grameen Bank in Bangladesh whose

founder, Nobel Prize winner Muhammad Yunus, pioneered microfinance loans for poor women in Bangladesh. There are now many similar schemes for poor people to help them start small businesses and lift themselves out of poverty and hunger. The Grameen Bank operates 1,092 branches in 36,000 rural Bangladesh villages, providing credit to over two million of the country's poorest people. It has loaned more than US$2 billion. This new banking system providing unsecured credit to the poorest of the poor began as an action-research project at Chittagong University and later grew into a full-fledged bank. Grameen Bank's patrons are 94 per cent women who have an unparalleled repayment rate of 98 per cent.

Likely Directions

To help poorer countries, the emphasis must be on strengthening local capacity and infrastructure and thinking about how to provide aid in a way that does not undermine local producers and traders. The way ahead becomes clearer and, with appropriate adaptations, applies to countries rich and poor.

The Possibility

- Bioregionalism, working with natural advantages, will be the basis for the global economy
- "Cheap food", not really cheap, is over; good food will be the name of the game
- Global collaboration and co-operation will be seen as essential to survival
- Global trade will focus on high FEET (Foreign Exchange Earnings per Transport tonne) and whatever cannot be produced locally
- Inhumane, industrialised rearing of cows, pigs and hens is over

- Local food shops, selling good, mostly local, food, will become more important
- Minds will change – food diversity, food security and ecology will become mainstream
- Organic and eco-agriculture will play a much greater part; industrialised agriculture and food will play a lesser part; it looks unlikely that GM in its present form will contribute
- Smaller scale or intermediate technology, agriculture and distribution systems will grow
- Supermarkets will adapt, change their distribution systems and source locally and nationally; some may become market halls for local food suppliers
- Unfair competition against small retailers and "bearing down" on small suppliers will be addressed
- We'll consume less meat and dairy
- We'll go back to eating in season – except for luxuries – and more home cooking.
- We'll grow more food in gardens, allotments, community food gardens, market gardens and farms again
- Wealthy nations will stop plundering the rest of the world.
- World farmers, especially smaller ones, will get a fair deal

We need a transformation from Stupid to Not Stupid economics. One thing is certain: we are entering an era in which everything will change dramatically. Simple-minded "solutions" will not work. The way forward will be much more complex and diverse than dogmas such as free market competition, sourcing for lowest cost, free trade and continuous economic growth. Ways forward will emerge through embracing diversity, sharing and collaboration. This will require Subsidiarity at global, national, bioregional and local levels. Instead of being dominated by multinational corporations, governments and global bodies must represent people's interests. And, maybe we'll all be happier, healthier and live a saner life at a saner pace!

Global Action: Take personal action and lobby and demonstrate to get our governments, politicians and global institutions to do the right thing. Target the next UN Summit and Common Agricultural Policy (CAP) to ensure it works for, not against, social, health and environmental benefits and global trade reform. Use: Ethical Consumer, Food and Water Watch, GM Freeze, Jeevika, Janadesh - Retrieving People's Dignity through Land and Livelihood, La Via Campesina, Practical Action, Slow Food, Vandana Shiva, World Hunger Project. World Family Ning contact: louisishere@msn.com

Local Action: City Farms and Community Gardens, Community Gardens, Community Supported Agriculture; Compassion in World Farming, Country Markets, Farmers' Markets; Farmers' Supermarkets NEF, Food and Mental Health, Friends of the Earth, Garden Organic, Guerrilla Gardening, Landshare – making spare land available for growing food, Schools Organic, National Farmers' Retail & Markets Association (FARMA), Organic Farmers and Growers, Organic Targets Campaign, Sustain – supporting good food, children's food, food in cities, London's Food Link, Soil Association, Sustain and Transition Towns Network.

Further reading:

- FEET Index
- Desai, P and Riddlestone, S, 2002, *Bioregional Solutions: For Living on One Planet (Schumacher Briefing no 8)*, p 59, Green Books, UK.

Chapter 13:

Sustainable Cities, Towns and Communities

June 2009

What sustainability means, localisation vs. globalisation, hi tech vs. low tech, positive models, many good things are happening

> *All truth passes through three stages. First, it's ridiculed. Second, it's violently opposed. Third, it is accepted as self-evident.*
> **Arthur Schopenhauer**

Cities and towns are now our major habitat

In 2007, the Earth became an urban planet, more than half its population living in cities. By 2060, over 60 per cent of the population will live in cities. Of the 2.2bn increase in population forecast by the United Nations Environmental Programme (UNEP), 2.1 billion will live in urban areas. Already in the UK, 90 per cent of us live in urban places.

People like living in cities. *"Cities are good for us,"* as Harley Sherlock said in his valuable book of that title but only if they are designed for people, not just for the benefit developers. Young people, especially, like cities because of the buzz, the excitement, the diverse opportunities for work as well as abundant social and leisure pursuits. Older people like them too. That said, many cities produce huge social problems, pollution, gross inequalities, poverty and lack of opportunity.

In many ways, cities are more sustainable than other places. The issue is to make cities more sustainable. Towns are basically mini-cities and the same principles apply.

In the following section, I am indebted to the *Ecologist* special issue "Sustainable Cities: rethinking sustainable building" for many insights.

What is a Sustainable City?

In his book *Creating Sustainable Cities* Herbert Girardet describes his vision of cities for people:

Cities for People

- Involve the whole person – mind, spirit and body
- Place long-term stewardship above short-term satisfaction
- Ensure justice and fairness informed by civic responsibility
- Identify the appropriate scale of viable human activities
- Encourage diversity within the unity of a given community
- Develop the precautionary principles, anticipating the effects of our actions
- Ensure that our use of resources does not diminish the living environment

(Adapted from Girardet, H, 1999, *Creating Sustainable Cities*, Green Books)

His superbly illustrated *Cities People Planet: Liveable Cities for a Sustainable World* is a "must read" for anyone wishing to help create a sustainable city, town, district, village, neighbourhood or community.

Another inspiration is Richard Rogers' vision, abbreviated here:

The Sustainable City

- A Just City
- A Beautiful City
- A Creative City
- An Ecological City
- A City of Easy Contact and Mobility
- A Compact and Polycentric City
- A Diverse City

Adapted from Rogers, R, 1998, *Cities for a Small Planet*

A Polycentric City is one with multiple centres – main centres or sub centres or both. That is one of the attractions of London with its villages. The same principle needs to apply to towns beyond a certain size i.e. beyond what is a comfortable walking distance for people of most if not all ages.

We know intuitively what a sustainable city is. We sense "spirit of place". Sustainable cities and towns are the places we want to live in, be young in, bring up our family in, create a business in, work in, retire to, visit or go to for a holiday. Some, like Ludlow, are expensive because of their desirability. Incidentally, despite many protests, Ludlow citizens were unable to stop Tesco from spoiling part of their town, endangering what makes it attractive. Others like Llandidloes in Wales are not expensive, particularly if they do not have a railway station. Living in such places often means a lot of driving. They are communities offering the characteristics mentioned in Happy Planet indexes. They give a sense of well-being, partly because so much is uniquely local; partly because they are places people are proud of, where they are aware of their roots and their past. The scale is human and there is texture, craftsmanship and art in buildings and pride in manual achievements. Local materials and traditions add to their uniqueness.

People want to live in places that are alive and good for people of all ages, not ghettos for any group in society, where there is an exciting variety of good building from various periods including modern. Such cities are very much lived in, not full of great ugly blocks resembling fortresses built to exploit the location and make the maximum profit, not dreadful ugly areas from which nature has been excluded and people feel alienated. There are individual shops and places to eat, rather than international chains, contributing to, rather than extracting wealth from, the local economy. They are cities for people, not for cars and big noisy vehicles. You can tell: people look happier. You can see it in their faces.

Amongst many examples are Brighton, Barcelona, Edinburgh and Montpellier. People enjoy themselves outside, sometimes in gardens in the middle of wide streets or tucked into unexpected corners. Fitness classes are held in the central square of Montpellier. They have sustainable transport systems, trams in Montpellier, cycle lanes and cycles to borrow or hire in Bristol and Barcelona. They are good to walk and live in. They have markets, good local food, mixtures of old and new. I think of smaller places in Italy like Lucca and Spoleto in parts of which cars are excluded. They are holistic and exemplify Herbert Girardet's and Richard Rogers' models.

What we do not know intuitively. The places we live in must now have low ecological and carbon footprints. That is the huge challenge facing us. There is a limit to what individual citizens and citizens' organisations like a Transition Town can do. ***Only government and councils*** can provide the infrastructure and services necessary to help our towns and communities adapt to climate change and Peak Oil: better transport, more room for cyclists and pedestrians, ways of reducing congestion, better waste disposal for small businesses, better town planning, better design and building of sustainable developments including up-to-date heat and power and space for vegetable growing and wildlife. Woking, Sutton, Bristol and Nottingham are shining examples.

The destruction of our towns, cities and communities

"Clone town Britain" has already been described. Beautiful, historic, homely small-scale areas in our towns and cities, with small shops, where people feel a sense of community and roots, are destroyed without our agreement. It is an outrage when, in order to meet imposed regional targets, the wishes of citizens are ignored and unsustainable, out-of-scale, poor quality developments are created, lacking proper infrastructure, or adequate consideration of the limits of the ecosystem and the needs of people facing Peak Oil and climate change.

Something similar to the Haussmannisation of Paris in the nineteenth century happened in UK after World War Two. But the results were not good. Post war redevelopment went too far and was a huge disappointment. "Slum clearance" and redevelopment destroyed more of Georgian and Victorian London than Hitler's bombs. Swathes of potentially sustainable communities were levelled. "Clone Towns" were inflicted on almost every town and city by multinational chains, superstores, supermarkets – ugly roads too. New Labour planned to demolish 250,000 houses in the North of England, and build a million new homes in the North and South of England. Is this the right way to go? We have had an increasingly strong conservation movement since the sixties e.g. the Victorian Society and other pressure groups like the Homes under Threat (HUT).

The Sustainable Communities Act, if adopted by councils, and the coalition's Big Society vision, giving more power to citizens, can help communities halt this damage and become more sustainable. Pressure works.

What kind of world do we want to build?

In Chapter 11, I argued that vast new developments, regeneration schemes, privately managed and policed, are a threat to democracy and civil liberties. I drew attention to the growing trend towards the gated communities in Britain with "hot spots" of affluence and "cold spots" of exclusion. These reflect a post industrial economy in which there are on the one hand increasingly wealthy, high earning, knowledge workers in globalised financial services industries and, on the other, rising numbers of "excluded" people on very low pay, of whom 2.7m are on sickness benefit or have dropped out of the system into the "black economy".

Worsening the gap between two societies. Schemes like these worsen the gap between two societies making nonsense of government targets and expensive measures to reverse these trends and overcome poverty. This is another example of "system blindness". We have seen vast new developments, regeneration schemes, *"retail-led development"*, *"malls without walls"*, described by New Labour as *"urban renaissance"*. Most vast retail projects create bland, characterless environments and drive out small businesses. Enabled through Business Improvement Districts (BIDs) introduced in the Local Government Act 2003, they were justified on the grounds of efficiency (i.e. shops of 3,000 sq metres are far more efficient than the average size of 500 sq metres). Is efficiency all that life is about? Is the nation's life about shopping, spending and big business, rather than the well-being of all its citizens and small, local business people?

Anna Minton, in her RICS report, commented:

> *This means a further boost for big retailers operating in sterile, privatised enclaves where several activities are banned – from rollerblading and skateboarding to handing out leaflets – while the spontaneous organic life of the city that encourages people to stroll*

and linger is squeezed out.

Lost opportunities to create exemplary sustainable cities and communities. In encouraging schemes of this kind, Girardet's and Rogers' vision of sustainable cities and communities was set aside. The advice of respected sustainability advisers was ignored. Government was more influenced by McKinsey's. We lost opportunities to create exemplary sustainable cities and communities comparable to those in other countries. New Labour was conned. It needed values based on whole system thinking.

Anna Minton quotes Jan Gehl, the architect credited with turning around the city of Copenhagen: *"If you asked people 20 years ago why they went to central Copenhagen, they would have said it was to shop. But if you asked them today, they would say it was because they wanted to go to town [to take in the atmosphere]."* She says Gehl's focus on creating public space has been remarkable for the Danish capital, with four times as many people spending time in the city. Its thriving public life is widely acknowledged as something to emulate. Other Scandinavian cities, such as Stockholm and Gothenburg, offer a similarly appealing environment.

Britons love the public squares and piazzas of cities in mainland Europe. While the rhetoric of government proclaimed a similar cafe-style urban renaissance in towns and cities, policy headed in the opposite direction towards *"retail-led development"* i.e. *"shopping makes places"*, meaning shopping in large chain stores. Articles on Anna Minton's website, in particular *Political Footfall* and *Can We Banish Fear and Loathing from the City? From shopping malls to gated communities, our city centres are turning into secure enclaves that erode trust,* reveal how the UK is failing to learn from mainland Europe how to make cities attractive for reasons other than chain-store shopping.

In Paris, French policy makers became so concerned about

the British experience, described as *"la Londonisation"* that they have introduced planning regulations specifically to prevent it. About half the shops in Paris will have restrictions placed on them to prevent changes of use. A food shop remains a food shop and a bookshop or a greengrocer cannot become part of a mobile phone chain. The French are in the vanguard against a trend predicted by the French sociologist, Henri Lefebvre, more than 30 years ago. He warned that treating a place simply as a product, with the aim of extracting the maximum return from it, would lead to the creation of many identical units of similar places, what we now call "Clone town Britain". If we don't act, shopping streets like the Lanes in Brighton will become the exception.

Independently owned shops are hubs of community life. Not only can small-scale shopping be cheaper; there is a growing body of evidence that the replacement of independently-owned shops, which have often been the hub of community life for a generation or more, isolates people and increases depression.

> *This should surely not be surprising, given that it is everyday experiences – such as talking to someone or exchanging a smile in the local shop – that adds up to quality of life in a local community. As in northern Europe, having a thriving public life in cities does not depend simply on the types of shops but on the approach to the place as a whole and what a successful place is seen to be .*

I am indebted to Anna Minton for her insights.

London is a wonderful city that people love to come to, especially young people, from all over the world. They say it is tolerant of diversity, exciting and good to live in. But it has problems on a vast scale of which many visitors may not be fully aware: an enormous eco-footprint, it is wasting vast amounts of energy and spewing out CO2 on a grand scale; pollution, both noise and air; massive waste and unbalanced land use.

Additionally, there are extreme differences in wealth and living conditions that, up until now, have been growing rapidly. Some areas breed hopelessness, anger, crime and violence.

As cities grow bigger, their footprint enlarges. London used to be more self-sufficient in food and materials. It had market gardens which used "night soil". It did more recycling – look at the wood from battleships used to build the interior of Liberty's great store. It had a growing empire supplying it with materials and unimaginable things to consume – a quarter of the world labouring to create wealth for its citizens in Queen Victoria's time – the Royal Albert Hall for instance. Slaves in plantations helped build Bristol and Liverpool. Now London's size is far surpassed by huge new cities in India and China.

London's "great stink" in 1858 was so bad that debates in the House of Commons were halted. Something had to be done about the stench and threat to health. Justus Liebig proposed a system that would reclaim precious plant nutrients and restore them to the land – nitrogen, potash, phosphate, magnesium and calcium. His scheme was discarded in favour of Joseph Bazalgette's solution, which was to pour human waste into the sea. That is what most cities do today. Berlin chose a wiser solution and reclaimed its sewerage for about 100 years until 1985 when it was abandoned because of industrial contamination. We need to use our "night soil" again in a better way. Technology has mastered how to extract precious water **and** nutrients from sewage and return them to the land.

Good Models – study what works

Innovative leadership

BedZED, the Beddington Zero Energy Development is one of the most important exemplars for large to small-scale development, a ***"must see"*** for anyone concerned with sustainable developments. The story of BedZED exemplifies a key message: A few inspired leaders who collaborate with each other bring about paradigm change. That message will recur throughout these models.

It is an environmentally-friendly, energy-efficient mix of housing and work space at Beddington, in the London Borough of Sutton. People come from all over the world to see it. It demonstrates the possibilities for mixed housing and office development. It is holistic in that it attempts to embody every aspect of what sustainable living means. It was built for and is occupied by typical "ordinary" people, many of whom have become more environmentally aware as a result of living or working there. Sutton, an exceptionally enlightened borough council, is now embarking on an eco-refurbishment project, whose progress is well worth following.

BedZED is the first large-scale "carbon neutral" community i.e. the first not to add to the amount of carbon dioxide in the atmosphere and was built from 2000 to 2002 on reclaimed land sold by the Borough of Sutton to the Peabody Trust at below market value. It comprises of 82 houses, 17 apartments and 1,405 square meters of workspace. Fifty per cent of homes are allocated to low income families.

It shows how the demand for housing can be met without destroying the countryside or damaging the environment. It shows how an eco-friendly lifestyle can be easy, affordable and attractive, something that ordinary people will want. BedZED offers a myriad of energy and resource saving measures, including maximising water reuse, reducing waste and decreasing energy consumption. Social provisions include a nursery, after school clubs, a medical centre, an organic café, bar, shops, Internet access and workspaces. It incorporates up-to-the minute thinking on sustainable development and demonstrates the technical possibility and economic feasibility of building without degrading the environment, instead improving and enhancing it.

BedZED was built from natural, recycled and reclaimed

materials, sourced locally when possible, to keep its carbon footprint low. Rooftop gardens and standard gardens provide places for residents to grow their own food. Waste-water recycling and low-flow appliances help conserve water. Super-insulated homes retain heat, and a centralised Combined Heat and Power plant (CHP) reduces the energy needed to warm the homes. Originally it was intended to provide its energy from renewable sources generated on site from a power station using bio-mass. However, teething problems with a small plant like this have not yet been overcome. The houses embrace passive solar energy with south-facing terraces for maximum sunlight and heat gain while offices, which often use air conditioning to counter overheating, stay cooler on the north side of the building. The home ventilation system uses wind cowls to let in air while preventing heat loss in winter.

Lifestyle changes as well as architecture are also a part of BedZED's environmental strategy. The community encourages people to buy local, organic food or grow their own in the community gardens. Easy-to-use, home recycling bins cut down on waste. BedZED offers pedestrian walkways and cycling, and bus and train stops within walking distance. Carpools and a car club cut down on personal car use.

With its colourful and contemporary style, it is an exemplar, both visually and in terms of its social and environmental sustainability credentials. Its 'pedestrian priority' streets, utilisation of electric vehicles, generous covered bicycle storage and balconies and gardens for every home are features which take the garden city ideal into the 21st century.

The project's inspiration came from the environmental development organisation BioRegional, which also plans to develop the adjacent landfill site into a working landscape to showcase sustainable land-based industries, such as urban forestry and lavender cultivation, and provide public green space and wildlife habitat.

BioRegional is a world-wide organisation. Its ten principles are:

BioRegional's Ten Principles

1. Zero carbon
2. Zero waste
3. Sustainable transport
4. Sustainable materials
5. Local and sustainable food
6. Sustainable water
7. Natural habitats and wildlife
8. Culture and heritage
9. Equity, fair trade and local economy
10. Health and Happiness

Here are more exemplars. You can use your browser for more information. There are countless examples, in the USA for example, left out for lack of space.

Countries

Denmark, Germany and Sweden. Denmark was the first country in the EU to introduce a tax on CO2, and it now generates almost 20 per cent of its electricity needs from wind power. Denmark is also one of the world's leaders in combined heat and power generation as well as in harnessing energy from biomass. Denmark passed a law forbidding the construction of nuclear power plants. Germany has led the way in Europe in almost every respect: research, far-sighted development of waste disposal, energy saving and alternative sources of heat and power. Sweden has set an ambitious goal to achieve a completely oil-free economy by 2020 without building more nuclear power plants.

Cities, Towns and Communities

- **Brighton and Hove** a mixed-use development in the New England Quarter, offering 172 eco-homes plus office spaces and areas for community use.
- **Bristol** is Britain's first dedicated cycle city. Government is investing £100m to turn one city and 11 towns into centres of urban cycling. Between 3 per cent and 4 per cent of trips in Bristol are already made by bike, or approximately 12,000 journeys a day, a figure that has increased by 12 per cent in the past year. The city's target is to increase cycling by 30 per cent by 2011.
- **Curitiba in Brazil** embodies four exemplary features: First, a rapid bus transit system on dedicated highways that is so attractive, fast, frequent and reasonably priced, that it has got people out of their cars in a city with the highest car ownership in Brazil. Trade downtown has benefitted as a result of this and pedestrian zones. Bicycle paths have also been created. Second, a flood defence system created by forming beautiful lakes and parkland areas. This has paid for itself as valuable homes have been built beside these attractive areas. Third, a "Waste is Gold" scheme which has not only solved the city's waste problem but given poor migrant people work and self-esteem. Again, it has paid for itself. Finally, new homes have been built for poor people that also incorporate work spaces and training has been provided – another social problem solved. Lessons are to be learned: the power of visionary, creative and collaborative leadership; getting things done quickly; a holistic approach; overcoming initial resistance by demonstrating benefits and addressing concerns quickly; using what exists – minimising demolition and new build; schemes that pay for themselves and solve more than one problem. Curitiba has become an inspiration in North America and

elsewhere. See the video: *A Convenient Truth: Urban Solutions from Curitiba, Brazil.*

- **Dongtan in China.** Arup, with advice from Herbert Girardet, is helping create Dongtan, the World's first sustainable city. A multi-billion pound contract with British engineers will create a string of "eco-cities": large, self-sustaining urban centres – throughout China, of which this is the first. These are intended to be self-sufficient in energy, water, and most food products and with zero emissions of greenhouse gases in their transport systems. Dongtan will be a vibrant city with green "corridors" of public space and a high quality of life for residents of all social classes. Farmland within Dongtan will grow food using organic farming methods. A network of cycle and footpaths will help achieve close to zero vehicle emissions.
- **Havana.** Cuba is well known for its pioneering work in adopting positive Climate Change and Peak Oil policies for saving energy and growing food organically. Havana is a model for "sustainable city", urban agriculture, local, organic food growing on every bit of spare ground. About 90 per cent of Havana's food supply is now produced in and around Havana, half in the city. Much of the food eaten by citizens is grown by communities, hospitals, old people's homes and schools in beautiful organopónicos, enriched with compost from city waste. Surplus food is sold in community markets. There is a marvellous video about this entitled *The Power of Community,* visit Cuba Organic Support Group and Sustainable Cities.
- **Masdar** near Abu Dhabi claims that it will be the world's first carbon-neutral city.
- **Merton Council and Sustainable Merton** have produced a Sustainable Strategy covering energy, planning and development, waste, transport, water, biodiversity and

environmental awareness raising, procurement and fair trade knowledge. The Merton Rule standard has been adopted by many others.

- **Sherwood Energy Village (SEV),** is particularly interesting because it was created by active members of a mining community following the closure of the pit with the loss of 600 jobs in 1994.
- **Sustainable Cities Website** describes several innovative city projects including ***New York's*** tidal energy harvesting, including two large-scale farms in the East Hudson River; ***Cairo's*** modernising and sanitising of its already very resourceful waste collection system, which is founded upon the recycling efforts of a poor class known as the Zabbaleen; ***Vienna's Bike City*** housing project, focusing on the needs of bicycle users, shifts money that would have been spent on cars to community areas, green space and other facilities that improve the standard of living; ***Malmo, Sweden*** which regained its original attractive status after adding green roofs and open storm water management. Three projects in ***Copenhagen*** – one to reduce noise and pollution on a street; another at the University, called the Green Lighthouse showing the world the incredibly high energy saving potential of buildings, helping maintain energy use lower than 2020 regulations require; thirdly the city and harbour area plan to create an entire new district covering an area of two to three hundred hectares in a capital city. ***Samsoe Island in Denmark***: A model in self-sufficiency, Samsoe converted the island's energy production from oil and coal to renewable energy. Local involvement has created a "social energy movement"; new transport solutions using biogas, waste dump gas and rapeseed oil and plans for electric cars. The island produces more electricity than it needs and exports excess energy to the mainland. Samsoe

Energy Academy shares its knowledge and experiences with the world.

- **Vauban district, Freiburg, Germany** with the following features: liveable streets; transportation encouraging car-free living and placing restrictions on private automobile ownership; design of a "neighbourhood of short trips", or high density; an ecologically-friendly district heating system with renewable energy sources; a mix of social classes and priority for private developers and co-ops over corporate investors.
- **Woking Borough Council** is a microcosm of what can be done, like BedZED, another "must visit" for any local government leader, officer or councillor. Woking Borough Council has cut carbon-dioxide emissions by 77 per cent since 1990 using a hybrid-energy system involving small private electricity grids, combined heat and power (CHP), solar photovoltaics (PV), and energy efficiency. It has made the town centre, housing estates, and old people's homes energy self-sufficient. If the UK grid went down, they would have their own heating and electricity year-round. The technologies work in harmony. CHP units generate heating when needed in winter and electricity along with it when the PV is not working optimally. PV generates a lot of electricity in the summer, when heating is not needed and CHP cannot generate much electricity. Because the use of private wires is so much cheaper than the national grid, the whole package costs fractionally less than the equivalent heating and electricity supply would cost from the big energy suppliers. This ingenuity needs to be compared with what nuclear has to offer.

Buildings

- Brighton and Hove Library, Elizabeth Fry Building at UEA, the Zuckerman Institute for Connective

Environmental Research (ZICER) building on the same site, Evelina Children's Hospital – children were involved in its design by the Prince's Foundation for the Built Environment, the Natural House at Building Research Establishment Innovation Park, PassivHausUK, Active House producing more energy than it consumes, Susan Roaf's Oxford Ecohouse, the Welsh Assembly Building (Senedd) an "exemplar" in terms of environmental design, sourcing and construction.

Summary

These are the features exemplified in many of these examples we need to adopt everywhere with the emphasis on refurbishing and adapting what we already have. Visionary thinking and belief in possibilities are needed to make them happen together with the support of local, national and regional government and global institutions.

A Holistic Approach for Sustainable Cities, Towns and Communities

Based in their biosphere and ecosystem

- Cities, towns and regions based on their biosphere
- Nature co-exists with humans in a city
- Sourcing biomass, food, fuel and materials as locally as possible

Buildings

- Carbon neutral, low energy buildings
- Emphasis on Refurb rather than demolition and new build
- Local vernacular building
- Longevity: buildings that will last for 200+ years and

meet the needs of Climate Change

- Traditional design, using natural breathable materials, that works in hot or cold weather
- Natural ventilation, solar gain and night-time cooling strategies
- Passive solar design for heating and cooling living spaces*
- Simplicity vs. Complexity: hi-tech can be short-lived, unreliable and expensive to maintain

Communities for well-being

- Diverse, mixed income population
- Leadership and collaboration at every level, involving everyone
- Environments and spaces where people of all ages can intermingle and enjoy themselves
- Local shops, diverse high streets in walkable neighbourhoods in which people connect
- Mix of old and new buildings and, in cities, high and low-rise areas, sympathetic in scale.
- Parks and gardens
- Streets for people, not traffic, safe for children to play and peaceful for residents
- Support for diverse needs at all stages of life

Culture, heart, body and soul

- A diversity of faiths and spiritual needs are met
- Local art, dance, drama, exercise, film, music, performance, recreation and sport
- Diverse therapies and forms of meditation

Food and health

- Food grown locally, not using agrichemicals or industrial methods, by farmers, in gardens, allotments, community gardens and public spaces; emphasis on food in season
- Gardens combine flowers, fruit, and vegetables with outdoor eating, relaxing, exercise and games.
- Housing developments provide space for these needs
- Health prioritised and pollution minimised
- Local shops, independent shops, busy markets, farmers markets and food co-ops
- Reconnection with healthy food, how it is grown and cooked

Heat and power

- Combined heat and power
- New development should only take place when housing and workplaces are planned as mini energy, cooling, heating and generating stations

Infrastructure

- Local mini heat and power stations
- Building projects pay for themselves and achieve more than one purpose
- Nearby infrastructure including shops and public services such as education and health facilities provided within walking or cycling distance
- Residential and commercial development (including eco-housing) only takes place when there is existing or planned infrastructure: transport, nearby shops and services, social services within easy reach, walkability, street connectivity* * and full ecological and green-

house emissions reduction measures

Local works

- Local shopping, local materials, local sourcing, local economy and local work

Transport

- Car sharing and communal car hire
- Fast, affordable rail connections between towns and cities; high speed for long distances, eliminating air travel for such journeys
- Location and transport efficiency
- Priority given to walking, continuous cycling networks and attractive, frequent and cheap public transport
- Rapid, reliable, regular bus or tram transit that is more attractive and cheaper than using private cars
- Street design forces drivers to respond to an urban environment

Waste treated as gold

- Reduction of waste and promotion of recycling within the community
- Use of human waste for fertiliser
- Implementation of water conservation and flood safety measures

Various Sources include: *Ecologist*, June 2009, *Sustainable Cities – a Greener Urban Environments*, special issue with articles by Hank Dittmar, Carolyn Steel, James Hulme, Pat Thomas interviewing Dr David Strong, Bill Dunster, and Twin Cites Study

* **Passive solar building design** aims to maintain interior thermal comfort throughout the sun's daily and annual cycles

whilst reducing the requirement for active heating and cooling systems. Passive solar building design is one part of green building design, and does not include active systems such as mechanical ventilation or photovoltaics.

* * **Street Connectivity** refers to the directness of links and the density of connections in a path or road network which help bring about human contact. Street Connectivity is defined in Online TDM Encyclopaedia.

Conclusion

The essence of cities, towns, communities and buildings fit for the 21st century is they are holistic and in harmony with nature. We should remember that we live at a time when the Earth's resources are more precious than ever before and millions of lives, including our children and their children, depend on our using them sparingly. We need to recycle, repair and reuse wherever possible. We need to employ the simplest technology fit for the purpose and solutions that will last. This means turning for inspiration to how our ancestors made buildings cool in summer heat and warm in winter cold.

Some valuable concepts underlie the simplest ways of creating sustainable habitats. Amongst these are ***Muda***, a Japanese concept, which Dr David Strong describes in the interview in the *Ecologist*. Muda is about elegant simplicity eliminating waste and complexity. It is about doing more with less. Carolyn Steel advocates communities created on ***"Sitopian"*** lines. The word is based on two Greek words, *sitos* meaning food and *topos* meaning place. It is a state of mind that results in recreating our habitats in ways that value food and base it locally. Empires and cities that did not follow this principle often did not survive.

Resources: BRE Trust/ Building Research Establishment, CABE the Commission for Architecture and the Built Environment, Campaign for Better Transport, Cycling

Demonstration towns, Farm Crisis Network, Global Action Plan's EcoTeams, Natural England, Homes under Threat – helping people save their homes from demolition – Sylvia Wilson sylvia@homesunderthreat.co.uk, Soil Association, Sustainable Energy Academy – transforming homes, Sustainable Travel Towns and Transition Towns.

Further reading

in addition to those already mentioned:

- Day, C, *Places of the Soul: Architecture and Environmental Design as a Healing Art*, 2008, and *Consensus Design – Socially inclusive process*, 2002
- Elsevier and Forum for the Future's Sustainable Cities Index.

Chapter 14

The Possibility of Peace

August 2009

Ending war, violence and the threat of nuclear annihilation

It is time to end war

The subject of this chapter – the possibility of peace – is the most ambitious. Can we really end war? Will it work? I hope to show that ending war is entirely possible and you can play an important part in bringing it about. In the face of climate change, Peak Oil, rising world population, wasteful and unequal consumption of the Earth's resources, increasing poverty, starvation and extremism, conflicts and wars are inevitable – unless we act differently.

We have to accept that, with the probable exception of WWII, force rarely works. The enormous weaponry of the great powers is useless in the face of today's challenges. The availability of nuclear weapons to terrorists is an inevitable and frightening prospect. "Wars" on terror, and drugs do not work. The lesson of history is: ultimately we have to talk with "extremists". Drugs must be legalised. Ultimately, we'll need to engage with the Taliban in Afghanistan, Hamas in Palestine if settlements are to be reached and Al-Qaeda if their campaign of terror is to be ended.

The time has come to resolve conflict by means that do not involve violence. It is perfectly possible.

The following is proposed:

A Paradigm Shift

- **We have to address the global system.** A critical mass that recognises systemic change is needed. Continuous growth is unsustainable and unjust. Western addiction to consumerism perpetuates an insecure and unsafe world
- Ending poverty and the economic and social injustices at the root of hostility and many conflicts
- An emphasis on what works
- Putting major resources into conflict prevention, reconciliation, trust and peace-building rather than military interventions. Whilst slower, it is more effective, and costs less in lost lives and destruction
- Enabling people on the ground to empower themselves to resolve their problems and conflicts and tackle corruption, instead of imposing solutions.
- Ending the threat of nuclear weapons through urgent action to bring about nuclear disarmament
- Strictly controlling the sale of arms
- Preventing, through international collaboration, resource wars that will loom large in the future
- Taking steps to limit the size, power and influence of large corporations and prevent their abuses
- Making the UN democratic and giving it more power
- Providing citizens with constitutional powers to gain control of their governments and prevent war being declared without fully informed consent
- Practising ethical foreign policies are ultimately in our best interest
- Learning to respect our differences
- Accepting that discussions need to take place with all stakeholders; excluding "extremists" does not work
- Addressing terrorism and the causes of terrorism non-violently

Conflict prevention and resolution

Sir Jeremy Greenstock, UK's Permanent Representative to the UN in the lead up to the Iraq war, is reported as saying governments need to relearn an understanding of the limits of power, broaden the means of tackling conflict and modify their attitudes to the use of force. They should support the UN at all times. Positive News, Spring, 2007 contains short articles, including one about the World Court Project UK which is attempting to bring legal pressure on nuclear armed states through the World Court and Rethink Trident.

The Ministry of Defence spends £33bn annually on the military, almost 10 per cent of all the tax we pay, yet only about 3 per cent of this sum is spent on conflict prevention. How much better it would be to spend the major part of these resources on promoting peace and reconciliation and policies of global economic and social justice. The UK is far behind other nations such as Norway, Canada and Germany in building resources fit to help in conflict prevention and resolution.

Scilla Elworthy, member of the World Future Council, says:

> *Since the early 1990s almost twice as many wars have been ended by negotiated settlement rather than by military victory. Yet peace-building efforts receive negligible funding; for every dollar spent on conflict prevention around the world, nearly two thousand times as much is spent on defence and the military.*

Increasing UK Security through non-military prevention and resolution of conflict. The evidence demonstrates that non-military conflict prevention and resolution is far more effective than military intervention. This case is made convincingly in Scilla Elworthy's comprehensive paper, *Increasing UK Security through Non-military Prevention and Resolution of Conflict,* delivered to the All-Party Parliamentary Group on Conflict Issues (APPGCI). Here is a brief summary and edited extracts from that paper. However, it is well worth studying in full.

What does war prevention mean? While the term is in common currency in Europe, it is still unfamiliar in the UK and more so in the US. It means the systematic use of proven, non-aggressive methods to prevent or stop killing:

What War Prevention Means

- Peace-keeping
- The introduction of trained inspectors to detect and report killing, ethnic cleansing, torture, rape and other forms of violence
- Civilian protection
- Control of arms entering the region
- Incentive schemes to collect weapons
- Law enforcement
- Bringing warlords and militias under control
- Track II or "back channels" diplomacy
- Muscular support for locally-based opposition to dictators
- Providing independent information daily
- Training of mediators and bridge-builders
- Active reconciliation measures

The report points out the fundamental inconsistencies in British policy, how Britain falls behind other countries and the EU in allocating resources to peace-building and training people in these skills. Whilst force is sometimes needed, research shows that in general, prevention and peace-building are not only more successful but far less expensive.

A fundamental inconsistency in British defence policy. MoD emphasises the importance of conflict prevention activity supported by confidence and security building measures to help create transparency and trust. It vaunts its efforts to counter the threat from the proliferation of conventional arms whilst at the same time spending some £426m to subsidise British arms sales. The UK regularly achieves second or third place in sales of arms to developing countries.

The main response to terrorist attacks, especially from the United States, has been military action in Afghanistan, the extension of military bases into Central Asia, support for counter-insurgency activities in numerous countries and the war with Iraq. Others have taken quite different approaches to problems of political violence and conflict, approaches that seek to prevent conflict while understanding some of its root causes. In particular, there is a growing understanding of the classic cycle of violence. This cycle is evident in the Israeli-Palestinian conflict, in central Africa and repeatedly in different regions of former Yugoslavia; if unbroken, this cycle ensures that conflict follows conflict.

Break the cycle of violence. A key part of conflict is the cycle of violence. Scilla Elworthy argues that, to break the cycle, effective intervention must address the physical, the political and the psychological security of people trapped in violence; all are equally important, and one without the other is insufficiently strong to break the cycle. In every case, the people involved in situations of violence must be supported in the development of their own resources for transformation.

What works: grounds for hope

It always makes sense to study what works. It is easy to feel hopeless about the enormity of the challenges that face us in transforming the human addiction to war and violence. After all, there never has been a time when there were no wars. We need the encouragement of successful initiatives that provide grounds for hope, and the inspiration of good news.

Evaluation and cost effectiveness: "bang for the buck".

Recent experience both in Afghanistan and Iraq has conclusively demonstrated the need for greater emphasis on non-military measures in Britain's defence and foreign policy forward planning. These measures are relatively cheap as well as cost-effective ways of preventing war, reducing the destructive effects of conflict, or enabling those caught in a cycle of violence to break out of it.

From the available figures it appears likely that non-military interventions, while slower, not only tend to cause less destruction than bombing or armed intervention, but also work better in saving lives. They are definitely far cheaper. In 1999 the Oxford Research Group examined 240 cases of non-violent intervention in conflict in different parts of the world and the fifty most effective of these in *Conflict Prevention Works: 50 Stories of People Resolving Conflicts*. These case studies show that small groups of highly motivated people, determined not to use weapons, can achieve extraordinary results in preventing or stopping killing. These interventions cost little. Of the examples mentioned above, successful third party mediation between Renamo and Frelimo in Mozambique in 1989-92 cost approximately $350,000; the gun return scheme organised by businessmen in El Salvador (1995-1999) cost $1.3m; and the task force set up in former Yugoslavia in 1999 to forge effective, united democratic opposition to Milosevic cost $240,000.

The removal of a dictator and installation of democratic process is a monumental task, as in the case of Slobodan Milosovic. Bombing failed to remove this dictator, while support for local democratic opposition succeeded.

Scilla Elworthy demonstrates how the money to be spent by Britain on 232 Eurofighters at a cost of £80m each could be put to far better use to:

- put another 1000 peacekeepers into Afghanistan
- organise negotiations with warlords to bring militias and

opium production under control
- support local initiatives to restore law and order outside Kabul
- set up liaison centres all over Iraq to enable people to get help with the daily trauma which engenders hatred for the occupying forces – civilians murdered,
destroyed homes, arrested relatives, lack of food and employment.

The £426 million per annum used to subsidise arms exporters could be used to:

- set up gun collection schemes in every single country where there is local killing, including Sudan, DR Congo, Colombia, Indonesia, Somalia, Afghanistan, Nepal, Sri Lanka, Uganda, Rwanda, Burundi, Angola, and Nigeria
- introduce effective boundary controls on gunrunning, with severe and enforceable penalties
- fully support the EU commitment to develop a "Civilian Crisis Management Capacity" by providing training for civilians ready to join.

This is not to say that military intervention is never necessary, but to date the value of non-military measures has been insufficiently recognised and that very substantial savings can be made by investing in them.

An All-Party Parliamentary Group on Conflict Issues (APPGCI) was set up in 2007 to study conflict issues at the suggestion of the Ministry for Peace in 2007. The APPGCI provides a forum where Parliamentarians, government officials, NGOs, academics and others come together on a regular basis to share ideas and thoughts about the challenges of non-violent approaches to managing conflict. To follow the activities of the APPGCI go to Conflict Issues.

Scilla Elworthy founded the Oxford Research Group (ORG) in 1982 to develop effective dialogue between nuclear weapons policy makers worldwide and their critics. For this work she was awarded the Niwano Peace Prize in 2003 and nominated three times for the Nobel Peace Prize. In 2003 she founded Peace Direct to fund, promote and learn from peace-builders in conflict areas. Both are described below.

Oxford Research Group (ORG): Its purpose is as follows:

> *ORG works to promote a more sustainable approach to security for the UK and for the world. We seek a shift in global priorities away from militarism, and towards security based on justice, human rights, prevention of conflict and fair distribution of the world's resources. Regardless of what current projects we work on, our long-term goals are always the same: to encourage and promote a deep shift in the way that people think about security, based on the understanding that lasting security is not attainable through military means. Developing long-term 'sustainable security' for everyone means understanding the root causes of conflict, and promoting dialogue rather than confrontation as the means to a truly secure world.*

Its key principles are dialogue, respect, prevention and pragmatism. ORG stresses the importance of building relationships and trust. Its two main programmes are Global Security for the 21st century and Human Security and the Middle East.

Global Security: *Central to this programme is an on-going critical analysis of the current 'war on terror' which shows how acutely the current approach to security is failing, and how it is in danger of distracting world leaders from the far more deadly and unavoidable threats posed by climate change, resource competition, poverty and marginalisation, and global militarisation. Linked to this analysis are a range of initiatives to shift thinking towards non-military conflict prevention, and the protection of innocent life.*

Middle East: This is seen as the major flashpoint threatening global security.

> *The premise of a human security approach is that no political or strategic goals can be pursued that ignore basic human needs for safety, well-being and livelihood. People on the ground, and their legitimate aspirations, should come before all other political or strategic considerations. We work on two primary implications of this approach. First, in negotiations, a way needs to be found of allowing all voices to be heard and respected. Solutions which exclude significant constituencies are doomed to fail. We provide forums in which groups who disagree may begin to build dialogue and find common interests. Second, in military interventions, those who plan and execute them need to find ways in which operations protect, respect and include local populations, rather than alienating them. Our work with Western militaries offers contexts in which fresh thinking can be undertaken about what is to be learned from mistakes made in recent interventions.*

If you wish to promote peace, through lobbying your MP for example, you need to be well-informed. ORG provides reliable reports and articles. It is a valuable source about the situation in the Middle East, Iraq, Iran and Afghanistan.

Oxford Research Group recently launched a new website: Sustainable Security – Global responses to global threats (Sustainable Security). This website is part of a larger programme, *"Moving towards sustainable security"* begun in 2006. The project has involved publications, consultations in different parts of the world, and a series of publications. Sustainable Security intends to be an important platform for promoting a better understanding of the real threats to global security in the 21st century and the policies that should be implemented to address those threats at their root cause. The website is organised to highlight four interconnected drivers of global insecurity:

- Climate Change
- Competition over natural resources
- Global militarism
- Poverty and marginalisation

Peace Direct is another key organisation with similar principles, such as working with local people in peace-building. Peace Direct say that peace cannot be built by politicians alone and 50 per cent of conflicts start again within ten years of a peace agreement being signed. The root causes have to be addressed and local people and leaders involved who are trusted and really understand the issues.

Peace Direct want to change the world by changing the balance of power and resources between local people and outsiders so that local peace-building is central to all strategies for managing conflict. They believe local individuals and organisations have knowledge and social capital which outsiders cannot access, and which are essential to achieving lasting peace. They maintain and provide the evidence that if local initiatives are adequately funded prospects for peace will increase and peace-building be done more cost effectively. So Peace Direct needs to work with others to:

- fund local peace-building
- demonstrate the effectiveness of local peace-building
- make it easy for people to find out what local peace-building initiatives exist
- increase our knowledge about how "outsiders" can work effectively with "local initiatives"
- get the public on board
- build coalitions of local peace-builders in conflict areas which can have greater strategic impact

Peace Direct are working in Sudan, Sri Lanka, Zimbabwe, Nepal, Afghanistan, DR Congo, Somalia, Kenya, Columbia and Newham, East London.

You can sign up for their regular monthly newsletter and provide donations as its resources are extremely stretched.

Responding to Conflict (RTC) is an independent peace-building organisation that has worked since 1991 to support people and organisations in transforming violent conflict and building lasting peace. They believe local people are best placed to find their own ways of dealing with conflict.

RTC provides training and professional development and a variety of consultancy services in the fields of conflict assessment, conflict transformation strategies and methodologies, facilitation and mediation, and organisational development. They also design and manage long-term programmes and provide on-going support to their partners.

RTC has established itself as a leader in the field of conflict transformation and has trained practitioners from more than 70 countries including those from some of the world's most violent conflicts. They have provided specialist advice and consultancy services to the governments of the UK, Australia, Japan, the United Nations Development Programme, and leading International NGO's and charities such as Oxfam GB, Christian Aid, AGEH, Care International, CAFOD, the American Friends' Service Committee and a variety of Red Cross national societies. RTC has designed and managed long-term programmes in the Middle East, the Balkans, East Africa and South East Asia. They are currently developing new programmes in Nepal, Kenya and the Middle East.

Their handbook *Working with Conflict: Skills and Strategies for Action* is acknowledged as a key resource for practitioners, trainers and academics throughout the world and has been translated into 6 languages. They need support and you can learn from their newsletter.

Unlock Democracy argues and campaigns for a vibrant, inclusive democracy that puts power in the hands of the people. In a fully functioning democracy, declaration of war is far less likely to occur. The decision to send troops into armed conflict is one of the most serious that any state can make. That this decision-making process is unaccountable and cannot be effectively scrutinised, is quite simply unacceptable. A short version of Unlock Democracy's *War Powers and Treaties Consultation* was provided in Chapter 11. To bring an end to war one of the most effective things you can do is to strengthen the UK's democracy through Unlock Democracy.

An example of what works

Kenya – a Citizens' Agenda for Political Dialogue following the post 2007 Election Crisis in Kenya. The following example shows the strength of citizens' actions. Although the conflicts in Kenya are not over, the following provides an example of how major violent conflict can be resolved, albeit not perfectly, as a result of an initiative by a citizens' coalition. This initiative followed the atrocities and destruction committed after the disputed election in December 2007.

A coalition was formed of Concerned Citizens for Peace, Kenya Private Sector Alliance, the National Council of NGOs, Peace and Development Network – Kenya, the Media Council of Kenya, Maendeleo ya Wanawake representing Partners for Peace, Federation of Kenyan Employers, the Global Call to Action Against Poverty, and the Kenya Association of Manufacturers among others. The coalition put forward an agenda which formed the basis of an agreement which ended violence. This is a shorter, edited version.

A Seven Point Citizens' Agenda for Peace, Truth and Justice

1. **Restoring peace, reconciliation and national healing initiatives.** All actors to work co-operatively to bring an immediate end to the violence, enable peaceful political activity, actively engage in reconciling communities and encourage peace initiatives.
2. **Trust and confidence building for the political players.** Deliberate efforts need to be undertaken to rebuild trust and confidence between and among political players to enhance the capacity for dialogue and constructive engagement.
3. **Election closure.** The disputed presidential poll has to be brought to closure if Kenyans are to have faith in the electoral process. This will require some form of agreement on the final presidential poll.
4. **Composition and duration of a Government of National Unity** – a grand coalition or Government of National Unity will command a significant popular mandate and be well placed to set the pace for tackling some of the deeper issues that have led to the current crisis.
5. **Priority agenda for the Government of National Unity** – Key among the items to be included in the priority agenda include:

- Constituting a body to carry out a comprehensive review of the election process
- Constitutional reforms to address some of the deep-rooted issues
- Administrative and legal reform to address the weaknesses identified in the electoral process
- The return of internally displaced persons and recon-

struction

- Priority initiatives to deliver equitable economic growth
- A comprehensive framework to address land issues
- An anti-corruption agenda and a robust, transparent Public Accountability framework
- Establishing the truth of the allegations of all forms of ethnic cleansing and genocide by both PNU and ODM with a view to restitution and justice

6. **The next Presidential and/or National Elections.** The timing of the next Presidential and/ or National Elections should be agreed as part of the negotiated settlement.
7. **Global agenda to restore international respectability.** A global agenda shared with all stakeholders should be agreed to form part of efforts and reclaiming our pride of place among nations.

The two contestants formed a power-sharing agreement. Mwai Kibaki's Party of National Unity became President and Raila Odinga of the Orange Democratic Movement became Prime Minister. This partnership has not fulfilled the hopes of citizens, and Kofi Annan, former UN Secretary General who brokered the peace deal, has warned Kenya's leaders that they are "losing momentum" in delivering the badly needed reforms to address Kenya's underlying problems and failing to face up to the big decisions needed to bring about change. However, at least peace has been established. It is to be hoped that citizen pressure will ensure that the necessary action will be taken.

Resources for action and to increase your understanding of non-military strategies to prevent and resolve conflict: CND, Campaign Against Arms Trade, Conscience's Peace Tax

Campaign, Darfur Peace & Development, Landmine Action, Ministry for Peace, National Campaign for a Peace Tax Fund, Washington, DC, Network for Peace, Open Democracy, Oxford Research Group, Peace Pledge Union, Peace Tax International, Reprieve, Responding to Conflict, Rethink Trident, RoadPeace included as a road peace campaign, Sustainable Security – Global responses to global threats, The Elders, founded by Nelson Mandela, UN Conflict Prevention Framework Team, Unlock Democracy – War Powers and Treaties consultation, World Future Council.

Chapter 15

After Copenhagen – Opportunities and Challenges

March to October 2010

Acknowledgements. I am indebted to the Schumacher College course: *After Copenhagen – Opportunities and Challenges,* March 2010 and contributors including Ian Christie, Clare Short, Miriam Kennet, Alex Randall and Lotta Hedström whose notes of his talk augmented mine. Thanks also to Alice Cutler's article *Copenhagen Chaos* published in *Ethical Consumer* March/ April 2010; the International Institute for Environment and Development (IIED) *COP15 Review and Analysis;* the BBC Website and the Copenhagen Accord Wiki.

What happened?

The chaotic UN Conference on Climate Change in Copenhagen (COP15*) 7 to 18 December 2009 was a huge disappointment, especially after all the hopeful worldwide campaigning by millions of citizens and NGOs (* known as COP15 because it is the 15th Conference of Parties since the first held in Berlin in 1992).

In the run-up to the summit, there had been a great spirit of optimism. Campaigns like *Age of Stupid* had rallied thousands of people. Many hoped that COP15 would lead to a legally binding international treaty with corresponding targets and actions to limit global warming to 2c above pre-industrial temperatures. This figure is widely regarded as the absolute minimum if disaster is to be prevented. However, during the summit, small island nations and vulnerable coastal countries demanded a binding deal to limit emissions to a level preventing temperature rises above 1.5c.

But the demands of millions of campaigners were not enough.

The Copenhagen Accord

On the final Friday evening, after almost two weeks of little progress, an accord was drawn up by a core group of twenty-five heads of state, so-called "friends of the chair", mainly from developed and leading developing countries.

This meeting was held in secret in a room separate from the rest of the conference. The Copenhagen Accord was based on a proposal tabled by a US-led group of five nations, including China, India, Brazil, South Africa and the EU. Essentially it was a deal between the US and big emerging nations. The Accord is extremely weak, with no legally binding targets or plans. China, heading towards becoming the dominant world power, would not agree to anything that would jeopardise its economic development, largely based on abundant coal, nor would it agree to verification. But it would fulfil its previously stated commitments. China's position tended to be supported by India. Europe wanted a 30 per cent reduction in CO2 emissions by 2020 and a deal with legally binding targets. Brazil was prepared to make strong commitments. US President Obama had wanted emission reduction targets by large emitters and internationally verifiable actions. However, he said that if they had waited for a binding agreement no progress would have been made. Clearly he was also constrained by what was possible to enact back home in the US House of Representatives and the Senate.

One commentator, present in the room, said that China wrecked the talks and China's Prime Minister Wen Jiabao humiliated Obama by not attending himself, sending his deputy instead, and he aimed to put Western nations in the wrong. However, it appears that he did not actually receive the invitation to this core group meeting. China has since pledged to lower its carbon dioxide emissions per unit of gross domestic product (GDP) by 40 to 45 per cent by 2020 compared with 2005 levels. At the end of January Wen also wrote to UN Secretary-General Ban Ki-moon and Danish Prime Minister Lars Lokke Rasmussen, stating that China highly commends and supports the Copenhagen Accord. It is better to keep an open mind and trust people's integrity.

Development debt of developed nations. The essential difficulty was the failure of "developed nations" to recognise their "development debt" to the rest of the world and the latter's insistence that its development prospects should not be damaged by the payback costs of the ecological damage caused by Western development over the past 200 years. Mo Ibrahim, Sudanese-born entrepreneur, was quoted in James Robertson's Newsletter January 2010 as saying:

> *Africans account for 13 per cent of the world's population and are responsible for less than 4 per cent of carbon emissions. That is our carbon credit. It is the only basis for any carbon trading that makes sense.*

The Copenhagen Accord recognised the scientific case for keeping temperature rises below 2c, but does not include the commitments necessary to achieve that aim. The agreement pledges US$ 30 billion over the next three years, rising to US$100 billion per year by 2020, to help poor countries adapt to climate change. Under the Accord developed countries also offer to pay them to reduce their emissions from deforestation and degradation, under a scheme known as "REDD". A Copenhagen Green Climate Fund would be established "to support projects, programme, policies and other activities in developing countries related to mitigation." The Accord called for "an assessment of the implementation of this Accord to be completed by 2015 including consideration of strengthening the long-term goal," for example, to limit temperature rises to 1.5 degrees.

The Accord was only "noted" by 110 remaining, many of whom were outraged by its inadequacies and the exclusive process by which it was reached. Amongst these are those nations likely to be worst affected and least able to pay for the necessary technological measures needed to reducc climate change, largely caused by the richest nations, or to mitigate the consequences.

Climate Scoreboard estimates that business as usual will lead to a 4.8c rise in temperatures and the Accord proposals 3.9c. Others say we'll be condemned to an average temperature rise of 3c to 3.5c. As these are global averages, some countries will face far greater increases. Unless further action is rapidly implemented, vast areas of the world will become uninhabitable with easily imagined consequences.

When the whole of humanity is in a situation of extreme peril and action is urgently needed, this was an astonishing though predictable result. Essentially most countries put their short-term national interests ahead of the long-term future well-being of the entire planet.

"Peak Everything". However, it is not only climate change and Peak Oil that threaten the future of humanity. Natural gas is probably 10 to 15 years away from a peak. Phosphorous and potash are starting to fail to keep up with growing human demand. Fish are under extreme pressure. All the provisions of nature are in decline whilst our population and demands are increasing. We must rapidly move away from endless growth and consumption. We need a complete change in our values and personal identities. Our children and future generations will suffer dreadfully. We need a forum to address "Peak Everything" says Ian Christie. Bold action by governments is needed to redirect economic activity and manage the necessary transition towards prosperity without growth. Only governments can institute the national and international measures needed to provide the necessary direction and framework for business corporations. That is exactly what the USA and Britain rapidly did in WWII. It led to an almost overnight redirection of manufacturing from peacetime production to the war effort. We need this now!

On the positive side, COP15 was clearly an important step. For the first time representatives of 193 nations, including 110 world leaders, met with climate change as the single issue. Climate change has clearly become central to the political thinking of almost every country. Public awareness has massively increased. Green Growth has got into the prevailing economic talk, though not the need for steady state economics on a finite planet. However, it is barely mentioned by political leaders in the current campaign for the UK parliamentary elections.

In the run-up to Copenhagen, there had been major campaigns around the world by NGOs; governments and large corporations and many governments announced substantial low-carbon measures. These will continue. The European Union has set an example by committing to implementing binding legislation, despite no satisfactory deal at Copenhagen.

UN Secretary General Ban Ki-moon welcomed the US-backed climate deal in Copenhagen as an "essential beginning." But he said the Accord must be made legally binding in 2010. The International Institute for Environment and Development report described it as *"an open space waiting to be filled in."*

A summary of the Accord is available on Wiki.

The weaknesses of the accord. Earlier proposals, aimed to limit temperature rises to 1.5c and cut CO2 emissions by 80 per cent by 2050, were dropped. Many countries were prepared to co-operate, but not under the threat of legal sanctions. There is no quantified aggregate target for emissions reduction such as the 50 per cent by 2050 in early drafts. Countries are to be assessed globally. But no verification measures will take place in the developing world unless paid for by the developed world. There is very little detail.

The Accord relies on the implementation of national strategies within a policy framework with a progress review planned for 2015. Perhaps that is the most pragmatic way forward. But as countries will be free to make their own different pledges, it is unlikely that the necessary limitation to global warming will be achieved. As said above, so a temperature limitation of 3c or now seems more likely. Some fear the rise will be 6c which will be disastrous.

The International Institute for Environment and Development (IIED) say, the Accord does propose short-term funding for adaptation in vulnerable countries but lacks essential details such as where the funds will come from and whether they will be loans or grants; the target figure of US$30 billion over three years from 2010 to 2013 is not adequate for 100 vulnerable countries with about one billion citizens. Tellingly, this is about the same amount that JP Morgan Chase bank will spend on salaries and bonuses in the current year.

The long-term finance of US$100bn a year by 2020 that developed countries pledged to mobilise jointly to address the needs of developing countries does not say how much of this money would be allocated for adaptation in vulnerable countries (as opposed to mitigation actions in less vulnerable countries such as India and China). Moreover, this amount is just half of what vulnerable countries need to adapt in the long term. The Accord makes no special provisions regarding technology transfer for the vulnerable developing countries.

Reactions. Lumumba Stanislaus Di-Aping, the Sudanese negotiator, said the Accord spelled *"incineration"* for Africa and compared it to the Nazis sending 6 million people into furnaces in the Holocaust.

About 50,000 environmental activists from regions of the

world most affected by climate change convened Klimaforum09, simultaneously with COP15, with leaders such as Dr Vandana Shiva and author Naomi Klein. A People's Declaration formulated at the People's Climate Summit and signed by nearly 300 civil society organisations calling for *"System change – not climate change"* was handed over to the Conference on December 18. This declaration opened thus:

> *There are solutions to the climate crisis. What people and the planet need is a just and sustainable transition of our societies to a form that will ensure the rights of life and dignity of all peoples and deliver a more fertile planet and more fulfilling lives to future generations.*

It called for:

- Complete abandonment of fossil fuels within the next 30 years
- Recognition, payment and compensation for climate debt
- A rejection of purely market-oriented and technology centred false and dangerous "solutions" such as nuclear energy, agro-fuels, carbon capture and storage, Clean Development Mechanisms, bio-char, genetically "climate readied" crops, geo-engineering and reducing emissions from deforestation and forest degradation (REDD), which deepens social and environmental conflicts.
- Real solutions to limit climate crisis based on safe, clean, renewable, and sustainable use of natural resources, as well as transitions to food, energy, land, and water sovereignty.

Indigenous rights organisation, Survival International, raised concerns about climate mitigation measures affecting the survival of tribal people as badly as climate change. Some developing countries, as already mentioned, are demanding reparations from the West. They argue that developed countries have been accumulating a climate debt for the past 200 years and it is their greed that has brought about the climate change crisis that will have the worst consequences for developing countries.

What went wrong?

George Monbiot described COP15 as *"a scramble for the atmosphere comparable in style and intent to the scramble for Africa."*

Conference processes were seriously flawed: undemocratic, unrepresentative, unfair to poor and small countries and chaotic. We must not let it happen again.

Accounts of what happened at COP15 differ widely.

Essentially, leaders at Copenhagen represented three interest groups: Wealthy developed nations trying to rise to the challenge but fearing the political consequences of climate measures on their economies, employment and affluent living standards; developing nations aware of the dangers of climate change to their countries but wanting to continue economic growth in order to raise living standards to Western levels; the poorest and most vulnerable countries threatened with massive consequences such as flooding, drought and complete annihilation. The latter are the least able to afford the measures to deal with the consequences of climate change for their people, for which the wealthy nations have been largely responsible over the past two hundred years.

These three groups had far from equal influence and resources. The developed and rapidly developing nations had large delegations; both Canada and China had over 200 people. Twenty-four countries had less than 8 delegates, most of them least developed or small island states. The European Youth Forum organised themselves to assist underrepresented delegations.

The absence of women at the top negotiation tables was

notable, apart from Angela Merkel and Conference President Connie Hedegaard, who somewhat mysteriously resigned, replaced by a man, partway through. In October, she had threatened to resign after complaining of being left out of an important meeting.

Some 20,000 people attended the event. There were 3,000-4,000 representatives of Parties' (Nations) negotiators. The rest were Business NGOs (BINGOS), Green NGOs (GRINGOs), Youth NGOs (YOUNGOs), Trade Unions (TUNGOs), Indigenous Peoples Organizations (IPOs), local government and municipal authorities (LGAM), Non-Governmental Observers and Media/Press following the proceedings and attending side events and exhibits.

Then there were the protesters. The Danish government had rushed through new repressive laws. There were mass "preventative" arrests. Protesters were treated violently and there were many arrests including media people.

The Bella Centre, thirty minutes drive from the city, lacked sufficient space to accommodate it all. Many people were accommodated far away from the centre. Consequently, some people slept on floors and settees. Outside the conference negotiations were many NGOs and protesters, together with some of the press and the media. Perhaps 40,000 people came, including the 20,000 attendees.

Arrangements were chaotic and contributed to mistrust. In the second week NGOs and key civil society organisations were unable to get in. On Thursday of that the Chief Negotiators for Brazil and for India were barred. The Chief Negotiator for the Indian Government was so upset with how he was manhandled that he couldn't think straight and, before putting India's representations to the conference, waited for about 20 minutes whilst he got his composure back! Brazil and India are not minor players. Arguably, Brazil's rainforest holds the key to human survival.

The main conference room was windowless, separating everyone from the environment and the biosphere on which all our futures depend, the main subject of the conference. The Northern elite mind is disconnected from Nature and the reality of life for billions of people in other parts of the world. Deep issues of personal identity are an obstacle to accepting the transformation in our way of life that is needed so urgently. Summits, deciding the fate of all life on the planet, should be held in places where people (and other creatures) are most vulnerable and where delegates can see the natural world outside, not in a windowless centre in an affluent city.

Here is an account of the negotiations based on IIED's report. In the second week, towards the end of the negotiations, talks were going on in two completely separate processes. First, negotiations among all 192 Parties to the United Nations Framework Convention on Climate Change continued. Second, and behind closed doors, a select group of about 25 world leaders came up with the Copenhagen Accord, to which most of the vulnerable countries had very little input. As 25 Parties agreed to the Accord, President Obama told the US media that a deal had been struck. The only trouble was that it had yet to be presented to and adopted by all 192 countries attending; so his announcement was premature and looked as if the US was trying to take undue credit. China, India, Brazil and South Africa formed a new block called BASIC. As the BASIC group took on the industrialised nations, the most vulnerable countries were squeezed out. As a result, the G77/China block of 130 developing nations may not survive. A new block representing poorer developing nations seems likely. Gradually they began to compromise. Prime Minister Zenawi of Ethiopia, representing Africa, made a deal with President Sarkozy of France and dropped the 1.5-degree target in exchange for a promise of funding for Africa. This split the Least Developed Countries (LDCs), most but not all of which are African, and left the small islands as the only nations hanging on to the 1.5-degree target.

The story of Kiribati is shocking and reveals the flaws in the conference process that led to unjust and disappointing outcomes. During the Schumacher College course, we listened to a first-hand account of the conference given by Alex Randall from the Centre for Alternative Technology. Alex and a colleague were to attend COP15 as representatives of CAT. Beforehand they noticed that some countries' delegations were enormous whilst others' were tiny. They decided to research which countries most needed help. They took the IPCC maps on hydrological collapse, matched them with density of population, low GDP per capita and the smallest negotiating teams. They e-mailed all those worst off countries to offer their services. Kiribati with only five representatives accepted.

Kiribati is a small island in the Pacific Ocean, facing annihilation. Their team was led by the Minister of Emigration, charged with evacuating the whole population if worst came to worst. It is not simply that the Island will disappear under the sea. Floods are becoming more and more frequent: from one every other year, to one every year and now every half year. Sea water penetration becomes too frequent for the land to recover. It becomes useless for crops and there is a lack of fresh water. Salt water intrudes into the aquifer in the middle of the island. People start to use other water sources that are polluted. Water-borne diseases increase and mortality rises. Madeira is another small island state making plans to evacuate large numbers of their people.

Delegation size was important because separate negotiations were going on day and night, eight to twelve at the same time, like finance, forestry, co-operation between developed/undeveloped counties, etc. Delegations must be able to follow them all or they miss decisions affecting their country. Meeting times and locations constantly changed so they struggled to know exactly where and when to be present. Massive documentation was produced which had to be read to watch what to argue against or for. Everything would be guesswork, unless you read everything thoroughly and summarised it. Even the BBC could not keep up with it. In the final three days there was nothing at all on the news screens. Increasing confusion resulted.

Because NGOs were excluded in the second week, Alex and his colleague would have been excluded too. But they asked to be included as members of the Kiribati team.

Countries like the USA, Canada, China and the UK with their very large and well organised teams could keep abreast of what was going on and create summaries of documents. They could catch up on sleep in relays. For inadequately resourced delegations from poor countries, desperately short of sleep, it became impossible to keep up. Having insufficient resources to cope with the mass of information was part of the unfairness for smaller and poorer countries. Some observers concluded that speaking at length was a deliberate tactic to exhaust other people. Towards the end of the summit, exhausted negotiators, without sufficient sleep, were taking critically important decisions affecting the future of humanity.

Small countries like Kiribati, with very different cultures, were at another disadvantage: they lacked the necessary tough negotiating skills. Kiribati's representatives were trusting and assumed people wanted the best for everyone whereas the culture of the Summit was adversarial and confrontational – a cross between the House of Commons and a courtroom. In the last three days they were exhausted and gave up. They sang songs and told stories.

Alex summed up the reactions as he saw them. Countries from the North said it was a step forward. Countries from the South said it meant the end of their countries. A great injustice had happened. There was a huge revolt. Basically the rich countries are forcing people to:

- Move from where they live
- Die prematurely from flood, loss of fresh water or food.

Failure to keep the temperature rise to 1.5c leads to death and forced migration. It amounts to genocide.

There are parallels between national and international politics. In both arenas, the interests of rich and powerful dominate and the whole system bears down upon poor people and poor countries. Government leaders, there to serve citizens and protect them from the abuses of power, whilst talking a good talk, are too frightened to take on the rich and powerful and tackle the fundamental injustices and unsustainability of the current system.

Nations have to transform the whole global economic system simultaneously. We have to pressure our national governments to act. But John Bunzl, leader of Simpol, says:

> *for me, the "bleeding rhino's head in the room" is that we are asking our leaders to dramatically cut emissions and yet we expect them to do so without significantly harming our national economies.*

It is unrealistic to expect them to do that unilaterally in a globally competitive economy. The risk is that unilateral initiatives will put those nations at a huge disadvantage. The whole global economic system, he argues, has to be changed simultaneously. Otherwise leaders will be committing economic and political suicide. Citizens need to pressure their governments to adopt the necessary policy changes simultaneously, thus removing the excuse they now make under pressure from their businesses and industries, that by adopting these policies before other countries do they will damage their economic competitiveness. Countries need to act in unison. His organisation provides the means for citizens to bring pressure to bear.

What Next

Most of the countries who endorsed the Accord want a binding treaty agreed by the next UN Summit. This will be held in the Mexican resort of Cancun in November and December, 2010. In the meantime there will be both UN and non-UN climate meetings. UN meetings were held in Bonn in April and the USA hosted the Major Economies Forum, a meeting of the 17 biggest-emitting countries shortly afterwards.

US "arm-twisting" tactics are resented and seen as a potential major stumbling block. For example, to placate domestic concerns about losing competitiveness, the US unilaterally demanded that China and other major developing countries should be subject to the same regime on verifying emissions curbs as industrialised nations. The US made it clear that countries not endorsing the Copenhagen Accord would be unlikely to receive US funding. It will withhold money from Bolivia and Ecuador because they did not endorse the accord.

Bolivia hosted the World People's Conference on Climate Change and the Rights of Mother Earth at Cochabamba, Bolivia from April 19 to 22. Over 15,000 people and up to 70 governments from all over the world were expected to attend. The event, supported by 241 partners from all over the world, was a response to the failures of COP15 It aimed to highlight the central role of peoples' movements and social movements in the climate struggle and the critical alliance that must be forged between movements and progressive governments.

The organisers also called for *"System change; not climate change"* and urged all members and friends to organize actions on Earth Day 22nd April to raise demands for climate justice and opposition to water and power privatisation projects that exacerbate climate change.

Their demands:

1. Northern countries give full reparations for the ecological debt and climate debit they owe to the South.
2. Northern countries undertake deep, drastic cuts of GHG (greenhouse gas) emissions.
3. Southern nations assert their right to develop and meet the needs of their people through a system that is ecologically sound, just, equitable and democratic.
4. An end to the policies, operations and projects of IFIs (International Financial Institutions) that exacerbate climate change, including water and power projects. Stop IFIs, especially the World Bank and regional development banks, from claiming major roles in addressing the climate crisis and using it to push more privatisation projects.
5. All governments to recognize and ensure people's rights and access to sufficient, affordable, clean, quality water and adequate, reliable, affordable, safe, clean and sustainable power services and energy.
6. All governments to recognize that the use of very critical ecological and environmental resources in water and power services necessitate that these services remain under the public domain, protected from intrusion by corporations.
7. Cancel all illegitimate debts claimed from the South as a major step towards enabling countries to deal with the economic and climate crisis.

Meanwhile President Obama challenged all Americans to celebrate the 40th anniversary of Earth Day by making their own lives more energy efficient, demanding more and sending their stories to the White House. *"It's clear change won't come from Washington alone, I want you to take action,"* he said in his video message, citing his efforts to create green jobs and a clean energy economy.

Deliberative and fully inclusive processes are absolutely

essential. Clearly future summits need to be far better organised. Confusion and poor communications were key factors in the failures. A way has to be found that puts poorer and endangered nations in a stronger position. This will eventually be forced on Northern countries. The UN needs to learn how to devise deliberative, democratic processes that are opaque and inclusive and enable all peoples to be properly heard and included in deciding ways forward that meet all needs. Large-scale whole system processes that are needed have been used widely and successfully in large corporations and communities for years, especially in North America. They are being used lower down in the UN hierarchy. The time has come to practise them at Summits.

Trust needs to be built between all participating nations. Trust broke down because of the undemocratic processes, such as major powers meeting behind closed doors from which poor nations were largely excluded. The North bringing pressure to bear on poorer nations with incentives to accept the accord had the same effect. In the long run "strong-arming" poor nations is counterproductive. Denmark and the USA are denying Bolivia and Ecuador climate aid following the Summit. The US decision will cost Bolivia US$3m and Ecuador $2.5m. Such behaviour breeds deep, long-lasting resentments that result in threats to the security of all of us. National leaders need to demonstrate complete integrity. If we are to survive as a species, national leaders need to move beyond bargaining and put the long-term well-being of the entire planet above short-term national interests.

Foreign and economic policy must be transformed. The survival of human civilisation is at stake. We have a choice. Everyone deserves the basics of human life. We have the technology and the means to achieve this. It is a moral issue. Instead of stepping in, imposing Western solutions and making money out of development, local capacity needs building everywhere.

> *The Arab/Muslim world is getting angrier. Yet we put our money into making it worse. We need to take on the whole underlying foreign policy.*
> **Clare Short**

We are spending enormous resources on wars; wasting money and people that could be applied to much greater effect.

> *The more equitable the world is the greater our guarantee of security. The possibilities of progress and development are enormous but we don't take inside our heads what this means. Development should be our central focus.*
> **Clare Short**

We cannot afford to disengage from politics. Historic change comes from mass popular movements. The poor are urbanising. This will give strength to popular movements. The Internet is providing people with the ability to rapidly inform themselves and each other. They can access and share information that corporations prefer to hide and governments censor what they do not want their people to know. It is enabling people to communicate, rapidly organise and work together in protesting, campaigning and demanding reform. We have far greater power than ever before to force governments to act.

We cannot afford to just focus on our own lives and local actions. We have to engage and fight for what we want if we want to survive. There is growing impatience with old-fashioned, adversarial politics that is superficial and focuses on short-term, ill-considered knee-jerk reactions, encouraged by irresponsible media dependent on shock headlines. We are media driven when we need honest, informed, dialogue. That requires truthfulness and integrity. There is a yearning for consensus, inclusive deliberative processes and values based policies.

Clare Short says her experience of politics is that:

> *It is almost never about leaders – it is about bottom up. We are in deep trouble. Politics is paralysed – people are disillusioned. Demoralisation is paralysing us – it can and must be done. There is a lot going for us – urbanisation could create the mass pressure for change. Politics is going to come alive again. We have the common sense within us – the elite are out of touch. We each have to find our place in this.*

Conclusion

In prosperous developed countries, like ours, climate change and the global economic crisis may turn out to be a blessing, a "godsend", if we see it so. It is curtailing our addictive consumption. We are, perforce, using and wasting less, less fossil fuel and other precious resources. The crisis may encourage us to take simpler pleasures that cost less, stay at home, make our homes and gardens nicer, and make do and mend. Recession may encourage us to live, buy, holiday and work local; and make better choices about when to shop local, when global and when in-between. It may also help us see the advantages of appropriate technology and when to use none, as Gandhi and Schumacher tried to teach us. For more affluent people, the fallout may be a blessing, clearing a space for them to start different enterprises and a different life that is more rewarding, more worthwhile. A clearing is often needed before something new can begin.

The consequences for the rest of the world are already devastating. It is much harder for the poor, wherever they are. There are legions of highly skilled, good people who have been working hard, keeping their heads down to earn a living, unaware until now of the harm they were doing. They could instead provide the resources for creating a new order. Our much abused farmers and the so-called "poor" in "underdeveloped countries" can feed the world, if we support them instead of grinding them down for the sake of so-called cheap food that isn't cheap at all.

Perhaps, at last, we will wake up to the fact that our enormous material prosperity has been at the expense of the vast majority. The poor have been left out, scarcely thought of. We eased our consciences through charities, whilst continuing our way of life, unwilling to take actions that would really make a difference. We turned a blind eye to what was going on overseas to provide our prosperity, unwilling to face inconvenient truths, including how our petrol and all those cheap products were provided at the expense of other human beings.

Perhaps "the universe" is trying to teach us something. We need to be open to its message: to survive, all human beings have to work together, care about each other, respect and value difference, find our common humanity and common ground, stop being greedy, grabbing resources, stop murdering each other on a massive scale, describing mass murder as war, and stop being violent in word and deed. We have to respect all nature, of which we are a part, as sacred. Otherwise we are likely to destroy ourselves. I believe the universe provides us all with what we need, including what we need to learn to fulfill our higher selves.

Action

We urgently need to campaign for decisive outcomes at the next UN Summit. Talks in Bonn, April 2010, intended to firm up actions to implement the Copenhagen Accord, which many smaller and poorer nations refused to sign, completely failed. As I write hopes are not high for the UN Summit, COP16, in Cancun, Mexico starting 29 November. The debt crisis is overshadowing everything. There is an impasse between the G20 and the poorer nations who have most to lose. We must put even more pressure on our governments and demand processes that properly include the poorer nations. Otherwise all of us will all lose. ***Support the following***: Via Campesina, Climate Justice Action Network, ALBA – the Bolivarian Alliance of the Americas, Greenpeace, Christian Aid and the Youth forum on climate change.

Chapter 16

What We Need to Do

August 2009 to October 2010

How we can make it happen; what you can do

> *You never change things by fighting the existing reality. To change something, build a new model that makes the existing model obsolete.*
>
> **Buckminster Fuller**

What we need to do

The whole of humanity needs to make a paradigm shift. The essential message is: we have to learn to live as part of nature and in harmony with one another.

This is a summary of what we need to do:

The Paradigm Shift

- Learn to live as part of nature, within Mother Earth's limits, and tackle the environmental crisis
- End the destruction of the ecosystem on which all life depends
- Embrace prosperity without growth
- Substitute well-being for GDP as the measure of progress
- Create a global economy that is fair to all humanity and puts an end to poverty
- Make democracy fully representative and participatory

at all levels

- Transform the way we do politics from an adversarial process to a consensus building collaboration in which everyone wins
- Recognise that injustice leads to violence and violence rarely works
- Invest in even-handed foreign policies and conflict resolution rather than war
- Collaborate globally to fairly distribute the planet's resources
- Create a new identity for ourselves, not based on power and wealth but living well and being stewards and servant leaders

This might sound idealistic or utopian. But as Satish Kumar says: *"Now is the time to give idealism a chance."* "Realism" has not done too well. Millions of people can exercise enormous power by lobbying governments and corporations and using customer choice.

Everything that is done in the world is done by hope.
Dr Martin Luther King

How we can make it happen

The strategies set out in Part Two are summarised here:

Strategies

- Green the world economy to tackle climate change, Peak Oil and ecological destruction
- Radically rethink what we mean by Globalisation

- Get control of big business and government at all levels and ensure they meet our needs, not their ambitions
- Create a new monetary system, not based on debt and sustainable, fair taxation, land value tax and citizens income
- Transform democracy at every level from global to local, giving power to people, providing real choice and government that serves citizens
- Apply the principle of Subsidiarity; not all problems can be solved locally
- Transform the way we feed ourselves – a real green revolution, eco-agriculture, food sovereignty and security
- Create sustainable communities, towns and cities and regions based on bioregionalism

What you can do

It is an enormous task: everyone is needed; there is no one way; all initiatives are needed. Friends of the Earth say:

> *Individual actions can only reduce one-third of carbon emissions. The rest is up to governments.*

We need to:

- *Act Local* – Change our communities and "Be the change".
- *Act Global* – Be activists and lobby government, global institutions and corporations and insist they change.

Act Local. Whatever you do a strategic approach is needed:

A Strategic Approach

Strategy

- Be clear that a paradigm shift is needed
- Declare the possibility; then work on how to make it happen
- Aim to engage everyone – "critical mass" is required. Identify and involve key stakeholders
- Vision – the power of declaring that something is possible. It needs to involve everyone
- Be clear about priority objectives
- Leadership is crucial, successful leaders are leaders of leaders and develop more leaders
- Organise. Also allow and encourage things to emerge and people to self-organise.
- Massive education and awareness raising is needed
- Uniqueness is important, everywhere is different
- Good models open our minds to possibilities, study what works and why

Influencing strategy and processes

- A paradigm shift requires new paradigm processes and structures for transformative meetings, train people in them
- Networking brings results. Neighbours, family and friends are important
- Pressures on most people are enormous, so focus on creating energy
- Respect and value difference in meetings

Thanks to Mick Crews for his valuable contribution to the thinking in this section.

Be clear that a paradigm shift is needed; change of this

magnitude requires a 10 to 20 year project. It is a massive challenge – a major change is needed in lifestyles, attitudes and how we define ourselves – our identities. A timescale of 10 or more years is required. Yet it is urgent.

Declare the possibility; then work on how to make it happen. Declaring something possible is at the heart of every extraordinary endeavour. US President John Kennedy declared that putting a man on the moon was not only possible but would be done within ten years. Problems and difficulties dissolve when people focus on possibilities and vision. That changes the mindset and turns obstacles into opportunities… Technology is not the issue; it is the way we think. One way of putting it all is: *"If we have a clear vision, the universe will conspire to support us!"* Synchronicity will kick in. In my experience this almost always works.

Aim to engage everyone. The transformation we need cannot be seen as a fringe project of eco-angels or greens. It has to be mainstream, involving everyone. There is an urgent need to develop awareness and help people see that they can and must get involved. We have to create a "critical mass". Wikipedia defines this as *"a socio-dynamic term to describe the existence of sufficient momentum in a social system such that the momentum becomes self-sustaining and fuels further growth."*

For a large-scale community initiative to succeed, it is essential to identify and engage all stakeholders. All the diversity of the community is needed, people of all cultures, political and religious viewpoints. Only in this way will we meet all needs. It is important not to underestimate opposition, those powerful vested interests, some local and some global, including "deniers". Respect, listen and learn from people who disagree with you. "Restraining forces" can be a gift – ignore them at your peril (Johnson, B, 1996). People who resist change often become strong supporters.

Vision and Mission. Exciting possibilities, passion and hope inspire and sustain us. Everyone needs their own vision of the community they want to create, brought together in a shared vision. The process starts with the leadership but the whole community needs to be involved. The mission is the long-term task. Here is the mission statement of Transition Town Totnes:

> *The mission of Transition Town Totnes is two-fold. The first is to explore and then follow pathways of practical actions that will reduce our carbon emissions and dependence on fossil fuels (getting to zero carbon is increasingly seen as a viable response). The second is to build the town's resilience, that is, its ability to withstand shocks from the outside, to be more self-reliant in terms of food, energy, employment and economics.*

The worldwide Transition Town Network's website is an invaluable resource.

Be clear about priority objectives. The objective is a sustainable community in which we reduce our carbon and eco footprints to 2 tonnes and 1.8 global hectares respectively. We need to create measurable or observable 10 to 20 year objectives, milestones ***and*** short-term wins that will encourage us. We need to act; pause to reflect, take stock and review; then continue; then repeat these steps.

Leadership is crucial and evident in all successful initiatives. Successful leaders inspire and enable. Often initiatives fail because there are too few leaders; they burn out and become exhausted and discouraged. Instead of defining their role clearly, some get too involved in doing. Paradigm change is too big for a project leader approach. Excellent leaders focus on their strategic role, being leaders of leaders, developing new leaders and giving them the freedom and support to lead others. They have high expectations of everyone and build good relationships. They involve people in building a shared vision to which all are committed. Roles are clearly defined. Every book about change I have ever read emphasises *"Communicate, communicate and communicate!"*

Organise and allow and encourage things to emerge and people to self-organise. A clear organisational structure is essential that takes care of the key functions, long-term and short-term, campaigning, global and local, doing ***and*** thinking, reflecting and learning. The different strengths and skills in a group find their place in such a structure. But it is equally important to enable things to emerge in self-organising, messy, chaotic ways.

Massive education and awareness raising is needed to create the tipping point at which human creativity clicks in and all the millions of changes, brought about by millions of people, lead to a transformation. There is a great need for a strategy to build awareness and engage as many people as possible by showing films and getting in experts for meetings. It also requires networking, making friends, being interested in their concerns, what they are doing and their thinking, listening more than you talk.

Uniqueness is important; everywhere is different. The essence of a sustainable city or town is that it is unique, created over time by its citizens to meet their needs in the unique bioregion in which it exists. Citizens know best. Equally, we need to see ourselves as part of a great global, national and regional endeavour.

Good models open our minds to possibilities – study what works and why. Excellent models inspire, expand our imaginations and make us aware of what is possible. We need to be creative and do it "our way" yet learn from good models. They save our having to reinvent the wheel, help us avoid unnecessary mistakes or missing opportunities to do something imaginative and bold. We need to learn how extraordinary achievements came about – mostly because a few determined people believed in the power of possibility. Merton, Taunton Deane and

Winchester Action on Climate Change show how citizens' organisations, working with their councils can create visionary strategies for a sustainable community.

Influencing strategies and processes

A paradigm shift requires new paradigm processes and structures for transformative meetings. We need processes that build consensus, not majority rule.

> *Consensus design is about everybody getting – if not what they originally wanted – what, after working together and listening to the whole situation, they have come to want.*
> **Christopher Day**

Every organisation needs to be good at handling the day-to-day and envisioning the future. These two different kinds of meetings require different processes, structures and skills:

- **Business meetings.** The traditional agenda structure will work with modifications.
- **Strategic meetings** need to engage heart, soul, body and mind, releasing the human spirit for co-creation.

Transformation is hard work. We need support with our feelings. Resistance and denial are big challenges. We all resist and deny; it's part of being human. Processes need to help people to think big, long-term and creatively. Edward de Bono's Six Thinking Hats can help. All this requires facilitation skills many of us may not have experienced. It helps to have someone in "consultant" or "facilitator" role, not otherwise involved, to focus on process and to observe, reflect, challenge and enable. Everyone needs to learn these roles by practising them in the group in turn.

Liberating, energising processes encourage people to get involved, not just through invitations to speak, but through the structure and processes of a meeting. People can be reluctant to try new things and cautious about engaging in public meetings. Chairs arranged in a circle, semi-circle or round tables of eight encourage participation. It's important to agree not to interrupt each other. One way is to use a "talking stick". While you hold it you have attention, unless you talk too long. Using such processes may seem risky but taking the risk is rewarding. Most people end up loving them because they are fun, they work and new possibilities open up. Good, easily remembered, simple processes for working together need to be learned by ***everyone*!** Train people in them. Vision, Commitment and Action (VCA) is a useful basic structure.

Structures for transformative public meetings. We need to learn how to help large groups of people, representing the full diversity of a community and all its stakeholders, enjoy co-creation. Participatory processes like Future Search and Open Space Technology that engage collective intelligence and creativity are widely used in companies and communities all over the world. My website offers articles about processes that involve people.

Creating vision needs to involve everyone. Many leaders of organisations make a simple mistake. They create a vision statement at a retreat; then hand it down to the workforce. It means very little. The process matters. Creating a vision must engage everyone, dreaming, creating a collective vision and strategy. People need to speak with integrity, do what they say they will do. It is important to hold an end of meeting review – to celebrate, reflect and learn from what worked and anything to do differently. Processes like these are essential if people are to have the energy and belief to achieve the "impossible".

Networking. Neighbours, family and friends are important. Friends and good neighbours are part of sustainability, part of our support system. We are part of one another's well-being.

Using our connections and making new ones is a powerful way of engaging people in transformation. A wise change agent I know talks of having two kinds of connections: close and loose connections. Inspire by being who you are. My neighbours, family, friends and acquaintances teach me a lot. Most ***do not*** want to hear from me about sustainability. My family are the same, having heard from me at length for many years. I have learned, painfully. People are different. It's best to be interested in ***their*** concerns and what they are doing. "How's it going?" Being the change has more power than words. People notice and get interested. It is the same in our transition town. It is as well to remember: everyone is on a journey.

My "shop local" policy is part of "being the change". I rarely use a car. Mostly I walk. The exercise is a bonus. Possibly I pay a bit more, but it saves fuel and I put my money where my mouth is! We go to an organic, biodynamic, ethical whole food shop supplied by small traders and co-operatives, local where possible, for almost all food and household products. On Saturdays we go to the market: Country Markets, the French delicatessen, the fishmonger from Suffolk, and the Farmers Market every third Sunday. We enjoy the high street and markets in our town as a social, community experience. We connect, meet and chat, getting to know new people this way. It's part of the pleasure of being a community. Only if we cannot buy locally do we go to any Big Co or the Internet. That's not much or often.

Pressures on people are enormous. It is important to acknowledge this. Most people are very busy, couples both working hard to earn a living, bring up children, be good parents, maintain friendships or support elderly relatives, singles too. The pressures can be extreme, at times unbearable. Many are just coping. Yet, it's extraordinary what they contribute, taking leadership and doing what they can to help create a sustainable community and fairer world. I am astonished by what people in Berkhamsted manage to do. They get exhausted. So it is important offer holistic processes that are enjoyable and release energy. I now use Satish Kumar's guided meditation, almost every morning.

Act Global

> *Whatever you do may seem insignificant, but it is most important that you do it.*
> **Mahatma Gandhi**

6.7 billion people have the power to bring about radical change. UN Climate Change Summit COP15 was disappointing. Hopes are not high for COP16. Lobbying brought key changes in the UK's Climate Change Act, helped bring about the UK Low Carbon Transition Plan and the *"Great British Refurb"*. We must continue to demand decisive action at UN Summits and other global gatherings. We need to insist governments devolve power to communities and provide the strategic support they need. The *"Big Society"* is an interesting idea. Read the Blog *Just how Big is the Big Society?*

Prioritise where to put your energy and money. Focus on the issues you are most passionate about and believe that will make the biggest difference. My top priorities are New Economics Foundation, Unlock Democracy/Local Works, WDM, CND, Peace Direct, Garden Organic, GM Freeze, Greenpeace, Soil Association, Avaaz, UKUncut, OneGoodCut and 38 Degrees. Use your browser:

Key Campaigns

- **A Just and Sustainable Global Economic System** ALBA – Bolivarian Alliance of the Americas, Avaaz, Christian Aid, Climate Justice Action Network, Greenpeace, International Forum on Globalisation, Jubilee Debt Campaign, People First Campaign, New Economics Foundation, Survival International, Stop Climate Change Chaos Coalition, Via Campesina, World Development Movement and Youth forum on climate change
- **Feeding the World** Compassion in World Farming, Ethical Consumer, Food and Water Watch, Friends of the Earth, Garden Organic, GM Freeze, Soil Association, Vandana Shiva and World Hunger Project
- **Global Governance** New Economics Foundation, One World Trust, SIMPOL, Tikkun – Rabbi Michael Lerner, World Development Movement (WDM)
- **Greening the Global Economy** Centre for Alternative Technology, New Economics Foundation, New Green Deal Coalition, Operation Noah, Stop Climate Chaos Coalition, (WDM), World Watch Institute
- **New Money, Debt, Citizens' Income, Fair and Sustainable Taxation, Land Value Tax** American Monetary Institute, Christian Council for Monetary Justice, James Robertson – working for a sane alternative, Land Value Taxation Campaign, Scottish Monetary Reform, Tax Justice Network, Tobin Tax Institute, WDM
- **Peace – Ending War and Violence** Amnesty International, CND, Campaign Against the Arms Trade, Oxford Research Group, Peace Direct, Peace Pledge Union, Peace Tax Seven, Responding to Conflict

(RTC), Rethink Trident coalition, RoadPeace – road violence

- **Sustainable buildings, cities, communities and transport** BioRegional, Campaign for Better Transport, Centre For Alternative Technology (CAT), Coalition of Campaign to Protect Rural England (CPRE), Keep Trade Local/Federation of Small Businesses Campaign, Local Works, New Economics Foundation Slow Cities and Transition Towns
- **Unlocking Democracy** Amnesty International, Electoral Reform Society, Liberty, Local Works, openDemocracy, Operation Black Vote, Unlock Democracy/2010.

Stop Climate Chaos is a coalition of over 100 organisations and their 11 million supporters, working together for positive action.

Further reading:

- Johnson, B, 1996, *Polarity Management: Identifying and Managing Unsolvable Problems,* HRD Press: Amherst, MA, USA. A simple explanation of polarity management is on my website with other articles.
- Nixon, B, *Making a Difference – Strategies and Tools for Transforming Your Organisation*, Kemble, Glos, UK.
- Thich Nhat Hanh, 1999, *The Miracle of Mindfulness,* Beacon Press, Uckfield East Sussex, UK.

References

Chapter 1: A Time of System Breakdown – but also of Hope

- *The Full Obama Interview* by Joe Klein in TIME, Nov 3rd 2008. Available at: http://www.time.com/time/politics/article/0,8599,1853081,00.html

Chapter 2: Understanding the Financial Crisis

- Peston, R. (2008) *The New Capitalism*, [PDF], BBC NEWS bbc.co.uk/robertpeston (Accessed 8 December 2008) Available at: http://www.bbc.co.uk/blogs/thereporters/robertpeston/newcapitalism.pdf
- Channel 4, *Unreported World, India Children of the Inferno*, Accessed: 17th April, 2009, Quicksilver Media/Channel 4. Available by inserting the title into your browser or at: http://www.channel4.com/programmes/unreported-world/episode-guide/series-2009/episode-7
- Monbiot, G, "The free market preachers have long practised state welfare for the rich", *The Guardian*, 30th September, 2008, page 33
- Davies, E, *The rocket scientists of finance they employed were amongst the cleverest people on Earth, but their technology was complicated and fragile. It was bound to end in tears.* Evan Davies, *City Uncovered*, BBC2, 14th January 2009. Available at: http://news.bbc.co.uk/1/hi/business/7826431.stm
- Monbiot, G, "You are being fleeced in the biggest, weirdest rip-off yet: a widened M25: a widened M25", *The Guardian*, 7th April, 2009, page 27

Chapter 3: We, 6.7 Billion People, Need to Feel Our Anger

- Minton A, 2009, *Ground Control – Fear and Happiness in the Twenty-First Century City,* Penguin Books, London & New York

Chapter 4: We Face the Biggest Crisis in Human History – Growth is Not Working

Section A: Climate Change

- MacKay, D, *Sustainable Energy – Without the Hot Air,* 2009 figure 20.23, page 128, and page 68, published by UIT, Cambridge, England. Also available as a free download for non-commercial use at: http://www.withouthotair.com/
  More figures are available from Wikipedia.
- MacKay, D, *Sustainable Energy – Without the Hot Air,* 2009 pp 129-130, Hydrogen fuel-cell cars; different forms of freight transport on pp 91-2, published by UIT, Cambridge, England
- Hutton, W, "Don't let the defeatists and cynics talk down Britain's need for speed", *The Observer,* 2nd August 2009, page 24

Section D: Poverty and Economic Injustice

- Hutton, W, "Of course class still matters – it influences everything we do", *The Observer,* 10th January 2009, page 32
- Minton A, 2009, *Ground Control – Fear and happiness in the Twenty-First Century City,* page 115, Penguin Books, London & New York

Chapter 8: Greening the World

- Sachs, W, Loske, R and Linz, M, editors, 1998, *Greening the North – A Post-Industrial Blueprint for Ecology and Equity,* Zed Books, London & New York.
- MacKay, D, 2009, *Sustainable Energy – Without the Hot Air,*

UIT, Cambridge, England, pp 212 and 214, published by UIT Cambridge, England

Chapter 12: Feeding the World

- Roberts, P, 2008, *The End of Food,* Global Health Watch 2: An Alternative World Health Report, Zed Books, London & New York

Other Books and Writings by the Author

Living System: Making Sense of Sustainability, 2006, *Making a Difference – Strategies and Tools for Transforming Your Organisation*, 2001 and *Global Forces: A Guide for Enlightened Leaders – what companies and individuals can do*, 2000, all published by Management Books, Kemble, Glos, UK and *New Approaches to Management Development*, 1981, Gower, Aldershot, UK. His many articles may be found on www.brucenixon.com.